# AFRICA
## *A Social Geography*

# AFRICA

## *A Social Geography*

by
### ANTHONY SILLERY

SECOND EDITION

A HALSTED PRESS BOOK

## JOHN WILEY & SONS
New York

First published in 1961 by
Gerald Duckworth & Co. Ltd.,
43 Gloucester Crescent, London N.W.1.

© ANTHONY SILLERY 1961, 1972

*Second edition 1972*

Published in the U.S.A. by Halsted Press,
a Division of John Wiley & Sons, Inc.,
New York.

I.S.B.N. 0 470–79169–1

Library of Congress Catalog Card No. 72–10687

PRINTED IN GREAT BRITAIN
PHOTOLITHO BY EBENEZER BAYLIS AND SON LTD.
THE TRINITY PRESS, WORCESTER, AND LONDON

# CONTENTS

# LIST OF PLATES

Between pages 68 and 69

## LIST OF MAPS

# PREFACE

IT has been well said[1] that modern books about Africa fall into two categories: those written by journalists who are chiefly interested in the continent under the impact of nationalism and have very little idea of its nature and of its past, and those produced by specialist researchers. The former class has perhaps too much influence, the latter comes too late for practical application. This book is an attempt to compromise. Many years spent in various parts of Africa give me the right to claim some first-hand knowledge of the country and of its people, and I have also devoted a considerable part of the last decade to the study of African history. At the same time I have been at pains to keep abreast of modern developments, and have watched with interest and understanding, though not always uncritically, the growth of the movement towards self-government which has resulted in the establishment of independent African governments in many former colonies.

This book is designed to present a picture of Africa as it is in the 1970s. The political tempo is so rapid that I have preferred to concentrate on those things which, if not immutable, at least change more slowly than politics. These include geography, ethnology, culture, economics and racial relations. Some emphasis is laid on history, since it is impossible to understand the present except against the background of the past.

Even if I tend to neglect politics, my subject is still so varied and so wide that it is impossible in the available space to deal with any aspect of it except in the broadest outline. The book is therefore not meant for the specialist, nor as a reference book for those seeking statistics or other detailed information. It is meant simply to be read by the general reader to whom I hope it will give some idea of Africa and of the people who live in it.

The first edition of this book was published in 1961. So many changes have taken place in Africa during the last decade that the process of bringing it up to date is almost like writing a new one. But although there are no doubt still many surprises in store, especially in the field of politics, there are signs that in the social and economic fields at least the graph of change is beginning to flatten out and the pace becoming steadier.

[1] In a book review initialled H.I. in *Corona*, January 1961.

One matter of orthography needs to be explained: When spelling Bantu tribal names it is usual nowadays to drop the prefix and use only the root; e.g. Ganda not Baganda, Chagga not Wachagga. I have followed no fixed rule, but have either kept or dropped the prefix according to which form I believe accords with common usage in each case.

Too much attention should not be paid to African statistics, especially population figures. At best these are only approximations, and probably wide ones at that. If it were possible by some magic means to discover exactly how many people live in the various parts of Africa, and how many cattle they possess, nothing would surprise me more than to find that my own figures, based on reputable reference books, were within 25 per cent of the truth. The same reservations apply, though perhaps in some cases with rather less force, to figures purporting to represent the areas of the various countries, and even to the geographical position of Africa itself: no two atlases agree on the exact co-ordinate of the continent's extremities.

A.S.

*Oxford*
  *December 1971*

# Racial distribution

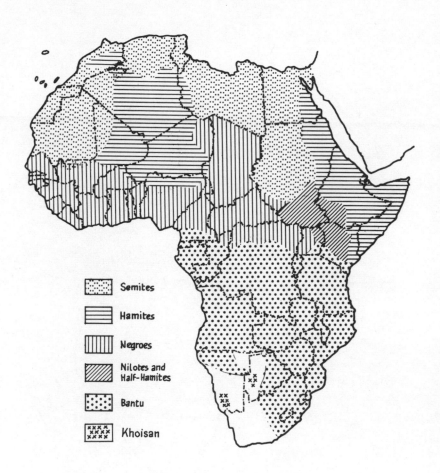

Semites

Hamites

Negroes

Nilotes and
Half-Hamites

Bantu

Khoisan

# Important Physical Features

CHAPTER ONE

## The Unknown Continent

THOUGH North Africa has been known to Europeans for thousands of years and the southern tip for centuries, it is only in the last hundred and fifty years or so that we have learnt what we now know about the rest of the continent. Up to the end of the eighteenth century a map of inland tropical Africa, if it was not 'a perfect and absolute blank', was largely guesswork:

> 'So geographers, in Afric maps
> With savage pictures fill their gaps;
> And o'er unhabitable downs
> Place elephants for want of towns'.[1]

The reason why Africa was for so long shut off from the rest of the world was no doubt largely that it is particularly well protected by Nature against penetration and settlement. In the north the Sahara Desert, though traversed by caravan routes in common use, was not adapted to regular large scale movement of peoples.[2] The African coastline affords few natural harbours, and much of it is backed by desert or semi-desert or by dense forest. The rivers are not easily navigable. Even the Nile is barred by cataracts which prevent easy access by boat to the upper reaches. The climate of the tropics was not good for Europeans and, before modern medicine, often fatal. Tsetse fly made animal transport impossible and in most parts travel was on foot with porters. The whole aspect was frankly unattractive and early European navigators like the Portuguese were well content to win footholds on the coast and sail on to the more accessible riches of the East Indies. Other Europeans who came later did little more than establish coastal trading stations. It was not until the late eighteenth century that Europeans set about seriously to explore the interior of Africa. By the end of the nineteenth century most of the blanks on the map had been filled in,

[1] Jonathan Swift, *On Poetry*.
[2] From the seventh century onwards Europeans could not in any case hope to penetrate from the north, since the whole of the Mediterranean coast was under Moslem control.

3

and the greater part of the continent had fallen under European domination.

## CONFIGURATION AND SPECIAL FEATURES

From its northern point, Ras ben Sakka, a little west of Cap Blanc in latitude 37° 20′ N, to its southern point at Cape Agulhas in latitude 34° 50′ S, the continent of Africa measures 5,000 miles. The width at its broadest point, from Cape Verde, 17° 33′ W, to Ras Hafun, 51° 25′ E, is 4,600 miles. The area is about 11½ million square miles. The shape is in one sense fairly symmetrical: on all sides the ground rises from a coastal plain to a plateau which runs like a backbone down the whole length of the continent. This plateau has great diversity of relief. Generally speaking the altitude ranges between three thousand and six thousand feet and is higher in the south than in the north. But there are in places great mountain masses which rise above the tableland, such for instance as the Ethiopian massif with peaks above 15,000 feet, and some of the mountains of East Africa which are considerably higher. On the other hand there are basins or depressions lying well below the general level, for example Lake Chad, the Congo basin and that which lies in the great bend of the Niger River.

Some time in the remote past a violent seismic disturbance accompanied by great volcanic activity caused huge fractures in the earth's surface. The result is a series of troughs, with sides more or less clearly defined, which is called the Great Rift Valley.[1] This is one of the most remarkable geographical phenomena in the world. The Rift begins near the mouth of the Zambezi River and runs northwards, including in its course the Shire River valley and Lake Malawi. North of Lake Malawi it branches, forming the Eastern and Western Rifts. The Eastern Rift goes through mainland Tanzania and Kenya, its path marked by a chain of small lakes, Manyara, Natron, Naivasha and others. It then runs through Ethiopia, cutting the Somali provinces off from the rest of the Ethiopian Empire. The Red Sea is the link that connects the Rift in Africa with its continuation through Palestine. The Gulf of Akaba, the Jordan Valley and the Dead Sea all lie in its bed, and it may be taken to come to an end in Syria, its total length 4,000 miles. The Western Rift branches off in a general north-westerly direction and contains the

[1] Also called the Rift Valley, or just the Rift.

stupendous trough of Lake Tanganyika and Lakes Kivu, Edward and Albert. It ends not very far north of Lake Albert and is thus much shorter than the Eastern Rift. Lake Victoria, which lies between the horns of the two Rifts, is not thought to be of tectonic origin. (*Plate* 36)

In Kenya particularly the Rift presents a most majestic spectacle, and no one who stands on its edge, say at the point where the main road from Nairobi to Kisumu plunges down into the valley, can fail to marvel at the vast forces which so affected the configuration of the continent.

If now we look at a map of Africa our eye will probably first be drawn to four, and possibly five, great rivers. The Nile, which once nourished one of the great civilizations of the world, flows into the Mediterranean and is in fact the only African river of any size with an outlet in the north. It has a length of more than 4,000 miles and may be said to begin at the Kagera River, which flows into Lake Victoria. It is a river, as we shall see, with a great and romantic past, and it plays an important part today, for both the Sudan and Egypt are dependent on it, and it is so far the most developed of the rivers of Africa. The Niger too has played its part in history, particularly in recent history. After taking an enormous bend through West Africa for a distance of 2,600 miles it flows into the Atlantic Ocean in the Bight of Benin. The great Congo River also empties into the Atlantic. It is nearly 3,000 miles long and has innumerable tributaries and a drainage area of nearly $1\frac{1}{2}$ million square miles. The Congo is navigable in many parts and carries heavy traffic. The Zambezi rises in Angola but runs south-eastwards, at one point tumbling over a cliff to form the Victoria Falls, finally to flow into the Indian Ocean 2,000 miles from its source. The Orange River, further south, is included with some hesitation. It is shorter than the others, being only 1,300 miles in length; it does not, like the others, flow regularly but is often dry or reduced to a series of pools. But since it has played a part in the history of South Africa and remains of no small economic importance, it deserves to be mentioned. (*Plate* 3)

The great lakes of Africa are all except one in the eastern and central parts of the continent. The largest in area is Victoria, of approximately 26,000 square miles, as a freshwater lake second in the world only to Lake Superior. It is on the Equator and forms the chief reservoir of the Nile, which leaves the Lake by the Ripon Falls at Jinja. Lake Victoria is enclosed by Uganda on the north and

west, Tanzania on the south and south-east and Kenya on the
north-east. It is a busy lake, with large populations on its shores
and many flourishing little ports. In many places it is also very
beautiful.

Africa does nothing by halves: after the second largest lake in the
world comes Lake Tanganyika, which is the longest, measuring as
it does 420 miles. It is also, except Lake Baikal, the deepest, sound-
ings of 4,708 feet having been taken. It lies in the Western Rift,
between Tanzania and Congo/Zaïre, and is narrow, being on
average only 30 miles broad. Lake Malawi, which lies between
Malawi and Mozambique or Portuguese East Africa, is 350 miles
long and has an average width of 30 miles. It is drained by the
Shire River into the Zambezi. Besides these three giants there are
other lakes, such as Albert, Edward and Kivu in the Western Rift,
Rudolf between Kenya and Ethiopia, Chad on the southern
edge of the Sahara, and many smaller ones in other parts of the
continent.                                                   (*Plate* 35)

Africa boasts some splendid mountains, though they are not the
highest in the world. Still, Kilimanjaro, 19,340 feet, in Tanzania,
the Ruwenzori range on the borders of Uganda and Congo/Zaïre
which has a peak of 16,794 feet, Mount Kenya itself, the Drakensberg between Lesotho and Natal and many lesser ranges, are
impressive enough.                                    (*Plates* 32–34)

## CLIMATE

Only in very limited parts of Africa are temperate conditions
resembling those of Europe to be found. Most of the continent is
hot, and the heat is associated with great humidity in some regions
and great aridity in others. The most remarkable thing about
African climates is their symmetrical distribution in relation to the
Equator. Each kind of climate has its counterpart or approximate
counterpart in the other, in the same position relative to the
equatorial belt. The various climatic régimes are not, however,
sharply distinguished one from another but shade off gradually,
each merging imperceptibly into its neighbour.

Beginning at the Equator we find three variations of what may be
called the equatorial climate. The first two are both characterized by
high rainfall, great heat and a steamy humidity. But whereas in the
northern part of the Congo basin the rainfall is evenly distributed
throughout the year, the Guinea coast and its hinterland has an

annual dry spell, and even drought. In both these regions the predominant vegetation is thick tropical forest. The third variation is that ruling in the plateau lands of East Africa where the temperature is comparatively cool owing to the high altitude, and the rainfall moderate. The vegetation is a parklike savannah degenerating to thornbush.

On either side of the equatorial belt there is a broad zone which represents the transition between the hot, humid belt and the dry heat of the northern and southern deserts. In the north this transitional zone stretches across the continent from Senegal to Ethiopia, and in the south from Angola to Mozambique. This is the 'tropical' or 'Sudan-type' climate, still very hot, but with a well defined season of moderate rain. In the northern zone the oppressive heat is periodically relieved by a dry wind which though very dusty is conducive to health. In the south there is also a well marked contrast between the cool and the hot seasons.

Next come the two deserts, the Sahara in the north and the Kgalagadi in the south. Exceptionally, their arrangement is not quite symmetrical for whereas the Sahara with lesser deserts covers almost the whole of North Africa and in parts reaches to the sea, the desertic regions of South Africa are confined to the western and mid-western parts of the sub-continent. The deserts are very hot in summer with dry scorching winds. In winter the nights are cold, with occasional frosts and there are sometimes cold winds by day. Rainfall is scanty. Vegetation in the Sahara is exceedingly sparse but in the Kgalagadi light rains produce a cover of grass nourishing to cattle, and great quantities of wild melons.

Last of all we come to the subtropical climates of North and South Africa, without doubt the most agreeable and equable climates of the continent. The winters are mild and rainy, the summers warm. Both these zones once had good forests but wasteful felling has greatly reduced them, especially in the south. Thicket growth has replaced forest where this has disappeared.

On the South African high veld there is another type of subtropical climate characterized by hot summers, cold winters and an unreliable rainfall which is in any case concentrated in a very short period. The vegetation is mainly grass and there is no forest. On the other hand the east coast of South Africa, subject to yet a third sub-tropical régime, is warm, has a heavy rainfall (Natal has a rainy season of nine months) and luxuriant vegetation.

## The People of Africa

This great continent has perhaps about 350 million people, all as varied as the physical and climatic conditions in which they live. They do, however, fall generally into a number of groups, each group having certain physical, cultural and linguistic characteristics which distinguish it from the others. Provided therefore that we remember that the ethnic frontiers are blurred, and that the dominant features of one group are often to be observed in another, we may divide the population of Africa into Semites, true Negroes, Hamites, Nilotes and Nilo-Hamites, Bantu, Khoisan, and Negrillos.

### Semites

The Semites are represented mainly by the Arabs, although not all who call themselves Arabs are of pure Arab stock. Indeed the term is sometimes applied to anybody who professes the religion of Islam, even though he may be quite negroid. It has thus very little ethnic significance but is useful in describing a large number of people of widely differing physical characteristics who are mostly Moslems and who speak Arabic. In Africa the Arabs of the north and east are those in whom the original strain is purest. The Arabs of the Sudan and those who are to be found as far west as Nigeria often carry much negro blood and are sometimes indistinguishable in appearance from the indigenous Negroes.

The Arabs of Africa are usually divided into three categories: the genuine nomads, the people of the camel, who are usually found in North Africa; somewhat less nomadic cattle owners; settled communities. How the Arabs came into Africa, and their impact on the people whom they found there, will be described later.

### True Negroes

The black people of Africa are all popularly called Negroes, but for ethnical purposes we may distinguish a particular type whom we may call true Negroes for lack of a more specific name. These are the dominant people of West Africa from the mouth of the Senegal River, about 16° N, to the eastern boundary of Nigeria. Their main physical characteristics are a black skin, woolly hair and a tall stature. The head is fairly long in comparison to its breadth, the nose is broad and flat, the lips thick and everted, and the features are often prognathous. These people were formerly organized in powerful and wealthy kingdoms with an elaborate apparatus of officials, a priesthood in the service of a complicated and often cruel religion, a strong military organization and a notable body of artists and craftsmen associated with church, state and the secret and semi-secret societies that are a feature of West African life. Although the old kingdoms and hierarchies have either disappeared, or, where they have survived, lost much of their power, the true Negroes still live in well organized communities and have a high standard of material and technical achievement. They give an impression of exuberant and full-blooded vitality and are in many ways the most advanced and ambitious of the dark-skinned people of Africa. Their economy is an agricultural rather than a pastoral one.

## Hamites

At some time in the very remote past Africa was invaded from Asia, possibly from southern Arabia, by a race we call Hamites. They were Caucasians and therefore belong to the same branch of mankind as Europeans. They also had strong affinities with the Semites. These Hamites came into Africa in a very long succession of waves. Some colonized the Nile Valley, others passed on into North Africa, while others gradually spread southwards into the heart of the continent. The last waves stopped, or were halted, in the Horn of Africa (the north-eastern tip, washed by the Red Sea on the one side and the Indian Ocean on the other) and now occupy the country that later became known as Somaliland. These, together with the Hamites of North Africa, are those who have best preserved their physical characteristics down the ages to modern times.

We may conveniently divide the Hamites into two main groups or branches:

(1) the Eastern Hamites, who include the ancient and modern Egyptians (allowing for strong infusions of foreign blood in the latter), the Beja, the Nubians, the Somali, the Danakil, the Galla, and, with some reservations, most Ethiopians.[1]

(2) the Northern Hamites, who include the Berbers, the Tuareg, the Fulani of West Africa and an extinct people of the Canary Islands called the Guanche.

So widely distributed, and over much of the continent so mixed is the strain, that it is not easy to give a description of Hamitic physical characteristics. Among the Eastern Hamites the build is

[1] See, however, pp. 147, 151.

fairly tall and often spare, the nose straight and sometimes aquiline, the lips thick, but not everted, the beard thin, the hair often frizzy but sometimes straight or wavy, and the skin variable in colour from yellowish to black. Many Hamites, especially the Berbers, are of distinctly 'Nordic' appearance, having long heads, narrow noses, and even in some cases white skins, blue or green eyes and fair hair. These are to be found alongside other types, swarthier, with broader noses, some with long heads and some with rounder heads, some with negroid characteristics.

There has in the past been a tendency among anthropologists to ascribe any signs of superior culture among Africans to Hamitic influence. 'The civilizations of Africa', wrote Professor Seligman, 'are the civilizations of the Hamites.'[1] This thesis is now under heavy fire. The advanced true Negro civilizations of West Africa are not Hamitic, and conversely there are a number of comparatively pure Hamites with no very impressive civilization. In our present state of knowledge we may accept the view that invading Hamites mixed with indigenous negroes to produce new strains; and that in some places they imposed themselves as a pastoral aristocracy on sedentary agricultural Negro populations. To go further would be to do injustice to people who have evolved spontaneous civilizations of their own.

## Nilotes and Nilo-Hamites

In the southern Sudan and in East Africa there are several peoples of considerable importance presenting a mingling of Negro and Hamitic elements and generally regarded as falling into two divisions, Nilotes and Nilo-Hamites. The Shilluk and Dinka of the Nile Valley, tall, long-headed and dark-skinned, are typical Nilotes and the division is represented as far south as Lake Victoria by the Luo or Nilotic Kavirondo. Nilo-Hamites include the Masai (known to even the most casual visitor to Kenya), the Nandi, the Lumbwa, the Suk, the Turkana, the Karamojong, probably the Didinga and Topotha of the southern Sudan and the Iteso of Uganda. They are fairly tall, fairly long-headed, often narrow-faced, with fine features and a skin (notably in the case of the Masai) that is somewhat brown. Nilotes and Nilo-Hamites are predominantly but not exclusively pastoralists, and devote to their cattle an almost religious esteem. This veneration extends to objects associated with cattle, such as milk and grass and some tribes will not kill cattle except on

[1] Seligman, *Races of Africa*, p. 85.

ceremonial occasions.[1] It must here be stated that the distinction between Nilotes and Nilo-Hamites is mainly based on linguistic grounds about which opinion is not unanimous.

## Bantu

This is really a linguistic term but is used ethnologically to describe a very large negro group whose languages have certain unmistakable common characteristics. Allowing for Nilotic and Nilo-Hamitic 'islands', the Bantu occupy the whole of the southern two-thirds of black Africa. Apart from the bond of language, they are diverse in appearance, and though all have certain common features, they differ considerably in their culture from tribe to tribe and from region to region. What link other than language, one asks, unites the aristocratic Bahima, true Nilo-Hamites in all but speech, the industrious and homely Sukuma, the handsome cattle-loving Kuria, the powerful, disciplined, warlike Zulu, the broken, partly islamized tribes of the coastal areas of East Africa, the intelligent, vocal, ambitious Chagga, the hardy, independent mountaineers of Lesotho? That certain very loose bonds do exist we shall see later. But spreading as they do over a great part of the continent (unlike the Nilo-Hamites and Nilotes whose habitat is comparatively circumscribed) the Bantu have been subject to a great variety of environmental influences that has caused a similar diversity in the characteristics of the various groups. Obviously, people living in arid plains will develop in a different manner to those living in swamps or mountains, while the presence of this insect or that, for instance the tsetse fly or the mosquito, will determine a whole way of life.

## The Khoisan

These are the Bushmen and Hottentots of South Africa. The Bushmen are the oldest indigenous race of Africa and were formerly widely distributed over the continent. Harried in the past by Bantu and European enemies they are now confined to the Kgalagadi desert and its neighbourhood.

Bushmen are short in stature, with a yellow or yellowish-brown skin, 'peppercorn' hair, prominent cheekbones, narrow eyes and very flat noses. One of their notable characteristics is the prominence of the buttocks in men and pronounced steatopygy in women. Further north, the swamp Bushmen of the Okavango delta

[1] Seligman, *Races of Africa*, Chapter 7, *passim*.

are taller and darker. Bushmen live in an exceedingly primitive way
and are almost completely unaffected by contact with higher
civilization. They obtain their livelihood by hunting and gathering
edible roots and plants, neither practising agriculture nor keeping
cattle. In spite of this precarious way of life, they are an exceedingly
merry people, much given to dancing and singing. Above all, the
race has produced a notable form of art, the so-called rock paintings,
scenes of people and animals and daily life executed on the rock
walls of caves. The colour is extraordinarily vivid and the pictures
themselves have high artistic merit, but the art has now died out
completely and the paintings we see today must be very old, though
exactly how old it is impossible to say. There are said to be over
50,000 Bushmen still in existence,[1] but the numbers are believed to
be dwindling. The conditions that made their life possible, unlimited space and plentiful game, are vanishing. The Bushmen
are becoming merged with other peoples by intermarriage and will
doubtless disappear as a race in the not distant future.   (*Plate* 7)

The Hottentots, whose habitat is now mainly South West Africa,
are the result of the mixture of Bushmen with early Hamites. They
are taller than Bushmen and differ from them in that they are a
pastoral people, possessing cattle and sheep. Their culture is
generally superior to that of the Bushmen but they do not appear to
have made rock paintings.

### The Negrillos

These are the Pygmies of the Congo forests. Their existence was
known to the early Pharaohs of Egypt but little is as yet known now
of their language and culture, although they are said to be excellent
dancers, singers, mimics and actors. They live mainly by hunting
and collecting and their way of life, primitive as it is, seems to be
ingeniously adapted to their environment.

### Non-African races

To complete the African scene we must make some reference to
those races which although comparatively recent immigrants have
now made Africa their home. The most important of these are
Asians and Europeans.

The Asians consist mainly of Indians and Pakistanis and are
to be found in Zanzibar, where they have been settled for a longer

[1] P. V. Tobias, 'On the survival of the Bushmen' (*Africa*, Vol. XXVI, No. 2,
April 1956).

time than elsewhere, on the East African mainland, and in Natal. They fall into two principal communities, Moslems and Hindus. There are also Sikhs, predominantly artisans, and Goans from Portuguese India, many of whom are office workers.

There is a whole European nation in South Africa and there are immigrant communities on the shores of the Mediterranean. Central Africa has a substantial population of British and Portuguese, while scattered about the continent there are innumerable groups, large and small, of European traders, officials, missionaries, miners and artisans of all kinds.

## African Culture

To the European explorers of the nineteenth century tropical Africa appeared to be savage and primitive, given over to tribal war and cruel superstition. With important exceptions the people lived in conditions of poverty and insecurity, lacking elementary amenities and struggling under difficulties for the essentials of life. The social and political organization seemed either excessively simple and backward, or, when more highly developed, barbaric and oppressive.

It is of course true that Africans were at that time comparatively uninfluenced by the outside world. Such contacts as they had had with higher civilizations in their more recent history had done them little good. What they had seen of Europeans or of Arabs, whether in the south, west or east, must have persuaded them that these were people to avoid. The only beneficial, or at least innocuous agents of European or Asian civilization were occasional Christian missionaries and the traders of many nations who usually kept to the coast. No doubt there was always some communication among the African people themselves, some interchange of ideas, some handing on of skills and practices from one community to another. Various crafts, the raising of certain domestic animals, the cultivation of certain plants, were at one time or another introduced from outside and in due course spread across Africa. But the breezes that blew from outside from the time of the Hamitic invasions, whenever that was, to the modern era, were very light and the culture that evolved over most of the continent, except of course in the Arab and European areas, was truly indigenous.

There are signs scattered about Africa that this ancient culture was not an unsuccessful one. Zimbabwe in Rhodesia with its

massive stone walls and towers, the most important of several such
sites in south central Africa, is now firmly believed to be the work
of a native race, and not, as was formerly held, that of Semitic
immigrants. At Engaruka in Tanzania there are the ruins of a
stone-built town large enough to have housed thirty or forty
thousand inhabitants. This too may be the product of a native
civilization. At Mapungubwe in the Northern Transvaal there is a
burial ground rich in golden ornaments and other metal objects
which seem to be of local inspiration and origin. There is no certainty in these matters and any conclusions must be tentative. We
shall perhaps never know for certain who built Engaruka and
Zimbabwe nor who was buried at Mapungubwe; nor shall we know
how and when and why their various cultures disappeared. But
these and other relics of the past do permit us to assume that at
various times there certainly existed south of the Sahara native
communities who had reached a state of civilization considerably
superior to that in which much of Africa was found by nineteenth-
century Europeans.[1]

   To leave the past and to come to modern times, African culture
varies enormously in kind and in quality from tribe to tribe and
from place to place, and ranges from that of the simple, primitive
societies of say, the pagans of northern Nigeria, to the highly
organized system of the Baganda. But it has enough aspects common to all regions and tribes to permit us to draw, in very broad
outline and with all possible reservations as to detail, a general
sketch of African culture as the first European travellers found it,
and as it still very widely is.

## RELIGION

   Most Africans believe in a Supreme Being, often associated with
the firmament. He is the creator of all things, but plays little part in
the life of the individual. Though there are some tribes who believe
in a personal God who answers prayers and grants favours, to most
Africans the Supreme Being is remote and impersonal and takes
little interest in His creation. From Him are derived numbers of
lesser gods, who may be graded in a descending scale and may be
associated with natural phenomena. By far the most important
aspect of African religion is a belief in mysterious and occult forces
that influence human life. These forces may reside in human beings,

   [1] Early African indigenous culture is attracting increasing attention nowadays,
but research in this field is still in the early stages.

animals or things and can be used to strengthen life and assure its continuity in descendants by observance of the correct ritual. Associated in some way with the life forces are the spirits of departed ancestors. Africans believe that the spirits of the dead have power to bring good or evil fortune to their living descendants. The ancestors must therefore be honoured and propitiated, it may be through the head of the family or through the chief or through priests. This belief was the reason why in some tribes it was thought necessary, when a chief died, to kill his servants and the women of the palace, so that they might attend their master in the next world. This idea is not of course peculiar to Africa, but seems to belong to mankind's common stock, different items of which keep appearing all over the world among people widely separated in space and time. It was also the custom from time to time to kill people in order that they might act as messengers to carry the news of the chief's activities to his departed ancestors. Fortunately most ancestor cults were not so bloody as these, and usually took, and still take, the form of invocation and an offering of food and of some small domestic animal.

The African also believes passionately in sorcery, which is the misuse of the life forces to bring harm to other people. Sorcery is regarded with the utmost horror, and to defeat it African society has provided itself with a class of persons whose profession it is to detect the sorcerer and to undo his spells. These are the witch-doctors, whose beneficent activities are often confused by Europeans with those of the very sorcerers whom the witch-doctors seek to frustrate. Allied to witch–doctors are other doctors who provide remedies for less personal disasters. In this category are the 'rain-makers', a most inappropriate term which they themselves would be the last to claim. All they purport to do is to ascertain why rain does not fall. This may often be because someone in the community has offended the ancestors, and the doctor will advise how the offence may be purged. He may also perform certain rites in order that the offended spirits may be appeased. 'Rain-makers' are therefore diagnosticians and intermediaries and nothing more. Other practitioners specialize in preventing plagues of various kinds, e.g. grain-eating birds, others, more positively, in ensuring supplies of food,[1] and the chief himself often carries out the rites designed to

[1] One chief whom I knew on Lake Victoria was a noted fish-doctor. His greatest triumph was when two or three fish fell from the sky. The rational explanation was that they were caught up and carried by a waterspout.

remove all obstacles to a successful planting and an abundant harvest.

## How The African Lives

It is impossible in one general chapter to describe the way in which all the people of Africa live, nor is it wholly necessary. We may disregard recent immigrants like Europeans who have brought with them the culture of their homeland and have merely modified and developed it in their new surroundings. Even the Arabs, who arrived many centuries ago, do not differ widely from Arabs of one sort or another anywhere else. We need therefore only concern ourselves with the Negroes between the Sahara and the Cape who have lived in the continent so long that they may now be called indigenous. They all have certain peculiarities of thought and behaviour that distinguish them from other races, and enough characteristics in common for us to be able to speak very generally of an African way of life.

### The Community

The great mass of these people belong to communities called tribes that may be large or small. Tribes are distinguished among themselves by language and by cultural differences. In one respect however they are all similar: they all have a well marked social structure. This may range from some simple organization of a few family heads, with perhaps one elder whom the others regard as their senior, to the elaborate machinery of the nation state, with a king at its head and around him justices, ministers, and representatives in many towns and villages. It must however here be said that African despotisms have in the past been rare. Tyrants there have certainly been, but on the whole the African system has usually contained safeguards against the unbridled and capricious exercise of power by one person. The chief is surrounded by well defined groups of councillors whose advice he is bound to respect. Most chiefs, however powerful, find it advisable to listen to what their councillors say.

In addition to his secular powers, which are political, judicial and social, the chief has religious powers as well. Many regard him as the intermediary between the tribe and the more powerful ancestral spirits; and it falls to him to perform the rites incidental to seed-time and harvest and to the other important events of the year. In some tribes the chief's person is the object of extraordinary venera-

tion; in others he inspires no more than the respect due to a social
superior.

It was inevitable that the tribal system should sooner or later give
way to some other form of political organization, and the process of
change has gained momentum in the last decade. The phenomenal
rise of the politician has caused the decline, indeed the disappearance
of the chiefship as an instrument of administration. At the same time
modern African governments, as a matter of policy, condemn tribal
sentiment as a threat to political stability and seek instead to foster a
sense of *national* unity and patriotism. There are many Africans,
mostly town-dwellers, who have long forsaken their ancient tribal
loyalties. But for the majority, local and traditional relationships
form the background of their lives. It is difficult for them to switch
their allegiance to the concept of a nation-state in the space of ten
years. The tribal spirit remains strong and forms the background to
politics in many areas.

Common to all African societies is a strong sense of community,
of communal existence and action, of collective responsibility. The
African does not regard himself primarily as an individual before
God and before man, as does a European. He is firmly embedded
in his family, and if not totally detribalized, in his clan and in his
tribe. Alive or dead his kith and kin are around him, concerned with
all aspects of his life, sharing his successes and his failures, his good
and his evil fortune, living in him as he lives in them. If an African
commits an offence, his community is responsible with him. If he
prospers and reaches a position of wealth and power, the family and
the clan will expect to benefit. This sense of community has many
admirable sides. The African tribe is itself a complete welfare service. The old are cared for and the needy are fed. Widows and
orphans are 'inherited' by some male relative whose duty it is to
look after them. As long as there is any food no one will starve. In
addition to these material advantages the tribe gives a feeling of
'belonging' to something ancient and respectable, of communion in
some continuing spiritual order, of balance and stability. The idea
of strictly personal responsibility, introduced by European missionaries, traders, administrators, lawyers, has done much to destroy
the communal conscience which admittedly tended to blunt initiative and progress and to foster an excessive conservatism. Nevertheless there are some who regret the passing of something that
modern Europeans are none the better for having lost: a sense
of obligation to something wider than the individual.

## Justice

African justice ignores the difference between civil and criminal law, and is based on the principle of redress and compensation. Thus if I injure a man in any way, whether by striking him, or by stealing from him, or by negligently letting my cattle eat his crops, or by failing to pay him a debt, his remedy is the same: I must make suitable payment in compensation for his injury or for his loss. Punishment in our sense is alien to traditional African practice except in witchcraft and perhaps in offences specifically against the chief. The distinction between crimes and torts has no part in African legal theory. This however, has changed under European doctrine and we now find the division between criminal and civil clearly marked in most African judicial systems.

## Subsistence

The evidence of travellers shows that at the time of the European penetration of Africa in the last century the people's subsistence was simple and precarious. In the course of the ages the African had managed to adapt himself reasonably successfully to his environment; but he had never learned to dominate it. He got his living partly from agriculture, partly from cattle raising, sometimes exclusively from one or the other, occasionally adding to his larder and his wardrobe by hunting wild animals. Yet only in the last pursuit was he really successful. In a continent where rainfall is either excessive or scanty, where the soil is on the whole rather poor, where soil erosion and soil exhaustion are widespread, where pasture is seasonal, traditional agricultural and pastoral habits tended to accentuate the adverse effects of these factors rather than to mitigate them. Among comparatively few Africans was it the practice to irrigate or rotate their crops, conserve the soil or fertilize it (except by wasteful cutting and burning of forest), store winter feed for their stock, or cull their herds. When the soil or pasture was overworked in one place, the African simply moved away from the desert that he had made and went to make one elsewhere.[1]

The neglect of elementary animal husbandry is all the more surprising because cattle play a vital part in African life. They are not only, or even primarily, regarded as an economic asset. They are

---

[1] There are of course exceptions. To quote one known personally to the writer, the people of Ukara Island on Lake Victoria use their land in a very efficient and ingenious manner.

a social factor of first importance. They constitute an essential ingredient in the institution of marriage as dowry paid by the bridegroom to the bride's family. In former Ruanda-Urundi the custody of another man's cattle established a feudal relationship between the two men. In many tribes cattle are the object of a cult and are regarded with almost religious veneration.[1] Many Africans will not sell cattle except when forced by dire necessity to do so, and do not habitually slaughter them for food. The result of this attitude is increasing pressure on scanty grazing and water. This is a commonplace of African agronomy and need not be laboured here.

In the domestic arts, houses were built with what lay nearest to hand, mud and sticks and grass, a ready prey for the white ants but easily built and easily abandoned. Clothes, if worn at all, were of simple, homely materials, such as bark cloth and hides, and here it may be said that by means of crude but very thorough processes the African contrived to make clothes that were both elegant and durable. Machinery in the modern sense did not exist. In one way only had the African risen above his circumstances. There is in him a boisterous vitality that has enabled him down the ages to triumph as a race (though many individuals succumb) over bad and insufficient food, disease, numberless germs and parasites, and all the disadvantages of a bad climate. To these are now added diseases acquired by contact with aliens. Before the coming of European government this vitality was the African's only protection. Now, while admitting that civilization brings ills of its own, we may expect that with European medicine to help him, and with education, child welfare guidance, and better economic conditions generally, the African will proliferate exceedingly.

*The Arts*

It is perhaps not too much to say that the African is the most musical person on earth. This does not mean that he has yet produced a Beethoven or a Bach, as far as we know. But it does mean that his whole being, his whole life, is permeated with music. There can hardly be an African who is not familiar with, and incapable of adding to the folk music of his community. It is a gift that is fostered at a very early age, and children of the tenderest years are expected to take part in music making, in singing and in dancing. New songs, new music are constantly being made, for the African sings about everything and about everybody. This racial trait persists

[1] Especially among the Nilotes and Nilo-Hamites (pp. 10, 164).

far from the ancestral homeland, and the Calypso of the West Indian is just another form of the same art which is practised in any African village at any time of day or night. Europeans have unwisely tried to teach music to these intensely musical people, but the African genius has been equal to the test and the children whom one might hear in school hours singing the Tanganyika national anthem to the tune of Clementine[1] revert quite naturally to the ancient musical themes of their race in their homes at night.

With music and singing goes dancing. Just as he always sings about his business, so is the African under compulsion to translate all his activities into rhythmic movement. An African dance is a thing of power, full-blooded, sensual, witty, dramatic; the movements are exuberant and often complicated; the rhythm of the dancers and the drums subtle and faultless. The effect is tremendously exciting—and quite inimitable. Modern European manifestations of the neo-African craze, from the early jazz of the 'twenties to the naïve wiggle-waggle of today, are sad imitations of the real thing.

In the plastic arts the true Negroes of West Africa are outstanding and the sculpture of Ife and Benin is famous. Some Bantu tribes of the Congo have produced a wealth of wood-carving. In other parts of Bantu Africa where the indigenous tradition is not so strong artists and craftsmen are coming forward under foreign influence. Recent years have witnessed the development in several parts of Africa of a literature European in language and form but African in inspiration. The ancient artistic tradition of Ethiopia expresses itself in painting, fine writing and illumination, architecture and music and is deeply transfused with Christianity. Ethiopian literature also finds its focus and inspiration in the Christian religion.

## African Languages[2]

Apart from European languages introduced by recent immigrants, the languages of Africa can be divided into five families: the Sudanic, the Bantu, the Hamitic, the Semitic and the Bushman.

The Sudanic family reaches in an irregular band across Africa from Cape Verde to the confines of Ethiopia, with a number of outliers in the territories of other families, such as Kunama in the

---

[1] This is a memory of the past.
[2] The reader who wishes to be more fully informed is advised to consult Werner: *The Language Families of Africa.*

north of Ethiopia, Luo at the north-eastern end of Lake Victoria, and Mbugu in Tanzania. This family comprises over two hundred languages, including most of the better known ones of West Africa, but not Hausa.

The Bantu family spreads over the whole of southern and central Africa, north-west as far as the Cameroon Republic and north-east to the Tana River. This enormous field is interrupted by enclaves of other languages to which we shall refer below, while there are also languages of a Bantu character, described as semi-Bantu, in the Sudanic area of West Africa. There may be as many as 250 Bantu languages and a great many dialects. Some of these languages differ from each other no more than, say, Italian from French but they all have unmistakable common characteristics and there is no true Bantu language that is not immediately recognizable as a member of the family.

The Ancient Egyptians spoke a Hamitic language. So did the Libyans and the Numidians and so do some of the people of North Africa today. Hamitic languages are now found in their purest form in north-east Africa, which is the home of several Hamitic peoples such as the Somali and the Galla. It should be mentioned that the Hamitic languages show some indications of a remote affinity with Semitic, as if in the very distant past they had been one branch which later became divided.

The most ancient African representative of the Semitic family is Ge'ez, the old liturgical language of Ethiopia. The most widely spoken is Arabic, which is the language of North Africa and of Egypt and has spread far south into the Sudan. Arabic has profoundly influenced the Hausa and Swahili languages of West and East Africa respectively, and is closely associated with the spread of Islam.

Finally, we come to the Bushman languages, spoken by the Bushmen of South Africa. These are politically unimportant, but, it appears, linguistically very interesting. One characteristic, a number of so-called 'clicks', sounds produced by the tongue, teeth and lips, has been much discussed. There are other tribes in Africa who use clicks: the Hottentots, the Zulu and the Xosa of South Africa, and the Sandawi of East Africa.[1] Comparatively little is known about the Bushman languages, and there may be little time left in which to study them. They seem to be giving way to the

[1] The Zulu and the Xosa may have acquired their 'clicks' from the Bushmen or the Hottentots.

C

languages of the surrounding populations, European and African, and will no doubt disappear altogether before very long.

African languages have for many years been a subject of study and research. Much of the pioneer work was done by amateurs, missionaries and administrators who needed to know the language of the people among whom they laboured and took the trouble to record it. Now African languages appear in the syllabus of universities in this and other countries, and trained academics have introduced to this study a whole apparatus of new techniques. African languages are now recognized as being highly organized and flexible, in many respects well adapted to render precise meanings, and often exceedingly melodious. Furthermore they are the vehicles of a very rich folk-lore. To speak an African language well requires time and plenty of hard work but the task is by no means insuperable. For those who intend to live and to work in Africa the effort is well worthwhile. To the missionary and teacher, the social worker, the engineer, the research student, the expatriate official and to many others, a command of the language is a tool of the trade. Others to whom this knowledge is not so important will be able, through communication with ordinary folk in the language of the country, to open for themselves a window on a new world.

## HISTORY OF AFRICA

### Ancient Egypt

Some five miles west of Cairo in the desert of Egypt stand three great pyramids. Weathered and rough and stripped of their former marble casing but otherwise intact, they still stand, grey and massive, constituting, with the Sphinx, the best known symbols of Ancient Egypt.

Though palaeolithic tools and neolithic graves have been found in the Nile valley, the history of Egypt begins 'officially' with Mena, first king of the first dynasty, who is also the first king of Egypt about whom anything is known historically. The division of the Egyptian kings into numbered dynasties is due to the historian Manetho (c. 270 B.C.) who wrote a history of Egypt from the records then in existence. His manuscript was deposited in the great library of Alexandria and is presumed to have been destroyed when the Moslems burnt the library in A.D. 642. Some fragments, however, copied by other historians, remain.

The authorities vary as to the dates of the earlier dynasties, some placing the first as far back as 5000 B.C. and beyond, and others as late as 3000 B.C. Whatever the date it is quite certain that the first dynasty marks, not the beginning of a civilization, but the continuation of one that is already well developed and already old. Carvers and gold workers were wonderfully skilful, hieroglyphic writing (the beautiful writing of Ancient Egypt) was coming into common use, and there was an advanced religion, with a well organized priestly hierarchy.

The practice of building pyramids, for a purpose that is still not altogether clear, was begun by the kings of the third dynasty. Zoser built the 'step' pyramid of Saqqara and Snefru built one pyramid at Medum and another at Dahsur. The three great pyramids of Giza were built respectively by three fourth dynasty kings, Khufu, Khafra and Men-Kau-Re.

Most of our knowledge of Ancient Egypt is derived from inscriptions and works of art in the tombs of the kings and nobles, from buildings such as temples and pyramids, and from papyri or from monuments. Many of the tombs so far uncovered—very few compared to the thousands that must still lie buried in the sand—had been rifled before they were found by archaeologists. Tomb robbery is a very ancient craft in Egypt and began in the time of the Pharaohs themselves. Nevertheless we have enough to provide us with much reliable knowledge of the history, religion and culture of this humane and artistic people, far more, for instance, than we have about our own ancestors of a much less remote period, who were neither artistic nor, probably, humane. Unfortunately these are matters on which we cannot dwell in a book of this kind, and those who wish to learn more about these people, their writing and painting, their art and science, their religion from which so much sprang, should consult one or two authoritative works on Egyptology and should also, if possible, see the Egyptian collections in the great museums of Europe or in the Cairo museum. It will be sufficient here to note that the Nile Valley, four or five thousand years before our era, was the nursery of one of the most remarkable, and certainly one of the most enduring civilizations ever so far evolved by man.

Egyptian civilization was carried by traders and soldiers far up the Nile into continental Africa. The ruins of Meroë, about a hundred miles downstream from Khartoum, testify to a culture closely derived from Egypt. The Meroitic kingdom, which occupied the country enclosed in the bend of the Nile between the fourth and

sixth cataracts, provided Egypt with its twenty-fifth or 'Ethiopian'
dynasty and rose to a position of great power and influence. It fell
from this position in the fourth century A.D. when Meroë was
destroyed by the kingdom of Aksum in what is now northern
Ethiopia.

The history of Ancient Egypt may be said to have come to an end
with the annexation of the country by Alexander the Great in
332 B.C. if indeed we do not date it two centuries earlier, at the time
of the Persian invasion. But even at the later date, the old religion
had enough vitality left to cause Alexander, no doubt as an act of
expediency, to travel to the Siwa Oasis and worship at the temple of
Jupiter Ammon. Perhaps from our point of view the most important
feature of the Ptolemaic period that followed was the inscription on
stone steles of a decree that special honours be paid to Ptolemy V.
One of these steles was the Rosetta Stone, found by a French
engineer officer not far from the town of Rashid or Rosetta in 1799
and now in the British Museum. The Stone is inscribed in three
characters, first the hieroglyphic, which was the old picture writing
employed for nearly all state and ceremonial documents intended to
be seen by the general public; second, the demotic, that is the con-
ventional, abbreviated and modified form of hieratic (a cursive form
of hieroglyphic which was in use in the Ptolemaic period); and
third, Greek. The hieroglyphic text corresponds to the last twenty-
eight lines of the Greek text, and since the Greek character was, of
course, perfectly known, the Stone thus provided the key to the
deciphering of the hieroglyphic.

As every schoolboy knows (at least every boy who has read
Shakespeare), the line of the Ptolemies ended with Cleopatra, and
Egypt became a Roman province. After many vicissitudes, a
weakened and impoverished country was easily conquered in
A.D. 639–640 by a Moslem army commanded by Amr ibn al Asi, a
general of Omar, the second caliph. At this stage, the beginning of a
new era, we leave Egypt for the time being and move westwards to
North Africa.

## Berbers and Carthaginians

The first people of North Africa of whom we have historical
knowledge are a race of light-skinned Hamites whom the Arabs
called Berbers,[1] who later provided Europeans with the name

[1] The etymology of the word is not settled. Some say it is derived from Arabic
'barbara', to talk noisily or confusedly, others favour derivation from a Greek and
Latin word describing anyone who was not a Greek or a Roman.

Barbary for the whole of the North African coast. Phoenicians began to colonize the coast about the twelfth century B.C., first founding settlements at Leptis, Oea, later Tripoli, and Sabratha in Libya, and then moving westwards to found their most important North African city, Carthage near modern Tunis. By the sixth century B.C. Carthage was the prosperous centre of Carthaginian power, wielding supreme influence from Syrtica in the east to the Straits of Gibraltar in the west. The Carthaginians were essentially sailors and merchants and their occupation of the coast was probably neither intensive nor continuous. On the other hand they undertook immensely long voyages. Carthaginian vessels sailed north as far as Britain for the tin of the Cornish mines and a Carthaginian admiral, Hanno, sailed round the West coast of Africa as far as Sierra Leone, calling at many places and founding towns on the way. Her wealth and power founded on maritime commerce, Carthage was mistress of the Mediterranean.

Much of the history of Carthage is the story of her wars with the Greeks in Sicily and with the Romans. The Sicily wars continued intermittently and with varying fortunes from the beginning of the fifth century B.C. for about 200 years. The mighty struggle with Rome, the so-called Punic wars, began in 264 B.C. and covered a span of 118 years. These were the wars that threw up one of the great figures of world history, Hannibal, the Carthaginian general (247–183 B.C.), a man of extraordinary character and powers of organization, no doubt the most dangerous enemy that Rome in her great days ever encountered. The Punic wars came to an end in 146 B.C. with the fall of Carthage to Rome and the total destruction of the city. The supremacy of the Mediterranean passed to Rome.

The early history of eastern Libya or Cyrenaica is different from that of other parts of North Africa. As in the rest of the region the earliest inhabitants of whom we have any record were Berbers. They seem to have been more or less continuously at war with Egypt, and Ancient Egyptian reliefs commemorating the victories of the Pharaohs often show Libyans in the most unfortunate situations—being hit on the head with clubs, crushed under chariots, or being led into captivity. There is no firm record here of Carthaginian colonization. Cyrene was founded by Greeks, who then built four more cities, Berenice (Benghazi), Barca (il Merj), Apollonia, and Teucheira or Arsinoë (Tocra). At the beginning of the third century B.C. the country became known as the Pentapolis from the federation of the five cities. Cyrenaica formed part of the empire of

Alexander the Great and after his death in 323 B.C. came under the
dominion of his successors in Egypt, the Ptolemies. The last
Ptolemaic ruler, Apion, who died in 96 B.C., bequeathed the country
to Rome, and it became a province of the Roman Empire. (*Plate* 70)

## The Romans in North Africa

The Romans tried at first to restrict the occupation of their newly
conquered territories to a comparatively small area round Carthage,
which they called the Province of Africa. But they soon found that
it is impossible to limit the responsibility of government at will, that
one commitment inevitably leads to another, and that no sooner has
one frontier been established than it becomes necessary to establish
another wider one to protect the first. After several conflicts with
rebellious tribes, Numidians, Garamantes and others, the Romans
extended their rule over the whole coast from Cyrene to the
Atlantic and southwards to the Fezzan.

The Roman domination of North Africa lasted for nearly six
hundred years and was a period of great material prosperity, as
many magnificent remains of towns and buildings testify. Agriculture and forestry were encouraged, public works developed, trading settlements grew into prosperous and beautiful cities, all under
the protection of garrisons deep in the desert at places like Bu
Ngem, Ghadames, and even Garama, the modern Germa, capital
of the powerful and warlike Garamantes. It is also worth remembering that North Africa gave Rome a great emperor, Septimius
Severus (A.D. 146–A.D. 211) who was born at Leptis.     (*Plate* 69)

North Africa's connection with Christianity is an early one. From
the many Jewish communities settled along the coast there was 'one
Simon, a Cyrenian, coming out of the country', on whom was laid
the Cross 'that he might bear it after Jesus', and in the account of
the Pentecost in the Acts of the Apostles men from 'the parts of
Libya about Cyrene' were among those who received the gift of
tongues. Tertullian, creator of Christian Latin literature, and St.
Cyprian, bishop and martyr, were both of Carthage in the Roman
province, while St. Augustine of Hippo, one of the greatest fathers
of the Latin Church, was born at Tagaste in Numidia.

## Decline and Fall

With the decline of the Roman power North Africa fell on bad
times. The troubles began in the fourth century with the rebellion
of the Donatists, a schismatic sect representing in some sort the

masses against Church and State. In A.D. 428 the Vandals with Genseric at their head poured into North Africa from Spain and occupied Carthage. The Donatists made common cause with them. Genseric had the sense to preserve the old administrative machinery and was thus able to maintain law and order, but the country was once more plunged into anarchy when he died in 477. A Byzantine army under Belisarius liberated the country from the Vandals but this victory brought no peace. The bridgehead of civilization in Roman Africa had always been a narrow one. Inland were savage tribes always ready to take up arms against the settled communities on the coast. As long as the Pax Romana extended as far south as the Fezzan, the inhabitants of the coastal towns could sleep sound in their beds. But those times were over. Now the barbarians of the interior watched the Byzantines and the Vandals at war and rose against the victor. The revolt was suppressed with difficulty and the Byzantines did what they could to reorganize the life of the province. Proper administration was re-established and Christianity, after its long subordination to the Vandals and their Donatist allies, was restored and extended to the inland tribes. But the spirit had gone from the place, the rulers had little faith in their task and the people were apathetic. When the Arabs invaded North Africa in 642 only the Berber tribes, with their passionate love of liberty, offered much resistance.

## The Arab Invasions

Until the seventh century the Arabs lived pretty well within the boundaries of Arabia, some as town dwellers, some as nomads in the desert. About 571 there was born among them a man named Mohamed who, proclaiming himself to be the prophet of the one God, founded Islam, 'submission' (to the will of God), one of the great religions of the world. After the prophet's death in 632 the Arabs, aflame with their new faith, burst out of their frontiers and poured into Africa. They invaded Egypt in 639 and subdued the country in 641. They met with little opposition. Egyptian Christianity was torn by dissensions, and its hold on the masses was certainly not strong enough to inspire in them a spirit of resistance. Similarly, when the Arabs resumed their westward march in 642 they easily overran Cyrenaica and Tripolitania. Here and there the Christians went down fighting (the town of Tripoli withstood a siege of six months before it was captured) but it was the Berbers who put up the most obstinate resistance, actually succeeding at one stage in

driving the invaders back to Egypt. But this success was only temporary and early in the eighth century the Arabs drove across the
country from east to west and in 711, strongly reinforced by
Berbers, invaded Spain and Portugal and there developed a remarkable civilization which has exerted great influence on all aspects of
life in the Iberian peninsula. The Arab conquest of North Africa
was completed in the eleventh century by two tribes of marauding
nomads from Arabia, the Beni Hilal and Beni Soleim. The Beni
Soleim stayed in Cyrenaica but the Beni Hilal passed on to the
west, harrying and destroying wherever they went. The devastation
that they caused was such that the country has never fully recovered
from it.[1]

Although the Berbers managed to an astonishing degree to preserve their purity of race and in some places their language, the
greater number in the end adopted the Arab religion, dress and
speech and many Arab customs. Christianity virtually disappeared
although it had survived further east in Egypt, and in Ethiopia
which was never conquered. The effect of the invasions was to
stamp North Africa indelibly with the Arab mark, and to turn it into
the Maghreb or western part of the Arab world.

## Morocco

The Arabs called Morocco Maghreb al Aqsa, which means the
Far West. It is a country of mountains and narrow plains with a
plentiful rainfall, very different from the country through which
they had passed on their long march from Arabia. Here they established the Idrisid dynasty, a branch of the family of the Prophet,
and contemporary with Haroun al Raschid, Caliph of Bagdad. Here
also they built the city of Fez, intellectual centre of the Maghreb.
In the eleventh century Morocco was invaded by the Almoravids
(al murabitun), Berbers and puritan Moslems, who built Marrakesh,
extended their rule as far as Algiers and overran Moslem Spain.
The Almoravids were succeeded by the Almohades who further
enlarged their dominions, making them stretch from the Tagus to
Tripoli. An empire so extended could not survive for long. In the
thirteenth century the Maghreb split into three parts. The governor
of the old Province of Africa proclaimed his independence and so
established the Hafsid dynasty; the Abd al Wahid dynasty took the

---

[1] 'The most serious consequence of the devastation was that enormous areas went
permanently out of cultivation and the desert crept in. Directly or through their
herds, these wild Arabs also destroyed most of the forests . . .' Bovill, *The Golden
Trade of the Moors*, p. 58.

central Maghreb round Algiers; and the Merinids succeeded the Almohades in Morocco. The present reigning dynasty in Morocco, that of the Filali, which originates from Tafilalet on the Saharan side of the Atlas Mountains, came to power in the seventeenth century.

## The Reconquest of Spain

The Arab occupation of Spain lasted for about 500 years. Spanish Christianity, where it did not compound with the invaders, retreated to the north where the idea of an ultimate reconquest was fostered and kept alive. The occupation was punctuated by frequent outbreaks of fighting but was on the whole marked by tolerance and a spirit of 'co-existence' on both sides. Tolerance, however, later gave way to fanaticism. On the Moslem side this was due to the coming of the Almoravids, who had no sympathy with Christians, and on the Christian side to the arrival of monks and warriors from France who communicated to the idea of reconquest the spirit of a crusade. In the thirteenth century the Christians vigorously assaulted Moorish Spain and by the middle of the century the kingdom of Granada was the only Spanish state under Moslem control. It survived for 250 years before falling to the Spaniards in 1492 after a hard-fought war. During this time there was steady pressure on those Moslems who remained in Christian Spain either to abandon their faith, or go to Granada, or leave Spain altogether. Many chose the last alternative, and in 1610 the remaining Moriscos, Moslems who had become converted to Christianity, were expelled from Spain.

## Trans-Saharan trade—the Empires of West Africa.[1]

Long before the dawn of Islam, the people of the North African littoral had traded southwards across the Sahara with the Negroes of West Africa, exchanging salt from the mines of Taghaza, Taodeni and Taotek for gold and slaves. This trade was carried by camel-caravan along recognized trade routes running from the cities of North Africa through the oases and the salt mines to the towns on the southern edge of the desert. There were three principal routes: a western one from Morocco to the great northern bend of the Niger and the country to the west of it, a central one from Tunisia to the country between the Niger and Lake Chad, and an eastern one from Tripoli and Egypt to Lake Chad. The trade they carried flourished

[1] Much of the material for this section comes from Bovill, *The Golden Trade of the Moors*, and Fage, *A History of West Africa : an introductory survey*.

down the centuries until the arrival of European traders on the
west coast and anarchy in the western Sudan[1] combined to
turn the direction of trade south towards the sea and commerce
with the north declined.

From about the beginning of the Christian era, North Africans
began to migrate across the Sahara and to settle in numbers north
of the Niger and Senegal Rivers, establishing dominion over the
Negroes whom they found there and gradually merging with them.
These migrations were intensified by the Arab invasions of North
Africa from the eighth century onwards, but in due course the
Arabs themselves came south of the Sahara, and the mixed people
of the region, products of the fusion between Berber and Negro,
became converted to Islam.

The outcome of these invasions from North Africa was a succession of great territorial empires in the country north of the West
African forest. These empires were founded either by the fair-
skinned invaders themselves or by Negro or semi-Negro peoples
who had learnt the ways of successful warfare from their contact
with North Africans. The secrets of success were a social organization of a military character and the possession of horses and camels.
The Negro tribes were no match for people endowed with these
assets, and the conquerors extended their empires rapidly, only
stopping at the forest, where cavalry was not effective. The earliest
of the empires of which we have any substantial knowledge is
Ghana, which may have been founded, perhaps by Cyrenaican
Jews, about A.D. 200. Ghana was absorbed into the Sosso Empire of
Kaniaga at the beginning of the thirteenth century, and Kaniaga in
turn was swallowed by the great empire of Mali, which reached up
into the Sahara and stretched from Futa Jallon in the south-west
to Gao on the middle Niger. Mali's greatest days were during the
first part of the fourteenth century, after which came a steady
decline; and as the greatness of Mali waned, so did that of the
Songhai kingdom of Gao gradually develop. Towards the end of the
sixteenth century, however, the Moroccans, not content with the
trans-Saharan trade, sent an army against Gao in the hope of securing the gold of West Africa at its source. The Songhai empire,
weakened by wars and dynastic quarrels, was no match for the
invaders and soon collapsed. But the Moroccans had quite misunder-

---

[1] 'Sudan' is used in this context to describe the great savannah belt that stretches
across the continent south of the great northern deserts from Senegal to Ethiopia.
The term 'western Sudan' covers broadly the sub-Saharan interior of the West
African region described in Chapter Seven.

stood the true nature of the wealth of Gao. This depended, not on possession of the gold mines, which were far away in the south, but on trade with the people in whose country the mines were. The Moroccans were in no position to conquer the gold-producing areas or to ensure the peaceful conditions necessary for the pursuit of the trade. Their victory was therefore a hollow one but the army managed to maintain itself in the western Sudan for nearly a hundred years, living on tribute from the local chiefs, electing its own pashas, and keeping up its numbers by recruiting Negroes. As time went on the authority of the pashas waned, the efficiency of the army decayed, and by the end of the seventeenth century such political authority as there was in the western Sudan had passed to powerful native rulers.

Between the Black Volta and the great bend of the Niger River a comparatively small group of invaders from the neighbourhood of Lake Chad, possibly refugees from Berber invasions, founded a number of states called the Mossi-Dagomba States. These were more stable than most of the great sub-Saharan empires and when the Europeans arrived at the end of the nineteenth century were still ruled by direct descendants of the men who had founded them 500 years before. Further east, other states were established by Hamite-dominated Negroes who spoke a language called Hausa. These Hausa states were conquered by Fulani between 1804 and 1810 in a *jihad* (war of religion corresponding to a crusade) and so became the Fulani emirates which the Europeans encountered when they entered northern Nigeria in the latter part of the century.

*Europeans in West Africa*

The title of 'Navigator' bestowed on Prince Henry of Portugal (1394–1460) was scarcely deserved, since the Prince himself never in his life went further afield than Tangier. Yet his services to African discovery can hardly be exaggerated. He drew together skilled geographers, founded a school of navigation and an observatory, and promoted and equipped expeditions to places hitherto unknown. During his life and after his death the Portuguese made a series of brilliant voyages of exploration down the coast of Africa, which towards the end of the fifteenth century were to take them round the Cape of Good Hope and into the Indian Ocean.

Henry's enthusiasm for exploration sprang from several motives. He knew all about the gold trade between West and North Africa and wanted to tap the source by out-flanking the Sahara. Then, he

hoped to find a way round Africa to establish contact with the
fabulous monarch Prester John of Ethiopia. Such a contact would
be doubly meritorious: in itself it would tend to the unity of
Christendom, and at the same time it would outflank the Moslems,
who stood astride the road to the east. Finally, Henry may have
been moved by sheer zeal for knowledge. The voyages initiated by
him were not isolated ventures, but formed part of a definite plan.
All the results were collated and compared, and each expedition,
armed with the accumulated experience of its predecessors, was
part of a scientifically organized system of exploration. As the
Portuguese pushed further south along the coast, so perhaps would
their plans develop and expand, until, with the rounding of the
Cape and with the Indian Ocean open before them, they had the
trade of the Indies almost within their grasp.

Meanwhile on the west coast Portuguese settlements multiplied.
They were usually small, consisting merely of trading stations or
off-shore islands, though at some places substantial forts were built,
as for instance at Elmina on the Gold Coast. Small as they were,
the stations had great commercial influence, and Portuguese trade
on the coast, especially on the Gold Coast, was of considerable
importance, and it was moreover a trade in which the Portuguese at
first had no rivals. This preponderance was of short duration. It was
challenged quite early by the Castilians and towards the end of the
sixteenth century several other European nations set out to break
the Portuguese monopoly and to establish trading stations of their
own. First the Dutch, then the English and the French, not to
mention Brandenburgers, Swedes and Danes, all threw themselves
into the contest with zest. Except for French attempts to develop
the trade of the Senegal River, European traders did not go inland
themselves, but contented themselves with establishing trading
stations on the coast. The main function of these stations was to
hold the slaves, who constituted the chief article of trade, between
their delivery from up-country by native slavers and the time when a
ship was ready to take them across the Atlantic.

The arrival of Europeans on the coast brought about a profound
change in the condition of the hinterland. West African contacts
with the outside world had hitherto been through North Africa.
The empires created and ruled by the Berbers and others stopped
short at the forest fringe, and though indeed the northerners visited
the forest peoples, it was only to trade and to raid for slaves and not
to settle. Now the direction of trade changed towards the coast, and

as the forest tribesmen flung themselves heartily into the slave-
raiding game they acquired firearms, became wealthy and strong
and founded states comparable with those whose connections were
with the north. Such, for instance, were Oyo, Ashanti, Dahomey
and Benin. Like the northern states, these were formed by comparatively small groups of alien immigrants, and their organization
was in many respects similar to that of Ghana, Mali and Gao. They
also had considerable resemblances one to another, since they were
formed from people with a common cultural tradition. And as they
rose by the Slave Trade, so by the same accursed traffic they fell.
Their frenzied participation in the Trade led them into ruinous
wars, corrupted their rulers, promoted internal divisions, decimated
the peasantry, and inhibited the development of any proper
economic order.

In 1578 young King Sebastian of Portugal, obsessed with the
idea of a crusade, dragged his reluctant people into a war with the
Moors of Morocco. He met complete defeat at al Ksar al Kebir
(Alcazar) where an army of 26,000 Portuguese was annihilated.
The King himself was killed and with him the flower of Portuguese
chivalry. The direct result was that in 1581 the Crown of Portugal
passed to Spain and the Portuguese overseas empire collapsed.
Though Portugal regained independence in 1640, she had already
been supplanted by the Dutch as dominant power on the west coast.
About the middle of the seventeenth century other European
nations, particularly the British and the French, were attracted by
West African trade. Following the Dutch example they created
national trading companies with charters giving them the monopoly
of their nation's trade on the coast. The Dutch lost ground to the
British and the French between whom there presently ensued a
bitter fight for world power. The consequence for West Africa of
the Anglo-French wars of the eighteenth century was that Britain
became the dominant power in West African trade.

It must be emphasized that this predominance was not accompanied by extensive territorial possessions. Competition between
the nations was for trade, not for sovereignty. In 1764 the British
made an unsuccessful attempt to constitute a crown colony, that of
Senegambia, but in the main European colonization was an affair
of forts and factories necessary for operating and defending trade,
on land recognized as belonging to the natives. The companies
regarded themselves as tenants of the local chiefs, without whose
goodwill and assistance trade could not be carried on.

## Arabs in East Africa

There is an early 'pilot' or guide to trade and navigation called the *Periplus of the Erythraean sea*, compiled about A.D. 80 by a Greek merchant seaman, which describes in detail the voyage down the Red Sea and the African coast of the Indian Ocean. Many of the geographical features mentioned in the *Periplus* may be easily identified, but the interest of the guide lies rather in what the author tells us of the politics and commerce of the day. We learn that the people were apparently of negroid stock and ruled by chiefs. But it also appears that these chiefs had long been under some kind of Arab suzerainty and that there was already a well-established trade carried by Arab and Indian ships between Africa, Arabia and India.

For several hundred years after the *Periplus* information about East Africa is scanty, but there is enough evidence to show that inter-continental traffic prospered and spread. Between the fifth and sixteenth centuries the Arabs were masters of the Indian Ocean. East African trade reached beyond Malaya to China and there was a large Arab 'colony' in Canton. Nor was the trade by any means one way. Indian ships called at East African towns, and although there is no certain evidence of *direct* contact with China, Chinese books often refer to East Africa and Chinese coins are found on the East African coast.

In due course, probably in quite early times, the Arabs proceeded from trade to colonization. We do not know when the first Arab settlements were founded or where, but the process was no doubt a gradual one. By the early middle ages there was already a string of Arab colonies from Mogadishu to Sofala, each one a city state usually at odds with one or more of the others. At no time was there anything like an Arab 'empire' of East Africa. The nearest approach to unity was 'the overlordship exercised for varying periods over a varying number of other towns by the one which happened at the time to be the strongest or the most aggressive'.[1] The unwarlike tribes of the coast submitted to the colonists without much difficulty. Intermarriage quickly took place and produced the Swahili, the mixed, indefinable people of the coast. The Arabs attempted no systematic exploration or colonization of the hinterland. Their only interest in the tribes of the interior was trade; and if in the course of their trading expeditions they established permanent inland settlements, these too were not for

[1] R. Coupland, *East Africa and its Invaders*, p. 26.

administration, nor for the establishment of plantations, nor for the exploitation of natural resources, nor for anything else but trade. Unhappily the principal and most valuable article of trade was slaves, of whom great numbers were taken to Arabia and India and a few as far as China.

As the years went by the Arabs of East Africa attained a state of considerable prosperity, living in large towns, wearing fine clothes and surrounded by luxury. The great Arab traveller Ibn Battuta, visiting East Africa in the fourteenth century, was most impressed by their wealth and civilization, describing Kilwa as 'one of the most beautiful and best built towns', and Mogadishu, where he was well entertained by its hospitable and pious people, as an 'exceedingly large city'. This advanced, if predominantly material, civilization was almost destroyed by East Africa's next invaders, the Portuguese.

## The Portuguese on the East Coast

The west coast of Africa, valuable as its trade proved to be, was only a stage in the Portuguese plan of expansion. In 1485 Diego Cão reached Cape Cross in latitude 21° 50′ S. In 1488 Bartholomeu Diaz, blown far to the south and turning back towards the north-east, found that the coastline was now running east. He had rounded Africa without knowing it. He got as far as Algoa Bay and sighted the Cape on the return journey. In little more than twenty years after this significant discovery the Portuguese had achieved the mastery of the east coast of Africa. The assault began after a reconnaissance by Vasco da Gama in 1497–99. First da Gama himself in 1502 compelled the Sultan of Kilwa to acknowledge the supremacy of the King of Portugal; in 1503 Ruy Lourenço Ravasco obtained the submission of Zanzibar. In 1505 a fleet of twenty ships under Almeida occupied Sofala and Kilwa and destroyed Mombasa; in 1506 another fleet of fourteen ships under Tristão da Cunha and Albuquerque persuaded Lamu to submit and destroyed Oja and Barawa, sparing Mogadishu only because the sailing season was drawing to an end and time was short. In 1507 Mozambique was built up into a permanent settlement, with church, fort, quarters for garrison and staff. By 1509, when a governor-general was appointed, occupation of the east coast was complete. Combined with footholds at the mouth of the Red Sea and in the Persian Gulf it assured the Portuguese command of the Indian Ocean.

The effect of the Portuguese conquests on the Arab colonies was disastrous. The Portuguese claimed and enforced a rigid monopoly of the sea trade of the Indian Ocean, the old Arab connection with India was cut, and even coastal shipping was made as difficult as possible. On land the Portuguese employed every effort to destroy Arab commercial relations with the inland tribes, but made no more impression themselves on the interior than the Arabs before them. The Portuguese conquests therefore, while destroying the wealth and power of the Arabs, had few positive results.

With the annexation of Portugal by Spain, and the collapse of her empire in the first half of the seventeenth century, the Portuguese lost their hold on the eastern trade. Their ejection from most of East Africa was soon to follow. The Arab communities had always hated their Portuguese masters and there were several revolts which were sternly repressed. But the serious, and in the end fatal, challenge came from the Omani of the Arabian coast. After intermittent hostilities that lasted many years the Portuguese were finally driven out of the whole of the northern part of East Africa. By 1740 they retained only the southern strip, now the coast of their present colony of Portuguese East Africa, while the old and now decayed Arab settlements in the north came under the control of Oman.

### The Dutch in South Africa

On the 6th April 1652 Jan van Riebeeck, under instructions from the Dutch East India Company to establish a revictualling station at the Cape of Good Hope for ships plying to and from the Indies, dropped anchor in Table Bay. He was to build a fort sufficient for eighty men, to plant a garden, and to obtain cattle by trading with the natives. His instructions were quite plain: the place was simply to be 'a depot of provisions for the ships' and nothing else.

Van Riebeeck found two native races in occupation of the surrounding countryside, the Bushmen and the Hottentots. Only the latter had cattle and it was with them that he had to do business. Trade with the tribes in the immediate vicinity was not altogether satisfactory, and in order to find fresh meat which he simply had to have in order to fulfil his duty of victualling the ships, van Riebeeck was constrained to send exploratory parties further and further inland. Thus in 1655 Dutch expansion in South Africa had already begun. In 1657 the Dutch East India Company—still for the purpose of ensuring supplies for ships—planted a few farmers near the settlement. They were to be free (that is to say they were not ser-

vants of the Company) but they were subject to various controls
which considerably curtailed their independence. These so-called
'free burghers' were intended merely to be purveyors to the
Company. It was not until twenty years later that the Company,
hitherto on the whole opposed to immigration, made any real effort
to encourage immigration and settlement. In 1679 and in the following years farms were given out in full ownership, the village of
Stellenbosch was founded, local government instituted, young
women were imported to provide colonists with wives, a group of
French Huguenots arrived and were gradually absorbed in the
Dutch population, and by the beginning of the eighteenth century
there were about 1,700 Europeans, men, women and children. As
early as 1657 van Riebeeck had tried to meet the demand for labour
by importing slaves and in succeeding years the number of slaves
owned by the 'free burghers' increased considerably. In 1717 the
decision was deliberately taken to develop the colony with slaves
rather than with free white labour. This decision was a fateful one
and had far reaching consequences.[1] Meanwhile the demand for
cattle encouraged cattle farming and as this is an occupation requir-
ing much land the colonists had to spread out to find it. Land was
unlimited then, the only obstacle to its peaceful occupation being
the Bushmen who were soon either killed or driven away. By the
end of the eighteenth century the 'refreshment station' at the Cape
had grown into a colony extending over a sizeable part of the modern
Cape Province with a population consisting of Europeans,
'coloured', as people of mixed descent were called, and an assort-
ment of other races at Cape Town; a number of settled farmers
cultivating vines and corn with slave labour in the neighbourhood
of the capital; beyond them the cattle farmers or Trek Boers,
wandering further and further afield in search of grazing and water
and game, with their families and their cattle and their Hottentot
herdsmen.

These Trek Boers were a peculiar people. They were of Calvinist
stock, like the other South African Dutch, and their religion
derived more from the Old Testament than from the New. They
came to compare their own wanderings with those of the Children
of Israel and hence to look upon themselves in some sort as a
Chosen People, while the African tribes with whom they came
into conflict fell quite naturally into the category of Amalekites and
Amorites and all the other *ites* whom the Israelites in their various

[1] pp. 72-3.

D

aggressions ousted from the Promised Land. They admitted no kind of equality with the coloured races, whom they regarded as classified by Providence to be servants for ever. Living a poor, hard, isolated life remote from towns, self-sufficient to a fault and masters of their own rugged environment, the Trek Boers resented any form of government control. All they asked was to be plentifully supplied with ammunition, otherwise to be left alone. These were the people who in due course came up against the Bantu tribes pressing south. It should here be noted that in many parts of South Africa the Bantu occupation is hardly older than that of the Europeans and in some parts more recent. The contact between Bantu and Boer had several important consequences. The first was that the old custom of roaming at will was checked. The Bantu were also farmers and the Trek Boers, who had long held the belief that all free men had a right to as much land as they needed, found that beyond a certain point any more land had to be fought for. This led to raids, counter-raids and wars, which had unhappy consequences not only immediate but also remote. For it is not too much to say that many of the racial complications from which South Africa now suffers can be traced back to the frontier conditions of a hundred and fifty years ago.

In 1795 the French revolutionary armies invaded Holland and Great Britain occupied Cape Town by arrangement with the Dutch King. This occupation came to an end in 1802. Four years later, Great Britain, at war with Napoleon and fearing lest the key to the sea route to India should fall into enemy hands, occupied the colony again, this time for good.

## The Slave Trade

It seems that slave-trading is endemic in Africa. The author of the *Periplus* tells us that slaves 'of the better sort' were exported to Egypt from Ras Hafun[1] and slaves were an important element in the Moorish trade between West and North Africa across the Sahara. They also made a large contribution to the prosperity of the Arab settlements in East Africa in medieval times. In the seventeenth and eighteenth centuries European trade with the west coast of Africa was practically synonymous with slaving. The Portuguese began it, but other European nations soon followed suit and in 1652 the British joined in when Sir John Hawkins sold 300 Negroes from West Africa to Spaniards in the West Indies. From

---

[1] On the eastern coast of Somaliland.

then on British participation grew under the highest auspices and by 1770 the British were carrying about half the total number of slaves taken across the Atlantic.

The sufferings of these unfortunate Negroes during the process of transportation were appalling. The direct route to the West Indies, the Middle Passage as it was called, lay wholly within the tropical belt, and the slaves were confined in a narrow space below deck in stifling heat, squeezed together like sardines, with bad food, and of course with no proper sanitation. Numbers of them died, and all arrived in a most miserable condition, only about 50 per cent of those transported being fit for effective work.

Nor were these poor wretches the only ones to suffer. One of the ways in which slaves were obtained was by inducing native chiefs to make raids into one another's country in order to take prisoners. This added the horrors of inter-tribal war to a trade that was already bad enough. During the slaving season the whole coast was a scene of terror and violence and devastation. It is curious that so loathsome a traffic should so long have passed uncensured. There were several reasons for this. One, of course, was that the ordinary Englishman knew very little about it. Africa and the West Indies were a long way away, and those who ran the Trade were at no great pains to give publicity to the detail of their proceedings. The good people of those days had more excuse for their ignorance of colonial affairs than we have for ours. Then, the Trade paid very well and was an important part of our maritime commerce. Not for the first time, nor for the last, was immorality justified by economic and political necessity. Finally, the people interested in the Trade were a powerful caucus, not lightly to be challenged.

Still there were protests, chiefly at first from Quakers and other religious people. In 1761 American Quakers went so far as to disown all Friends who continued to take part in the Trade. But the first really important victory for the Abolitionists was the judgment given in 1772 by Chief Justice Mansfield in the case of James Somerset, brought at the instance of Granville Sharp. The effect of Mansfield's judgment was that as soon as a slave set foot on the soil of the British Isles he became free. This was all very well for slaves who were able to reach England, but it did nothing to help those shipped direct across the Atlantic from Africa. Abolition of the Trade in British dependencies was due mainly to the efforts of Thomas Clarkson (1760–1846), William Wilberforce (1759–1833) and a small band of associates. Their task was a long and uphill one, for there was much prejudice to combat, strong potential allies to persuade, powerful interests to overcome. Victory came in 1807 when a Bill was passed which 'utterly abolished, prohibited and declared to be unlawful' any dealing in slaves among British subjects and in British ships.[1] In 1811 slave-trading became a felony punishable with transportation, and in 1833 the institution of slavery itself was abolished in all British colonies.

The abolition of the British Slave Trade and of British slavery did not destroy the whole of the system everywhere. It continued to exist not only in Africa and Asia but also in parts of the world ruled by Europeans,[2] in the Portuguese, Spanish and French colonies, in the southern states of America and in South America. It is true that all the nations formerly engaged in the Trade passed laws and made treaties for its abolition. But these engagements existed only on paper, and violations were frequent and regular. An Englishman may claim with pride that it was largely due to British interference with the shipping of other nations (to a degree far beyond international usage) that the Trade was finally stopped. The last bastions fell when slavery itself was abolished in the United States in 1863, in Cuba between 1880 and 1886, and in Brazil between 1883 and 1888. The abolition of Arab slaving from East Africa will be dealt with in a later section.

## West Africa in the nineteenth century

One of the results of the campaign against the Slave Trade was the founding of the British colony of Sierra Leone. This was originally a settlement sponsored by the Abolitionists of slaves freed in England by the Mansfield judgment and of American Negroes who had fought on the British side in the War of Independence. The first expedition, made up of Negroes and white prostitutes, failed for lack of organization but the second, conducted under the auspices of a company floated by the Abolitionists, was far better managed. A settlement was founded on the present site of Freetown and continued under considerable difficulties until 1808 when it was taken over by the British Government as the Crown Colony of Sierra Leone.

The Republic of Liberia owes its origin to a somewhat similar enterprise on the part of Americans. In 1821 the American

---

[1] The honour of being the first to abolish the Trade among their own nationals belongs however to the Danes, whose abolition law became effective in 1804.
[2] The word is used here in the racial and not the geographical sense.

Colonization Society obtained land at Cape Mesurado which became the site of Monrovia, and planted there and at other places on the coast numbers of free Negroes from the southern states of America. The Republic was constituted in 1847. Although the government at Monrovia claimed to rule the indigenous people on the coast and for some distance inland, it had in fact for many years practically no control over any but the coastal areas.

At the beginning of the nineteenth century there were three British settlements on the west coast. These were the Crown Colony of Sierra Leone, constituted in 1808, and the forts on the Gold Coast and the Gambia, administered by a company called the Company of Merchants Trading to West Africa. This company was wound up in 1821, and the Gambia and Gold Coast establishments taken over by the British Government to be administered by the government of Sierra Leone. From 1828 to 1843 they were again placed under a committee of merchants, whose representative, Captain George Maclean, was a man of outstanding character. Although his political authority did not extend beyond the coastal settlements, his reputation for wisdom and honesty enabled him to extend British ideas of justice over a wide area, thus bringing some order and stability to a much troubled country. The British Crown resumed control of the settlements in 1843, Maclean being made Judicial Commissioner, that is Chief Justice with a special responsibility for the administration of justice among the local tribes. The jurisdiction which had grown up under Maclean's influence was then confirmed and defined in a celebrated treaty with the local chiefs known as the Bond of 1844, in which the chiefs recognized that the first object of the law was to protect individuals and property, declared human sacrifices and other barbarous customs to be against the law, and agreed that crimes such as murder and robbery should be tried by British judges sitting with the chiefs, 'moulding the customs of the country to the general principles of British law'. In 1850 the British bought the Danish forts and in 1871 also bought out the remaining Dutch, thereby becoming possessors of Elmina, the fortress originally founded by the Portuguese.

From the early days of the century the European settlements and the coastal tribes around them had lain under the threat of the great Ashanti kingdom in the interior. Attacks by the Ashanti were frequent throughout the century until 1873, when an Ashanti army invading the British sphere was defeated, driven back, and followed up the next year to Kumasi, the Ashanti capital, by a British army commanded by Sir Garnet Wolseley. The Ashanti agreed to renounce far reaching territorial claims, to keep the road to Kumasi open to trade, to pay a substantial indemnity and to abandon human sacrifice.

Further west along the coast the British in 1861 annexed the island of Lagos, whose chief, though friendly enough, was unable to prevent his country from being used as a base for slave raiding. In 1885, at the height of the Scramble for Africa,[1] the belt of thickly populated forest country from Lagos to the Cameroon border was declared to be a British protectorate in order to forestall the Germans. This so-called Oil Rivers Protectorate, later the Niger Coast Protectorate, together with the Colony of Lagos, formed the narrow foothold from which the British presently advanced inland and created modern Nigeria.

The Napoleonic wars were not long over before French activity in West Africa began to revive. In 1817 France was able to regain some of her lost influence north of Sierra Leone. French merchants then turned their attention towards the south and from about 1838 onwards displayed considerable activity in those parts of the Guinea Coast which were not already under British influence. With the accession of Napoleon III in 1848 the French Government decided to develop the trade of the Senegal, and this policy found active expression from 1854 when French influence and power was extended up the Senegal River into the western Sudan. The Franco-German War of 1870–71 put a stop to the colonial expansion of France. This stop, as we shall see, was only temporary.

*The Exploration of Africa*

The nineteenth century was for Africa the century of discovery. When it opened, the Mediterranean coast was still largely the haunt of corsairs, a collection of closed little despotisms. Further east Nelson had destroyed the French fleet in the Battle of the Nile in 1798 and thereby foiled Napoleon's attempt to conquer Egypt. By 1801 the Turks, with British help, were again in control of Egypt, but their hold was precarious and did not last long. On the west coast the Slave Trade continued though its end was in sight, but several European nations maintained settlements on the coast for trading in other goods. On the east coast the Arabs were back in occupation of the northern part of their old empire. Ever since the Portuguese had been driven out the Omani Sultans of Muscat had

[1] pp. 52–3.

claimed overlordship of all these Arab settlements, but their dominion was still intermittent and shadowy. Though the nations of Europe had abandoned, or were about to abandon the Slave Trade, it remained an important occupation for Arabs, and Zanzibar was a vast entrepôt for the buying of slaves from the mainland and dispatch to Arabia and India. In South Africa the British were in Cape Town, and there were a number of settlements extending for some distance inland but the band of western civilization was still a narrow one. The interior of the continent was not of course entirely unknown. Ethiopia, the Blue Nile, the Senegal, the Libyan desert, the Congo, Angola, Mashonaland had all been visited at some time or other, in some cases as early as the fifteenth century, by European travellers, many of them Roman Catholic priests. Still further south, Dutch and English travellers knew the basin of the Orange River fairly well, and some had pushed beyond it. But there had been nothing in the nature of systematic exploration. This did not begin until 1788, with the founding in that year by the British of the African Association. The Association set itself to attack the problem of the Niger and sponsored several expeditions to that river from the north and from the west, of which the most notable were those of the heroic and ill-fated Mungo Park. Following the African Association, the British Government took up the quest and also sent expeditions, the most fruitful being that of Lander, the servant of an explorer named Hugh Clapperton who had died on a previous journey in Northern Nigeria. In 1830 Lander traced the Niger down to the ocean, thus solving the chief problem connected with that river. Further attempts to explore the Niger and its tributary the Benue followed, but met with little success until the expedition of Dr. W. B. Baikie in 1854. Meanwhile Major Gordon Laing reached Timbuktu from Tripoli in August 1826 but was murdered shortly after his arrival. Soon afterwards the Frenchman René Caillié performed the remarkable feat of reaching Timbuktu from the west, accompanying a caravan and disguised as a native. He continued his journey to Tangier where he arrived safely after extreme hardships. In 1850–55 the German Heinrich Barth, travelling under the auspices of the British Government with two companions who died during the journey, added enormously to current knowledge of the central Sudan. Other explorers, mostly French and English, penetrated inland from a number of points along the coast between the Gambia and Calabar, and some years later, in 1855 and again in

1863, the French-American Paul du Chaillu made important expeditions further south in the region of the Ogowe River.

The first half of the nineteenth century saw a considerable advance in the exploration of the Nile. The Scotsman James Bruce had lived adventurously in Ethiopia in 1769–72 and had seen the source of the Blue Nile. In 1821 the Frenchmen Cailliaud and Letorzek reached the confluence of the White and Blue Niles, to be followed in 1827 by Linant de Bellefonds, an emissary of the African Association. The German Rüppell visited Kordofan and travelled in the region of the Blue Nile between 1837 and 1839. Meanwhile explorers of various nationalities had been active in Ethiopia where by 1848 extensive triangulation had been done by the French brothers d'Abbadie, thus providing the basis for accurate maps. In the region of the Upper Nile an expedition mounted by Mohamed Ali in 1841 had pushed south to Gondokoro where in 1850 a permanent station was founded by Austrian missionaries.

The eastern side of Africa remained closed to European exploration a little longer than the rest of the continent, possibly owing to the fact that the coastal belt was already in the occupation of Arab colonists. In 1849 Dr. J. L. Krapf of the Church Missionary Society sighted Mount Kenya and in the same year his colleague Rebmann saw Mount Kilimanjaro. Rebmann's sight of Kilimanjaro, with Arab stories of great lakes inland, opened the possibility of a great field of exploration. The Royal Geographical Society sent first Burton and Speke (1856–59) then Speke and Grant (1860–63) inland from the coast opposite Zanzibar. The first of these two expeditions reached Tanganyika, Speke making a flying visit to the southern end of Lake Victoria; the second passed west of Lake Victoria, continued through Uganda, and at Gondokoro, on the way home by the Nile Valley, met Samuel Baker, who discovered Lake Albert, thus completing the broad outlines of the geography of the Nile. Meanwhile, further south, two German travellers came to unhappy ends: Albrecht Roscher was murdered in 1860 near Lake Malawi and Baron Karl von der Decken, after an unsuccessful expedition to Kilwa and a more rewarding one to Kilimanjaro, was murdered by Somali on the Juba River in 1865.

David Livingstone discovered Lake Ngami in 1849, reached the Zambezi in 1851, and in 1853 began a great journey that led him first to the west coast at Luanda then back across Africa. At about the same time Africa south of the Zambezi was attacked from the south-west by the Englishman Francis Galton and the Swede C. J.

Andersson, and later by Andersson alone. Other travellers in these regions were the trader James Chapman, the artist Thomas Baines, and the German geologist Carl Mauch, whose discovery of gold in the Tati area in 1866 caused a small gold rush. Livingstone's achievements received a most enthusiastic reception in England, and the British Government organized an expedition under him with the purpose of opening up the country to commerce in order to check the Slave Trade which still flourished under Arab auspices. The expedition lasted from 1858 to 1864 and though it was not by any means a complete success it added much to the current knowledge of central Africa, and by underlining the evils of the Slave Trade contributed in some measure to its ultimate disappearance. Livingstone went back to Africa in 1866 and struck inland from the east coast at Mikindani. In the following years, with dwindling resources and none but his African porters and servants for company, often hungry and often ill, but sustained by his faith and by his consciousness of divine guidance, he explored the country between the coast and Lake Tanganyika with wonderful courage and determination. He was very near the end of his tether when, on 10 November 1871, Stanley found him at Ujiji. Stanley had left the coast at Bagamoyo on 21 March and by ruthlessly driving his men arrived at Tabora on 21 June, both his European companions, Farquhar and Shaw, having died on the way. He found the countryside round Tabora disturbed by war between the native chief Mirambo and the Arabs, joined in on the Arab side and took advantage of a lull in the fighting to slip away and reach Ujiji by forced marches. His arrival with plentiful supplies gave Livingstone sorely needed relief, and these two men so dissimilar in character then spent some months together, even engaging in a joint exploration of the northern end of Lake Tanganyika. Had Livingstone returned to the coast with Stanley on 14 March 1872 it is possible that he might have lived. As it was he was determined to complete his exploration of the river system south and west of Lake Tanganyika. He parted from Stanley at Tabora and struck southwards down the eastern side of the Lake, his first goal being Katanga. But the effort proved too much for his ravaged constitution and on the morning of 1 May 1873[1] his servants found him dead in his shelter near Lake Bangweulu in an attitude of prayer.

[1] This is believed to be the right date, but it is not quite certain. The last entry in his journal is dated 27 April.

A government expedition for the relief of Livingstone had been organized and was assembling at Zanzibar when Stanley arrived at the coast. Whereupon, since it appeared that Livingstone had already been relieved, the expedition returned to England. But a second relief expedition under Lieutenant Lovett Cameron started from Zanzibar on 2 February 1873 and at Tabora met Chuma, one of Livingstone's servants, who, with his companions, was carrying his master's body to the coast. Cameron decided nevertheless to push on to Ujiji, where he mapped the greater part of Lake Tanganyika, and then crossed to the Atlantic coast near Benguela where he arrived in November 1875. Stanley's great journey in 1874–7 finally confirmed that the great river system which Livingstone had suspected was that of the Nile was really that of the Congo.

## The Great Trek of the Boers

The British Government, which ruled in Cape Town from 1806 onwards, was not popular with the Boers. These were people who were not amenable to government in any form, and this government had shown unmistakably that it meant to govern, and on new lines. Moreover, it was a government that tended more and more to come under the influence of the humanitarians. These were the people engaged in abolishing the Slave Trade and in preaching doctrines of native rights which to the Boers, who held as an article of faith that there was a gulf divinely fixed between the natives and themselves, was destructive of all security. Yet a third cause of restlessness was that even in the vast hinterland which the Boers at that time occupied, land in the quantities that they considered necessary for their well-being was no longer quite so freely available as before. One of the reasons for this was that the wars of the Zulu tyrant Shaka, like a stone thrown into a pond, had caused waves of Bantu migration in all directions, whole tribes being forced to flee to seek homes and land elsewhere. The competition between Boers and Bantu in the eastern borderlands of the Cape led to the so-called Kaffir Wars in which the British Government became automatically involved as the governing power, incurring great expense and considerable unpopularity. About 1835 these discontents came to a head and the Boers resolved to remove themselves from the reach of the British Government. By 1836 the Great Trek, which was to carry the European to the remotest confines of present South Africa and beyond, was in full swing. With all their possessions loaded on ox-wagons, women and children on the wagons and the men usually on horseback, the Boers trekked away to the Promised Land in the north. In the years that followed the trekkers spilled over the Vaal River into the Magaliesberg and Zoutspansberg, over into Zululand where one of their leaders, Piet Retief, was murdered with many of his followers by Chief Dingaan—the massacre was later amply avenged in the battle of the Blood River—up to the borders of Swaziland and of Portuguese East Africa. Thus in a very short time southern Africa became known as far north as the easterly bend of the Limpopo River. (*Plate* 9)

The Boers did not find the field entirely untenanted. There were already a considerable number of native tribes in most of these areas, sadly disorganized by the wars of the Zulus. There were also the Matabele, led by a dissident captain of Shaka named Mzilikazi, who had to be overcome before the trekkers could enter into enjoyment of the great plains that stretched between the Vaal and the Limpopo. Finally, there were the missionaries of the London Missionary Society, who had founded their mission at Kuruman in southern Bechuanaland in 1817, and had already, through David Livingstone, extended their influence at least as far north as the trekkers had extended theirs, and who, in the long run, were to become the most formidable opponents of all.

★ ★ ★ ★ ★

By the 'seventies all the great geographical problems of Africa had been solved, though there were still many blanks on the map. The course of the more important rivers and many of their tributaries had been traced; the great lakes were known; vast areas of land had been crossed and re-crossed by European explorers and mapped; there was a considerable body of knowledge about the inhabitants, climate, vegetation, fauna and natural features; there was already a considerable amount of literature about Africa, not of hunters' tales and travellers' fantasies, but sober accounts of people and places based on observed facts. About this time too, one kind of exploration came to an end. It was that prompted only by scientific curiosity, the passion for discovery for its own sake. With Stanley's journey down the Congo in 1874 there began the phase of political exploration which grew into the Scramble for Africa and ended in the partition of the continent between the Powers of Europe.

## The French in North Africa

Before European penetration of Africa became competitive—the Scramble began in the early 'eighties—there had been a substantial advance of Europeans in North and South Africa. By 1840, as we have seen, the Boers were across the Vaal and spreading about the high veld. During the following decade the French established themselves in North Africa.

Algiers was long the headquarters of the Barbary corsairs, who preyed on the shipping of every nation. By the beginning of the nineteenth century the former Turkish sovereignty had vanished and the coast was studded with a number of small principalities always on the verge of anarchy, with no resources other than the proceeds of piracy. Numbers of expeditions, English, Dutch, French, Spanish and American, tried unsuccessfully at various times to check piracy until 1830, when the French fleet bombarded Algiers into submission and the French occupied the town. They were not, however, able to assert their authority over the rest of the country until 1847, after a long war with the gallant and skilful Abd el Kader. So began the great French Empire in Africa.

## Egypt from the Middle Ages to modern times

The history of Egypt from the Arab invasions to modern times contains more than a fair share of unrest, assassination and massacre. The country was ruled at first by governors appointed by successive caliphs. During this early period the character of the Moslem occupation changed. The intention had originally been simply to establish garrisons but it was not long before the country was being systematically colonized. This period was also marked by a number of revolts by the Copts, all of which were suppressed, and by the spread of Arab speech at the expense of Greek. From 1352 to 1517 was the era of the Mamelukes, so-called because the sultans were drawn from the enfranchised slaves who officered the army. They made way for the Turks and Egypt became a dependency of the Porte. But the power of the Mamelukes was by no means destroyed and they were still in the ascendant when Napoleon invaded Egypt in 1798.

With the ejection of the French by the British and Turks in 1801 there began a bloody struggle for power between Turks, Mamelukes and Albanian soldiers, from which Mohamed Ali, an Albanian commander, emerged victorious. He killed off the Mamelukes, defeated a small British force and by about 1807 was the undisputed ruler of Egypt; though acknowledging Turkish sovereignty, he was virtually independent. He campaigned in Arabia, Greece and the Sudan, organized a strong but oppressive administration in Egypt itself, carried out public works at the cost of considerable suffering to the people, and started and encouraged the cotton trade. He died in 1849 and was succeeded by his grandson Abbas I who was murdered in 1854. Next came Said, a son of Mohamed, who in 1856 gave Ferdinand de Lesseps a concession for the construction of the Suez Canal. Said's successor Ismail was in some ways a progressive ruler, and did something to restore the administrative system, which since Mohamed Ali's death had fallen into anarchy. But the money and labour for carrying out the considerable public works which he put in hand were ruthlessly wrung from the miserable peasants to the point where there was nothing more to be got from them, while Ismail's own credit was so bad that he could not raise loans on the international market.

In 1875, to meet his needs, Ismail sold his shares in the Suez Canal Company to the British Government for four million pounds. Henceforward he found himself compelled to submit more and more to European control. Some of the courts of justice became international and finance came under the dual control of France and England. In 1878 Ismail made an attempt to return to his old autocratic ways but was immediately dismissed by the Turkish Government and replaced by Tewfik. In 1882 a programme of rehabilitation and reform begun by the British and the French was interrupted by the revolt of Arabi Pasha. This was put down by the British alone, the Sultan of Turkey having declined to suppress it and the French and Italians refusing to co-operate. Sir Evelyn Baring, later Lord Cromer, became British consul-general in Egypt in 1883 and instituted a series of reforms designed to introduce order and prosperity, and the elements of an independent, liberal government. Baring's appointment coincided with a successful revolt against Egyptian rule in the Sudan.

### Egypt in the Sudan—the Mahdi—Gordon at Khartoum

In 1820 Mohamed Ali ordered that Nubia, northern part of the Sudan, should be conquered, and this was accomplished in the following two years in the face of strong resistance from the Nubians. Having taken Nubia, also Sennar and Kordofan, the Egyptians set up a civil government which was unbelievably oppressive and corrupt. The Sudanese were plundered by their rulers, intolerable taxes were imposed on them and the Slave Trade became the country's chief industry, in which the government itself took an active part. In 1870 things took a turn for the better when Sir Samuel Baker arrived at Gondokoro as governor of the equatorial provinces under the Egyptian Government. He was succeeded in 1874 by Colonel ('Chinese') Gordon. Baker and Gordon both made strenuous attempts to stop the Slave Trade, but the authorities in Khartoum were inactive and gave them little effective support. Gordon left the Sudan in 1876 but in the following year he was given the governorship of the Egyptian provinces outside Egypt. He waged unceasing war on the slave raiders and in 1879, when his subordinate Gessi caught and executed Suleman Zobeir and other ringleaders, no less than 10,000 captives were released. But when Gordon left in 1879 all the old evils of Egyptian administration, weakness and corruption at the centre, extortion and venality on the periphery, returned with his successor Raouf Pasha. In 1881 Mohamed Ahmed, a man of Dongola, proclaimed himself to be the long-awaited Mahdi (guide) of Islam. The Sudanese, weary of Egyptian misrule, flocked to his standards.

By the beginning of 1884 the Mahdi was well on his way to becoming master of the Sudan. Alarmed by the annihilation in November 1883 of an Egyptian Army under Hicks Pasha, the British Government sent Gordon to effect the withdrawal of the Egyptian garrisons. Whether Gordon went beyond his instructions and attempted not an evacuation but a re-occupation is a matter of controversy.[1] However that may be, the situation worsened, Gordon was shut up in Khartoum with no chance of escape, and on 26 January 1885 Khartoum fell to the Mahdist host and Gordon was killed. A relief expedition under Lord Wolseley was too late to save him. The Mahdi died in the same year, having completely destroyed Egyptian power in the Sudan, and was succeeded by the Khalifa (Caliph) Abdulla, a military autocrat who ruled by fear. Public anger in England at the government's failure to save Gordon contributed to the fall of the Gladstone Administration in 1885.

## Arabs and British on the East Coast

The Arab Slave Trade on the east coast reproduced all the dismal features of the Afro-European trade from West Africa. The whole wretched process was repeated here, the raids, the inter-tribal

---

[1] The exact scope of his instructions has been the subject of discussion (see e.g. J. S. R. Duncan, *The Sudan*, pp. 34–7).

wars, the treachery, the massacres. The captives also suffered
appallingly on their long march to the coast. Roped together and
shackled to a beam, many of them died on the way and those who
fell out were left to die. On arrival at the coast they were shipped in
dhows to Zanzibar thence on to their further destination in conditions of hideous discomfort and squalor. 'The sights I have seen,
though common incidents of the traffic, are so nauseous that I
always strive to drive them from memory.' The words are Livingstone's and it was Livingstone who forced the horrors of the Trade
on to the conscience of his countrymen in a crusade which began on
his return from his crossing of Africa in 1857. His personality, the
prestige of his achievement, his heroic, dedicated life, kindled the
imagination of the British people. There was no need for a campaign
such as Wilberforce had been compelled to conduct to win popular
support. When the British Government set about to eradicate the
Trade in the Indian Ocean it had the full weight of public opinion
behind it.

During the first half of the nineteenth century the grip of the
Arabs of Muscat had been much tightened by Said bin Sultan, or
Sayyed Said, who, after usurping the sovereignity of Muscat and
devoting the first half of his reign to establishing himself firmly
there, spent the second in building up a strong political and economic position in East Africa. In 1840 he went so far as to move his
seat of government from Muscat to Zanzibar, from whence he
exercised sovereignty over the mainland. This sovereignty was
fairly firm at the coast but shadowy up-country. Said died in 1856
and was succeeded in Zanzibar by his son Majid, a shifty weakling,
who, after a troubled reign of fourteen years, died and was followed
by a younger brother named Barghash, a bold and resolute man,
who had plotted against Majid almost since the latter's accession.

Great Britain was fortunate in having in Zanzibar a succession of
brave and able consuls, men of the calibre of Hamerton, Rigby
and especially John Kirk. It was to them that fell the difficult and
delicate task of stopping the Slave Trade. The first policy was one
of restriction, slavery being limited to the dominions of the
Sultan of Zanzibar and export forbidden. From 1873 onwards
the aim became total abolition and this was practically attained in
the surprisingly short space of three years. By 1877 the inspiration
of Livingstone, the combined efforts of the British consuls, the
British Navy, and also, in the last phases, of Barghash himself, had
brought the Trade in East Africa virtually to an end.

## The Scramble for Africa

In the early 1880s there began a brisk international competition for colonies of which one aspect was the so-called Scramble for Africa. Hitherto rivalry in Africa had been primarily commercial, each nation striving to oust others from the trade of this area or that, and only rarely to impose an alien government on countries not suitable for white setttlement. This form of competition suited Great Britain very well. Her industries were second to none, her navy the best in the world, her merchants enterprising and ubiquitous. All that seemed to be necessary was the possession of a few forts and bases here and there to bolster commerce and suppress the Slave Trade; for the rest it was accepted that the unappropriated parts of the world would remain open to legitimate British trade indefinitely. The emergence of Germany as a world Power and France's recovery from her defeat of 1871 shattered these illusions. These two nations embarked on a purposeful career of overseas expansion, and it soon became clear that they intended to reserve the trade of their new dominions to themselves. At the same time the King of the Belgians set about to carve himself a private domain out of the Congo basin and Italy secured her first foothold in Africa at Assab on the Red Sea coast and from this small beginning developed an empire in the Horn of Africa. Great Britain, naturally averse to expansion, was compelled to join in, and through the agency of a number of brilliant individuals rather than by any vigorous action on the part of her government managed in the end to secure a substantial empire in Africa. Britain's participation was also determined by motives other than imperialist and commercial. The travels of missionaries and explorers had revealed not only the splendours of Africa but also its horrors. The opening up of Africa by the missionary, the soldier, the administrator and the trader went hand in hand with the abolition of the Slave Trade, the suppression of tribal war and the alleviation of much human misery.

The Scramble for Africa was marked by two important international conventions. The first was the General Act of a conference of Powers held in Berlin in 1884–85. This provided *inter alia* for freedom of trade in the Congo basin and for free navigation of the Congo and the Niger Rivers. The second was the Act of the Brussels Conference of 1889–90 which dealt mainly with slavery and the liquor traffic.

The Scramble lasted a little more than a decade. By the early

'nineties most of Africa had been divided among the Powers, and
the map of the continent drawn largely as it remained until 1914.
It was still a map lacking in detail, and in the following period
several important changes were made, as well as many comparatively small adjustments to territorial boundaries. Perhaps the
most important was the reconquest of the Sudan by the British
and the establishment of an Anglo-Egyptian condominium over
that territory. This coincided with the arrival at Fashoda on the
Nile of Major Marchand at the head of a French colonial force,
the spearhead of a thrust eastwards from Equatorial Africa. After
much friction an Anglo-French agreement of March 1899 de-
finitely excluded the French from the Nile basin and barred them
from any further advance from west to east. Other important
arrangements were those that took place in 1911–12, which resulted
in a French protectorate over Morocco, the cession by France to
Germany of a slice of Equatorial Africa which was added to the
German Cameroons, and the definition of the respective zones and
interests of Germany and France in and near Morocco. The final
act of the partition of Africa was when Italy, whose attempt to
conquer Ethiopia in 1906 had been bloodily repulsed at Adwa,[1]
comparatively easily possessed herself of Tripolitania and Cyrenaica
in 1911–12.

## Christian Missions

Africa is to all intents and purposes a modern mission field.
North Africa, land of Tertullian, St. Cyprian and St. Augustine,
has long been part of the world of Islam, and Christian evangelism
there is weak. Except for the valiant exertions of Portuguese priests
in the Zambezi and Congo fields, missionary activity did not begin
in Africa south of the Sahara until the middle of the eighteenth
century.[2] From that time it steadily expanded, with periods of
especially rapid growth in the 1880s and after World War I, until
now there are few parts of Africa without a mission belonging to one
or other of the Christian creeds. Indeed there are sometimes so
many different missions in a comparatively small area as to create
an impression of rivalry.

While the primary purpose of Christian missions is, and must be,
to bring men to the Faith of Christ, Africa is indebted to them and

---

[1] See p. 150 fn.
[2] The Moravians started work in South Africa in 1737 but the Dutch stopped
them.

E

to their supporters for immense services of an incidental kind. As
pressure groups or as individuals they have fought tyranny and
oppression, roused public opinion against scandals and abuses, and
stimulated valuable reforms. In the earlier days of European
expansion in Africa they provided the only social services that there
were. The only schools were mission schools, and the only European
medicine was that provided by the missionary, doing his best with
plenty of hot water and a few simple drugs. With the expansion of
government departments the missionaries are no longer the only
teachers and doctors, but their educational institutions are still
exceedingly important, and mission hospitals are in many places a
valuable part of the medical organization of the country. Christian
missionaries have also made a quite exceptional contribution to
African studies. They were often the first to record the customs of
the people among whom they lived, to learn African languages and
reduce them to writing. If against these services we set some insen-
sitivity to the value of harmless and ancient customs, too rigid an
attachment to the forms of nineteenth-century Christianity, a tendency to quarrel among themselves, and, occasionally, political
activities of a somewhat disingenuous kind, the balance of Christian
missions in Africa is still weighted very heavily on the credit side.

## Colonial Africa

The history of the various parts of Africa after the Scramble will
be roughed out in the regional chapters, but in order to save
repetition later it is opportune at this stage to make a few points of
fairly general application.

The various Powers adopted very different political and social
aims in the administration of their dependencies. The British, with
a long tradition of devolution and disengagement, made it their aim
to train the colonial peoples for self-government. Tolerant in
religion and politics and respectful of tradition they found no better
framework of government than that provided by Africans themselves. Purged of abuses, educated to meet the complex needs of the
modern world, African institutions would provide the basis of
future African self-government.

The French philosophy of colonial rule never included the concept of local autonomy. On the contrary, the underlying assumption
was that the colonies were actually or potentially part of France,
their people actual or potential Frenchmen. This principle was not
easily applicable to the extensive, remote and primitive territories

acquired by France in the late nineteenth century and the French were often driven to practices reminiscent of those adopted by the British. Nevertheless the theory of 'assimilation' was never abandoned, and it has certainly influenced the relations between France and her former overseas territories, in Africa and elsewhere, in the post-colonial era.

The Belgians placed no emphasis on political objectives, and appear to have followed the belief that the less the general public had to do with politics the better. Government was paternalistic and neither Europeans nor Africans had any franchise rights at all. On the other hand great importance was attached to economic development and the Africans were given considerable encouragement to participate in industry at comparatively high technical levels.

The Portuguese, like the French, dismiss the concept of autonomy but insist on that of 'identity'. There is close integration between the overseas territories and the metropolis, no colour bar, while Africans who fulfil certain qualifications become *assimilados* and acquire the status of Portuguese citizens of European birth. Unhappily the lack of facilities for higher education make those qualifications hard to acquire and the number of *assimilados* remains small.

The Germans appear to have entered on their overseas career with no colonial philosophy but that of direct rule through European administrators on simple forceful lines. Many of these administrators were inexperienced and of poor calibre, and their excesses led to several rebellions, of which the Herero rising in South West Africa was the best known example. These rebellions were repressed with great ferocity. Thereafter there were genuine attempts at reform which were interrupted by the 1914–18 war before their fruits could be known.

In the early days following the partition of Africa economic development was slow. All the facilities were lacking, labour was scarce and the distances enormous. In some colonies development was entrusted to monopoly companies who were granted powers of administration, in others very large blocks of land were given to planters, in others again the European trader provided the capital and organization necessary to foster peasant industries and bring their products on to the world's markets. It was not until after the Second World War that the conception of state initiative in planning and financing the development of backward areas was fully recognized. The result was that all colonial Powers launched development schemes designed to improve the economic position of their dependencies. The earlier British schemes laid no little emphasis on the promotion of 'welfare' and it soon became clear that the recurrent cost of numerous welfare projects would very soon cause such expenditure on welfare services as the local budgets would be unable to meet. In the last few years of colonial rule welfare was played down and emphasis shifted to the promotion of services calculated to create economies capable of bearing services of their own.

In the early 'sixties most of colonial Africa became fully independent. The courses which the various countries have followed since then will be described at appropriate places in this book. In the last part an attempt will be made to assess the whole situation as it appears at the end of the first decade of independence.

# The Rift Valley

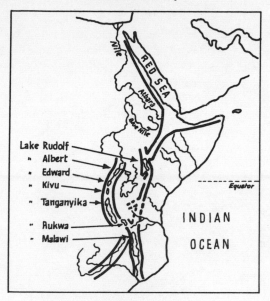

# Climatic Zones

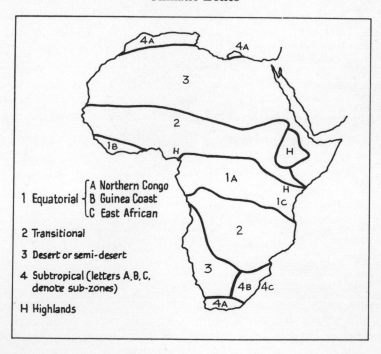

1 Equatorial
  - A Northern Congo
  - B Guinea Coast
  - C East African

2 Transitional

3 Desert or semi-desert

4 Subtropical (letters A, B, C, denote sub-zones)

H Highlands

# Natural Vegetational Zones

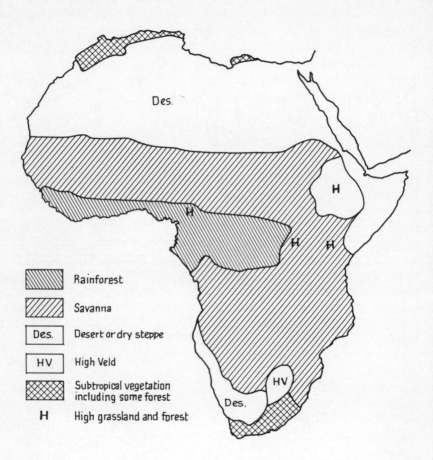

Des.

H

H

H

H

H

HV

Des.

Des.

| | Rainforest |
| | Savanna |
| Des. | Desert or dry steppe |
| H.V. | High Veld |
| | Subtropical vegetation including some forest |
| H | High grassland and forest |

# SOUTHERN AFRICA

SOUTHERN Africa for our purpose includes the Republic of South Africa, which until 1961 was a dominion of the British Commonwealth; South West Africa, formerly a German colony and now administered by the Republic; and Botswana, Lesotho and Swaziland, the first a republic, the other two constitutional monarchies.

The region is physically a plateau with an average height of four thousand to six thousand feet, enclosed by a great escarpment, tilting upwards on the eastern side and falling gradually away to the west. On the east and south-east the Drakensberg mountains represent the highest point of the escarpment, reaching an altitude of eleven thousand feet. In the west the edge is less distinct and the elevation only occasionally reaches six thousand feet. The plateau sinks west of centre to form the depression of the Kgalagadi, in altitude between two and three thousand feet, surrounded on all sides except the northern by a borderland rising to five thousand feet.

Between the escarpment and the sea the land drops in a series of terraces of varying width separated by mountain ranges running roughly parallel to the coast. These terraces are most clearly marked in the south, and form the Great and Little Karroo. The coastal plain is generally a narrow one except in the north-east where it widens out into Portuguese East Africa. The eastern coastal belt is well-watered and in places supports a luxuriant vegetation. On the Atlantic side the dry Namib desert, varying in width from thirty to eighty miles, stretches up the coast for 850 miles between the Orange and Kunene Rivers.

No mere physical description can do justice to the grandeur of southern Africa. From the hills and valleys of Natal, with their productive gardens, gracious towns and splendid beaches, to the Cape, with its immense coastline and wooded, fertile hinterland, the country is one of spectacular beauty; even the monotonous down-lands of Pondoland and the Transkei, the bare treeless plain of the Orange Free State, and the rolling steppes of the Kgalagadi and the Karroo, while not beautiful, have the majesty of unlimited space.

The climate varies throughout the region. On the east coast con-

ditions are tropical, with a fairly high temperature and a rainfall
heavy for this side of Africa (Durban receives over forty inches of
rain a year). But at Cape Town the climate is of the Mediterranean
type, with mild winters and no more than warm summers. This is
undoubtedly the most agreeable climate in Africa south of the
Sahara. Unlike tropical Natal and the temperate Cape the plateau
is a zone of extremes. The summers are hot and the winters chilly.
Rain is heaviest on the eastern, up-tilted side and dwindles in the
west, where droughts are by no means uncommon. The rains are of
short duration and fall in heavy showers. There are often violent
thunderstorms and at certain seasons high winds sweep across the
bare dusty plains. These conditions account for much of the pre-
vailing soil erosion.

The whole region has an area of over one million square miles. Of
this area the Republic occupies just under a half, and is geographically, economically and politically the heart and backbone of the
region.


## REPUBLIC OF SOUTH AFRICA

### History

The British Government's policy in South Africa from the time
of the Great Trek almost to the end of the nineteenth century gives
an impression of timidity and vacillation. On the one hand there
was reluctance to extend imperial responsibilities or to incur distant
and expensive commitments. On the other, the circumstances of a
large and warlike native population, a wandering body of land
hungry farmers, and in consequence a restless and turbulent frontier,
made impossible the favoured solution which was to withdraw and
leave the colonists to sort things out for themselves. Efforts to
compromise between the two extremes only bred chronic hesitation
and uncertainty which persisted until the time of the Scramble for
Africa, when Great Britain was forced by international considerations to take a more forceful line and to embark, still rather reluc-
tantly, on a policy of expansion.

The two dominant personalities in South Africa during the last
two decades of the nineteenth century were Paul Kruger and Cecil
John Rhodes. Kruger, President of the Transvaal, was the epitome
of the Boer frontiersman, powerful, simple and frugal in his habits,
religious, xenophobic, narrow, conservative and shrewd. Rhodes

was a manipulator and an amalgamator, a politician with a politician's standards of honesty, yet withal a man with a mission, placing all his wealth and power at the service of South African unity and the expansion of the British Empire in Africa. When gold was found on the Witwatersrand Kruger's rustic kingdom was invaded by gold-seeking foreigners or *Uitlanders* who demanded civic rights and seemed to Kruger to constitute a real threat to his government. To Rhodes, however, obsessed with his dream of South African unity, the *Uitlanders* were the instrument with which the unaccommodating Boer régime might be overthrown and the Transvaal brought into the comity of South African states. A force under Rhodes's henchman Jameson was assembled on the Transvaal border, a revolutionary conspiracy was fomented in Johannesburg, and on the night of 29–30 December 1895 Jameson set forth to march on Johannesburg at the head of his men. As everybody knows the Raid failed ignominiously, but its effects were nevertheless disastrous. The Boers were confirmed in their opinion that British imperialism meant to crush them and was prepared to resort to any means in order to do so;[1] British public opinion, in whose eyes Jameson was a hero, already suspicious of German manœuvres in South Africa, was further exacerbated by a telegram of congratulation which the Kaiser sent to Kruger. The Jameson Raid heightened tensions that were already high enough and increased the likelihood of the explosion that took place four years later.

The causes of the Boer War have been much debated and its course may be found in any book of South African history. To the modern Englishman, who has managed since then to struggle through two wars infinitely more bloody and more far-reaching, the Boer War, if he remembers it at all, seems little more than an affair of manœuvres with live ammunition. But it is deeply imprinted on the consciousness of South Africans of Boer descent and with the Trek is an important element in their lives.

Whatever the dispute about the origins and conduct of the war, it is generally agreed that the peace of Vereeniging, concluded between Great Britain and the defeated republics on 31 May 1902, was a generous one. Responsible government was promised as soon as conditions had become settled; the Dutch language was recognized as being equal with English, and Great Britain agreed to help in the reconstruction of the country. The ultimate flaw in the Treaty was

---

[1] The complicity of Joseph Chamberlain, British Colonial Secretary, has been much discussed but never proved.

that the native question was explicitly shelved until after the grant
of responsible government. However, insistence on a liberal native
policy at that stage would have probably caused a hitch and even a
breakdown in the peace discussions, and experience has since shown
that in any case the most firmly entrenched constitutional arrangements can be by-passed or abrogated.

The British undertakings were most faithfully observed, and
Lord Milner, the High Commissioner, whose actions have been
criticized as contributory causes of the war, found in post-war
reconstruction a field for his great ability.

In 1910, after some two years of negotiations, the four colonies
of South Africa, the Transvaal, the Orange Free State, Natal and
the Cape Colony were formed into the single Union of South
Africa. In 1931 the Statute of Westminster conferred on South
Africa, as on other dominions, virtual independence within the
Empire.

Since the Act of Union South Africa has fought by the side of
Britain in two world wars, and the personality of Jan Smuts, in his
younger days a commando leader against the British, and later a
British field-marshal and world statesman, kept the Union generally
in tune with the rest of the British Empire, though there were even
then admittedly some discordant notes. Since Smuts's fall from
office in 1948 and his death two years later, South Africa has been
governed by Nationalists, modern representatives of the Boers who
were defeated in 1902, and now called Afrikaners.

In October 1960 a referendum promoted by the South African
Government gave a narrow majority in favour of turning South
Africa into a republic. At the Commonwealth Conference in
April 1961 the South African Prime Minister announced that on
becoming a republic his country would withdraw from the Commonwealth. At the end of May 1961 South Africa accordingly
became a republic outside the Commonwealth.

## The People

The history of South Africa is one of conflict and though the
country is now a political unity and has been so for sixty years, these
discord between the different elements persist, and time has done
nothing to mitigate them. It is impossible to speak of 'the people of
South Africa' with any implication of common citizenship or of any
community of thought and outlook. There are several 'peoples of
South Africa', racially distinguished from one another and each too

often strongly in opposition to the others. They cannot therefore be considered under one comprehensive heading but must be described separately. The term European, while perhaps not strictly applicable to people whose homeland is Africa, will be used in the racial sense to describe South African whites.

## Europeans

The white population in 1970 was something under four million, having increased by 22·4 per cent since the last census in 1960. It is divided into two main sections, the Afrikaners and the English-speaking South Africans. What makes an Afrikaner is not easy to say, but generally speaking he may be regarded as the modern representative of the Boer, who speaks Afrikaans as his mother tongue. Afrikaans is derived from the Dutch of the original European settlers. It now shares with English the status of official language and indeed tends to become the dominant one. Official notices are printed in both languages, both languages are taught in the schools, and bi-lingualism is a necessity in any public appointment and a considerable asset in any other employment. Until the last twenty or thirty years the Afrikaners constituted the rural part of the population and the English-speaking South Africans the urban. This is no longer the case, as the Afrikaners have come into the towns and participate largely in urban industries.

Afrikaner farmers are hospitable, honest, thrifty, and conservative. As farmers the quality varies. Many of them are shrewd, hard-working and competent men, but there is a fairly large number who are not. The town Afrikaner of the upper or professional classes is able, urbane and cultured. The artisan, apart from politics, is like an artisan anywhere. Below the professional man and the artisan there is another class of urban Afrikaner drawn in part from unsuccessful farmers who have drifted to the towns and there become slowly industrialized. It is among these that many of the so-called 'poor whites' are found.

Most Afrikaners have considerable pride of race, of which one aspect is the conscious fostering of the Afrikaans language, culture and literature. The spirit of the Great Trek is very strong in them, and affects their whole emotional and cultural life. The 'kaffir', as the black man is still called, is usually an enemy, at best a problem, and the old intolerance of Natives, bred of frequent wars with Xosa, Zulu, Matabele and others, is now sharpened by fear of native competition, by anxiety lest the western way of life may be submerged in a rising tide of colour. Hence an uncompromising insistence on the colour bar and the rejection of any kind of equality between black and white. Almost all Afrikaners belong to one or other of the branches of the Dutch Reformed Church, which combines a sombre calvinistic theology with a taste for politics, into which too many *predikants* throw themselves with zest. His religion does nothing to mitigate the Afrikaner's intolerance in matters of colour.[1]

English-speaking South Africans are mainly townsmen and business men, engaged in industry, mining and in the professions. In Natal, however, and part of the Eastern Cape, the majority of farmers are English-speaking. It is largely to the English-speaking South African that the economic development of South Africa is due. 'The English-speaking South Africans were responsible for mining and industrial development, for railway construction, for the establishment of towns and cities, for commerce and banking, for shipping and for harbour construction—in fact, for changing South Africa from an agriculturally backward community into a semi-industrial modern state.'[2] They have also made a most important contribution to the educational and cultural capital of the country. Their attitude towards their African fellow-citizens, however, is much the same in essence as that of the Afrikaners, but they are more cautious than the latter in expressing their views.

*Africans*

The non-European population consists chiefly of Bantu Africans who number some fifteen million. They are divided into four main ethnic groups, Nguni, Sotho, Shangana-Tonga and Venda. The Nguni group, which includes the important Zulu and Xosa tribes, has its home in the east and south-east, in Natal and in the eastern Cape Province; the Sotho stretch in a broad band from the Drakensberg across the Orange Free State and the Transvaal to the Kgalagadi; the Venda live in the northern part of the Transvaal, and the Shangana-Tonga in the coastal areas on the southern border of Portuguese East Africa. It is, however, important to note that although we speak of the tribal home, only 41·7 per cent of the African population live in the native areas, or, as they are called, homelands. The others are to be found in towns and on European-

---

[1] It must however be said that the Dutch Reformed Church is particularly active in missionary work among non-Europeans.

[2] Marquard, *The Peoples and Policies of South Africa*, p. 72.

owned farms outside the homelands, most of them in the employment of Europeans.

## The Homelands

A 'Bantu homeland' is an area set aside for African occupation and represents at any rate parts of those areas in which the tribes were originally settled before being conquered by Europeans. The policy of establishing reserves in which Africans could live freely without exploitation or molestation by Europeans, was in fact strongly advocated by the early missionaries and other humanitarians, and it is now, some hundred and thirty years later, an important part of the theory of *apartheid*, which we shall discuss below.

The homelands are under the control of the Department of Bantu Administration and Development, and the day to day administration of the tribes remains in the hands of traditional chiefs. Special mention should be made of the Transkei, an area of 16,500 square miles north of the Kei River in the Eastern Cape, inhabited by Xosa, and constituting 'South Africa's most original contribution to the science of governing Africans'.[1] This territory enjoys a limited form of self-government under a cabinet headed by a chief minister and elected by a legislative assembly which is itself partly elected. The assembly has power to make laws on a fairly wide range of subjects but bills have to be transmitted to the Minister of Bantu Administration for assent. Although some ten per cent of officials in 1967 were white, the general policy in regard to the homelands is gradually to replace all white officials by black.

Since it is the avowed aim of the government to 'create self-governing Bantu national units' (see p. 73 ff.) one must presume that the Transkei will be the prototype in the transition of all homelands to semi-national status.

A first five-year plan for the development of the African areas was launched in 1961 and was completed in 1966. A second plan, of much wider scope, began in 1967. There are elaborate training schemes for African farmers and considerable sums of money are spent in the development of native agriculture and animal husbandry and the conservation of natural resources. It should be added that the homelands are not meant to be exclusively rural. A number of African towns have been established and more are planned. To divert African work-seekers away from existing cities, urban industry is

[1] Marquard: *op. cit.*, p. 110.

being offered substantial inducements to move to or expand on the borders of the homelands.

### Africans outside the homelands

Seven million Africans live outside the homelands and are to be found in every part of South Africa, most of them, as has already been said, in European employment. Rapid industrialization caused a large influx of Africans to the towns at a time when the Second World War had brought building activity to a standstill. The authorities were caught off balance, and although an ambitious housing programme was put in hand, shanty towns sprang up that were breeding grounds for disease and crime. The situation has much improved in recent years and many towns, especially the larger ones, have good African housing estates, with churches, schools, recreation halls, playgrounds and similar amenities, together with necessary services. South Africans claim that their industrial workers are better housed than those anywhere else in Africa and even better than workers in some European countries. Attention is now being given to the smaller towns, where conditions still leave much to be desired.

A third of the total African population is to be found on European farms, either as permanent or casual labourers or as squatters. Life on the farms is more spacious and in some ways more leisurely than in the towns. For instance workers are spared the long, overcrowded train journeys to work that are an uncomfortable feature of African urban life. Moreover employees are encouraged to bring their wives with them and the white farmers are usually kindly men who take a personal interest in their servants' welfare. But the wages are lower than in the towns, many of the adjuncts of civilized life are lacking and the type of work is by no means always of the kind to inculcate skill or industry. The urban worker is more likely than the farm labourer to acquire new techniques that he can use to improve, within limits, his situation in life.

### The Coloured People

Half-way between black and white, estimated in 1967 to number approximately two million, come the 'Coloured' people. They are of mixed race, descendants of marriages and less regular liaisons between Europeans and native Africans, Malagasy, Sinhalese and other eastern races. They are distributed over the country, but the great majority are in the Cape Province. They find employment as artisans in the building industry and to a very limited extent in other skilled trades, and in the professions as teachers and doctors. From 1853, when the Cape Colony first obtained representative government, to 1951, the Cape Coloured were on a common franchise roll with Europeans. In the latter year the Nationalist Government took them off, in defiance of one of the so-called 'entrenched clauses' in the South Africa Act of 1909. This cost the Coloureds considerable political influence. The Coloured vote was influential in many constituencies and decisive in several and would almost certainly be cast *against* the Nationalist party. Now the Coloured people can no longer take part in a general election, and whereas formerly they had a vote in a large number of Cape constituencies, they can now only elect four members. These measures aroused considerable anger in South Africa, not only among the Coloured people, whom it affected directly, but also among many Europeans, who thought that the Government had violated the constitution.

Though many Coloured people can aspire to situations in general beyond the reach of the black man, there is still much poverty among them and their housing is generally poor. Economically and politically poised as they are between the worlds of white and black, rejected by one and rejecting the other, they seem the more pathetic of the victims of racial separation.

It is perhaps convenient here to mention the Cape Malays, a group of about 65,000 Moslems whose ancestors came from the east, some as slaves but most of them as political exiles, intermarried with Europeans and others, but retained their religion. They are good craftsmen and shrewd business people and are therefore in fairly prosperous economic circumstances. Their religion, which encourages in its adherents a sense of superiority and exclusiveness, serves them as an armour against the colour bar.

## Indians[1]

The first Indians in South Africa were the indentured labourers who came to work in the sugar plantations of Natal in the 'sixties, when the British settlers could not get enough local labour. They were joined by their families and friends, and the community multiplied as Indians do, so that when free immigration was prohibited

---

[1] The word is used here to include all the people of the Indian sub-continent, whether Indians or Pakistanis. The more general term 'Asian', in the South African context, might cause confusion with other Asians, such as Malays.

in 1911 there was already a sizeable Indian population in the
country. In 1970 there were over 600,000 Indians in South Africa,
of whom about three-quarters lived in Natal and the rest in the
Transvaal and the Cape. They are not allowed to live in the Orange
Free State. The Indians are for the most part traders, and some
are market gardeners. Being very hardworking and thrifty, they
are prosperous as a community and many individuals are wealthy.
Socially, however, South African Indians are not readily assimilable,
as they have a natural gift for overcrowding under any conditions
and tend to create slums wherever they settle. In 1927 the South
African and Indian Governments came to an agreement called the
Cape Town Agreement to co-operate in an assisted emigration
scheme for Indians who wished to return to India. By 1947 some
15,000 Indians had taken advantage of the scheme but it was then
recognized that its possibilities were largely exhausted. The South
African Government now looks to the Group Areas Act[1] to confine
the Indians to specified areas. Outside the Cape Province, which
has always been more indulgent on colour questions than the other
provinces, the Indians have no political or municipal franchise.

ECONOMY

(i) *Mining*
     South Africa is almost synonymous with minerals and of all
South African minerals gold is pre-eminent. More than half the
world's supply of gold comes from South Africa, and the greater
part of this production is at present from the Transvaal. Gold was
discovered on the Witwatersrand in 1886[2] and soon attracted large
numbers of fortune hunters who built the village of Johannesburg
on this bare and windy ridge. Johannesburg is now a populous city,
centre of a great mining area which forms a crescent stretching a
hundred miles east and a hundred miles west before turning south
to run another hundred miles into the Orange Free State. Along this
crescent there are seven goldfields with fifty-one mines actively pro-
ducing and three mines still being developed. Three famous mines,
Crown, City Deep and Robinson Deep, are within three or four

---

[1] This Act, which was passed in 1950, empowers the Government to declare any
area a group area for European, Coloured, African and Asian. The intention is that
in due course the various racial groups will live in distinct areas, and property in
those areas may not be acquired by any member of another group. The Act has most
unfortunate possibilities for people like Indians who may be compelled to move
from some place where they probably have a valuable and long-established business.
[2] This is the date of the discovery of the main reef on the farm Langlaagte. Fred
Struben had found gold on the farm Wilgespruit in 1884.

1. TABLE MOUNTAIN. The flat-topped mountain (3,582 feet) which towers over Cape Town

2. JOHANNESBURG. An aerial view of the centre of the South African mining industry, which with over a million inhabitants is also the largest town in South Africa

3. VICTORIA FALLS. The greatest waterfall in the world. The falls are on the Zambezi and were discovered by David Livingstone in 1855. The road and railway bridge in the foreground crosses the chasm separating Rhodesia and Zambia.

4. KARIBA DAM. This dam is on the Zambezi downstream from the Victoria Falls. It is at present (1970) the largest dam in Africa.

5. COMMISSIONER STREET IN 1888. In marked contrast to No. 2, this photograph shows a Johannesburg street a few years after gold had been discovered on the Witwatersrand.

6. BOSCHENDAL HOMESTEAD. This building at Groot Drakenstein in the Cape Province is a fine example of the Dutch colonial style

7–9. Peoples of South Africa. A Bushman in the Kgalagadi (*top*); a Zulu boy (*bottom, left*); an Afrikaner farmer in Cape Province (*bottom, right*)

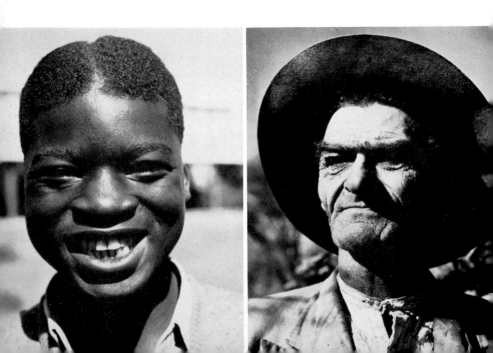

10–11. LESOTHO. A horseman at Mont-aux-Sources, 11,000 feet up in the Drakens-berg Mountains (*above*), and a mother with her child (*below*)

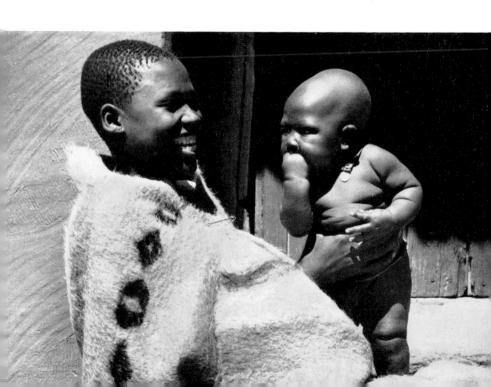

12. BOTSWANA. A camel patrol in the Kgalagadi

13. An African farmer in Rhodesia

14. ZIMBABWE. The ruins of a stone temple at Zimbabwe near Victoria, Rhodesia

15. "THE WHITE LADY". This beautiful 15¾-inch painting of a young woman appears among the rock-friezes in the caves of the Brandberg, about 100 miles north of Walvis Bay in South West Africa. Its origin and subject have been much discussed

16–18. GOLD-MINING IN SOUTH AFRICA. A shaft-sinking crew at work, filling the kibbles with blasted rock before it is hoisted to the surface (*above*); white and black miners removing the loose overhanging rock at the working face before drilling (*right*); drilling the gold-bearing rock before blasting (*below*)

19–20. Diamond-Mining in South Africa. White and black miners laying fuses in diamond-bearing blue ground at the Premier Diamond Mine (*right*); blue ground being loaded into trucks after blasting (*below*)

21–22. COPPER-MINING IN ZAMBIA. Norrie Shaft at Chibuluma (*above*), and the Chingola open-cast pit at Nchanga (*below*)

23. TEA PLANTATION IN MALAWI. Tea was introduced into Malawi in 1878 and has been grown commercially since the coffee crop failed in 1901. This plantation is in one of the main tea-growing areas, round the base of Mlanje Mountain, seen in the background

24. ALOES IN SOUTH AFRICA. A plant native to South Africa which yields drugs and fibres for nets and cords

25. THE ZAMBEZI NEAR TETE. Evening on the great river about 300 miles from the coast in Portuguese East Africa.

26. LUANDA WATERFRONT. The new houses give an almost Mediterranean air to the capital of Angola

27. THE ANGOLAN 'PLAN-ALTO'. The dramatic escarpment in western Angola as the mountains drop down to the sea

28. THE PUNGWE RIVER, RHODESIA, rises in the eastern mountains and flows into Mozambique

29–30. PEOPLE OF PORTUGUESE
AFRICA. A girl from northern
Mozambique has decorated her
face with white chalk for ceremonial reasons (*above*); these two
African girls of Angola show
strong Portuguese influence in
their dress (*right*)

31. CHILDREN OF ANGOLA. The little girl in the foreground shows clear signs of mixed ancestry

miles of the Johannesburg City Hall. In some places the reef is being worked at most prodigious depths. E.R.P.M., 11,301 feet, is the deepest mine in the world. In 1970 the yield from the South African gold mines was worth about £480 million.

Ninety-four years ago the little son of a farmer named Jacobs picked up a pebble on the banks of the Orange River. This pebble was found to be a 21¾ carat diamond.[1] Diamondiferous pipes were later found at Kimberley and the foundations were thus laid of an industry that provided the money for the conquest of Central Africa and for the development of the gold mines of the Witwatersrand. The principal diamond mines in South Africa are those round Kimberley, the Premier Mine near Pretoria, and Jagersfontein in the Orange Free State. Alluvial diamonds are found in or near the Vaal River west of Kimberley, in the south-west Transvaal, and at the Orange River mouth. The 'Cullinan', weighing about 1½ lb., and the largest white diamond ever discovered, was found in the Premier Mine in 1905. An alluvial stone, the 'Jonker' Diamond, 726 carats, about the size of a hen's egg, was found near the Premier Mine in 1934. The industry is very closely controlled in order to prevent a glut that would lower prices.

Apart from gold and diamonds, South Africa is a major producer *inter alia* of platinum, antimony, chrome, manganese, vanadium, asbestos and uranium. In all more than fifty minerals are mined in South Africa, and total production accounts for something like half the mineral output of the whole African continent. There are huge deposits of coal and iron ore, most of them easily accessible and extensively used in local industry, only a fraction being exported. In 1966 mining began on a large mass of low-grade copper ore at Phalaborwa in the north-eastern Transvaal. This will be one of the biggest open-pit workings in the world. One mineral that South Africa has not so far discovered is oil. In spite of vigorous efforts no significant quantities have been found. A certain amount, however, is produced from coal.

## (ii) *Manufactures*

The manufacturing industries of South Africa received a strong

[1] The official year book quotes a letter in the *Diamond News*, October 1956, which states that a Captain Richardson of the 86th Regiment, which was stationed at Cape Town in 1797, acquired a 56¼ carat diamond for a guinea. In 1810 an Irish traveller, William Hume, purchased another Cape Diamond for £10. (*State of the Union, economic, financial and statistical yearbook for the Union of South Africa, 1959/60, p. 169.*)

impetus during the Second World War when it became difficult, if not impossible, to obtain certain kinds of goods from overseas. The most important development is the steel industry. The government-sponsored ISCOR (Iron and Steel Industrial Corporation), which uses local iron and coal, expects to produce 5,100,000 tons of steel annually by 1971. The textile industry is also an exceedingly flourishing one. Other important manufacturing industries are metal engineering, chemicals, printing, vehicle making, stonework, and the heat, light and power industries.

### (iii) *Agriculture and Animal Husbandry*

The first European farmers in South Africa were agriculturalists who planted wheat and vines in or near the Cape Peninsula. Then, as settlement spread to regions too dry for agriculture, the pioneers took to cattle raising. The vine still dominates agriculture in certain areas of the Cape Province, and South Africa produces a variety of wines of good quality. There is also a fruit farming industry of comparatively recent growth but of considerable importance. Sugar cane production is a major industry in the coastal belt of Zululand and Natal. Tobacco is another successful economic crop, growing well round Rustenburg in the Transvaal. By far the most important cereal is maize, a most valuable staple food for the Africans. It is grown by both whites and blacks in the 'maize triangle' of the Transvaal and Orange Free State. Well behind maize come wheat, oats, sorghum, barley and rye. The cattle and dairy industry caters entirely for local consumption and there is no surplus for export. There are about 15 million cattle in the country in European and African hands. The basis of all beef and dairy stock is the Afrikander, a type evolved by selection from a native variety.

Of greater importance than cattle are sheep, which were first imported into South Africa from Holland in 1654. Eighty per cent of the sheep are now merinos which were found at the beginning of the nineteenth century to be well adapted to South African conditions. Wool is the most important agricultural product in South Africa and comes second only to gold as an export commodity. Most of the wool clip comes from the Cape Province, notably from the Great Karroo, which is particularly well adapted to sheep rearing.

Agriculture in the Bantu homelands suffers from the usual defects of African agriculture, and production is lower than it need be. The staple crops are maize, millet, sorghum, beans, and sweet potatoes.

REPUBLIC OF SOUTH AFRICA

Cattle are of considerable social and ceremonial importance and quantity is generally preferred to quality. As a result cattle are poor and small, though there are exceptions.

Mention should here be made of the Orange River Project. This is a vast scheme to utilize the waters of South Africa's greatest river for irrigation, town supplies and the provision of power to industry. The plan envisages three major reservoirs, nine smaller dams or weirs, a tunnel 51½ miles long, twenty hydro-electric stations and many thousand miles of irrigation canals. Present estimates of cost amount to £500 million or more and the project will take more than thirty years to complete. It is expected to make a most important contribution to the nation's economy.

(iv) *Communications*

South Africa has an even coastline and first-class harbours are consequently few. The river estuaries are almost all blocked by sand-bars and there is a dearth of sheltered bays. However, such harbours as do exist are very good. The two busiest are Cape Town and Durban and these are followed by Port Elizabeth, East London and Mossel Bay.

The discovery of diamonds and gold was quickly followed by extensive railway construction and South African Railways now link the interior to the ports and serve all the more important areas in the country. There is a line from Cape Town to the Botswana boundary which links South Africa to the Central African system. Good road transport services provide feeders to the railway in the rural areas. There is also a comprehensive system of air services which serves many important centres in the country and links South Africa with the outside world.

*The Economy and The People*

The economic development of South Africa springs in large part from the exploitation of minerals. Mining has led to the building of railways, the establishment of industries, the growth of towns, secure markets for the products of agriculture. The social effects have been no less dramatic. The countryman, both black and white, has come to the towns in great numbers. This has resulted, in the African, in a decay of the old simple morality, and the loss of his tribal loyalties. Though this may also to some extent be true of the European it has also in his case had a further, political, effect. Whereas it was formerly broadly true that the Nationalist party was predominantly a rural party, relying for support on the Afrikaner farmers, this is no longer the case. The Afrikaner has invaded, and now threatens, the urban constituencies that the United Party once regarded as safely theirs. It is therefore probable that unless there is defection within their own ranks or serious civil commotion the Nationalists will continue to govern the country for many years to come.

Of the half million Africans employed in the mining industry less than half come from the Republic. The others are from neighbouring territories. There are three forms of contract. Under the contract system proper the minimum period of engagement is 180 shifts. The prospective employees are medically examined and attested at some centre in their own country, and are then conducted to the mine of their choice at the expense of the industry. Here they are again medically examined, and those rejected are sent home, also at the industry's expense. The second form of contract is the 'assisted voluntary system', whereby men are accepted after a medical examination in the Republic or in one of the adjacent territories and undertake to apply for employment at a mine within thirty days. They receive an advance of travelling expenses and they choose their own mine after a short initial period of engagement. Their travelling expenses are refunded to them if they complete a continuous working period of 180 shifts underground. Finally, men who make their own way to the mines are engaged under the 'voluntary system'. Many of those falling within the last category are employed on surface work. Life in the compounds is monastic, and, one would think, drab and dull, food is scientifically planned and well prepared, hygiene is carefully observed, and medical attention is very good. The compound managers are men especially chosen for their experience of Africans and knowledge of African languages, and are at pains to keep their charges in good heart and free from worries. The mine labourers are usually healthier at the end of their contract than at the beginning of it and the fact that they return to the mines time after time seems to show that the work is not uncongenial. Three quarters of a million Natives are in other industries. Here the wages are considerably higher than in mining, and the Native has some hope of attaining at any rate semi-skilled status in his employment. On the other hand conditions are not always so secure, and the employee may be put to many inconveniences, such, for instance, as difficulty in finding somewhere to live, that are absent from the mining industry.

With the importation of slaves for service with the early settlers, the Dutch East India Company laid the foundations of the South African labour system, wherein the heavy work is done by Africans. If at that time the decision had been taken to import and encourage white workmen, the southern tip of Africa might have become a white man's country, built, like Australia, Canada and New Zealand, by white men's hands. In South Africa the white man considers himself to be exempt from hard physical labour, this being regarded as the lot of the black. The South African industrial economy is thus divided in two horizontal layers, one on top of the other. From the head of some mining concern right down to the foreman controlling a small gang of 'boys', it is the white man who directs, and the black who does the physical work. In the trades the industrial colour bar operates to reserve skilled occupations to Europeans, and in spite of the economic disadvantages of this arrangement in the face of rising costs the European trades unions see to it that this remains so.

*Problems of Race*

The South African attitude towards colour is partly a product of history. The first Africans whom the early immigrants saw were Hottentots and Bushmen, and they recoiled from any suggestion (such as was made by the missionaries) that they could have anything in common with people such as these. The early period of settlement was followed by one of expansion, and in expanding, the settlers came into conflict with the Bantu tribes. There was hardly a time, up to quite late in the nineteenth century, when there was not a native war going on somewhere. Thus the African came to be regarded as the enemy, temporarily suppressed, no doubt, but only waiting his chance to follow a new Shaka, a new Dingaan, in a war against the whites. To the fear of rebellion and massacre must now be added that of economic and political competition. Admit the blacks to full commercial and political equality, say the whites, and they will swamp us by sheer weight of numbers. Finally there is the atavistic aversion, sexual in origin, to social contacts with people considered racially inferior.

These factors have created a colour bar which excludes the nonwhite from all participation on equal terms in white society. Black may not live with white, nor eat and drink with him, nor study, work, play, bathe, or travel with him, or go to the same places of amusement, nor worship God with him, nor even shake him by the hand. The black man's only place in white society is that of a servant or an unskilled worker.

The policy of discrimination against people of colour has provoked much criticism in a world where the majority of people are coloured. Such criticism may come ill from some countries where conditions except among the ruling classes are much worse than in South Africa. Nevertheless many of the charges are well founded, and South Africa, quite convinced that she is the only one in step, has tended in reply to turn in more and more upon herself.

The theory of *apartheid*, which means 'separateness', is not, like the colour bar, in essence an assertion of superiority. It merely implies that white and black shall live apart. As the guide book blandly says, 'It is intended that as the non-Europeans develop their own residential areas, they will themselves staff their offices, schools, police force, hospitals, etc. with opportunities of advancement not hitherto open to them.'[1] Whereas the colour bar is designed to protect a privileged position, *apartheid* is a plan whereby two races may live beside each other without friction.

The Afrikaner is not naturally a good 'mixer' with other races, be they white or black, and *apartheid* is nothing new. It is clear that the Boers who trekked away from the Cape Colony in 1836 did their best at first to avoid entanglements with Africans. For a number of reasons they did not succeed, and even those who went furthest afield in their search for empty land soon found themselves in alliance or at odds with native tribes. If the Boers had been a nation of smallholders and South Africa had remained a poor agricultural and pastoral country, some kind of segregation might perhaps have been possible. As it was, every Boer regarded a farm of 6,000 acres at least as his birthright, and was bound therefore to enclose native holdings, whose original owners became dependants and squatters; and the revolution brought about by mining brought Africans in thousands, and then in millions, into the industrial areas to live cheek by jowl with the white man. *Apartheid* was designed to re-create segregation between the races and to arrest a process which South Africans consider demoralizing for the African and threatening to the European. The African's proper place is with his tribe in his homeland. His government is not parliamentary democracy, but traditional tribal government. He does not therefore need the franchise. Where African populations are unfortunately completely divorced from tribal life and have no other

---

[1] *Year Book and Guide to Southern Africa, 1959* (Union Castle Line), p. 24.

possible home but the town, arrangements will be made under the Group Areas Act,[1] for them to live in their own areas, some distance from those in which the European lives. Meanwhile—and this is no invention of the Nationalists—the Africans in towns are subject to a number of petty restrictions, the most irksome of which are the pass laws. These involve Africans in frequent conflicts with the police, choke the courts with technical offenders and fill the gaols with people who are not really criminals.

Apart from the vexatious and often tragic incidentals of South African racial policy, *apartheid* in practice has contradictions which render its achievement impossible. It may be arguable that polarization, as the proponents of *apartheid* contend, is the only way to prevent friction between the races. But to this extreme South Africans do not go. The white man has now become so accustomed to the African as the basis of his whole structure that he cannot do without him. While preaching segregation, South Africans apply part-integration. A simple case is that of the black nursemaid in a European family, integrated as part of the household during the day, but required at night to repair to a native township. On the grand scale, it is absurd to pretend that the mass of black workers in the towns, on whom the economy so much depends, belong to some different society. There are African families that have lived in the cities for three or four generations and have no ties at all with a Bantu homeland. These people cannot possibly think of their destiny except in the context of white civilization. The process of westernization has gone too far to be reversed and to them 'separate development' has no meaning. Would it not be better if South Africans, like the Portuguese, would go even half-way to meet 'assimilated' Africans and recognize a special civil status based on qualifications?

As to the homelands, *apartheid* is precluded by physical conditions alone. The units are too scattered and too poor to give the African a life of true prosperity and independence, however sincerely the government, and particularly the officials on the spot, may strive for his betterment. To provide the necessary resources the map would have to be redrawn so as to give the Africans say five times as much land as they hold at present, in homogeneous blocks. This operation would involve the transfer not only of bare acres but also of economic assets. It would have to be recognized that mines, ports, railways and so on would be included and that arrangements would have to be made to work them for the benefit of the new owners. Some people,

[1] See p. 68 and fn.

including at least one African, have suggested, perhaps not quite seriously, that the solution to South Africa's problems lies in partition: the country to be divided roughly into two parts, one white, one black. Once the land transfer had taken place, the European would work his own patch like other people, by the sweat of his brow and without black labour. This would be true *apartheid*, and it is inconceivable that any South African government could even propound the beginning of it and survive.

Since *apartheid* is ruled out, what is left? Nothing but a revolution within the present structure. The races may remain where they are alongside each other, their lives inextricably intertwined, but two forms of colour bar at least must be abolished, the industrial and the political. In industry Africans could reach a high rung of the ladder and nothing should be done to prevent them from doing so. In politics, though one would not wish to dogmatize on the question of a common roll, a way should be found whereby Africans may be represented *by their own people* in the highest councils of the land. The removal of industrial and political disabilities should of course be accompanied by the abolition of discriminatory legislation and also by a total change in white social attitudes towards blacks. Personal relations between races are difficult to govern by law and it is probably impossible to legislate effectively for them. Nevertheless this, a reform in behaviour and outlook, could be the most beneficial of all.

### The Republic

The referendum which turned the Union into a republic was for white people only, which means that thirteen million of Her Majesty's subjects were removed from their allegiance in proceedings in which they played no part, and in many cases against their will. It must be said at once that the referendum turned much more on domestic matters than on the issue of monarchy or republic, and the result may be read as a vote of confidence for the native policy of the government. In fact the change can have made no difference to the Africans themselves, since the power of the British Government to influence native affairs in South Africa could not have been weaker than it already was. At the same time doubts cast upon the Nationalists' claim that the Republic would make possible a united South Africa by removing the 'colonial' loyalties of the British section were not confirmed, since the two white sections are held together by their attitude to colour, and the Commonwealth is not an issue now.

The Republic represents the triumph of Afrikanerdom. Liberal voices with a few brave exceptions are muted, and flirtations with multi-racial ideas are firmly suppressed by the régime. Paradoxically any existing threat to the government comes not from the left but from the extreme right, which denounces present Nationalist policy as too liberal.

Meanwhile South Africa is riding high on a tide of prosperity, and the closing of the Suez Canal has restored some of the early strategic and commercial importance of the Cape as a half-way house between east and west. The country is self-sufficient in a way that we in Great Britain can hardly imagine, and if oil should be found, will become even more so.

## The Future

We deceive ourselves if we think that the Afrikaner's ideas on colour will be gravely shaken by world opinion. His convictions are in-built and he regards them as the very condition of his existence: unlike the more shallow-rooted settler communities in other parts of Africa, he has no other country to which the wind of change could blow him.

Afrikaners have always regarded themselves as a small proud nation, fated perpetually to battle alone against a great hostile power. The old enemy came successively in the guise of a missionary, a British governor, a capitalist, a soldier, a politician. Now he is embodied in the whole disapproving world. Other white South Africans are less rigid and more willing to make concessions here and there. But most of them stop short of anything that might upset the balance of power. At the same time all sections of the white community point to the good social services that are provided for all races, particularly medicine. They claim with justice that for the blacks especially, these are the best in Africa.

Nevertheless the South African Government is very conscious of the country's political isolation and is making cautious efforts to break it down. The Republic's immediate neighbours, Lesotho, Botswana and Swaziland are quite co-operative, while Malawi is friendly. Towards the end of 1970 amicable talks were held with the Malagasy Republic (Madagascar). At the same time there were signs of lessening hostility in some parts of francophone Africa.

The operative factors in all this are trade and commerce, since there is no country that does not stand to gain from economic ties with South Africa. Granted this, it may not be too much to hope that warmer relationships with the rest of Africa will have a moderating effect on native policy within the Republic.

For the moment, however, those who look for a better deal for South African blacks may find grounds for optimism in the evasion by the whites themselves of the dottier provisions of the *apartheid* laws. Even more important factors for change lie in the very prosperity that South Africa enjoys. There is an acute shortage of skilled workers in industry and in the professions. In spite of job reservation in favour of whites, non-whites are finding their way fairly steadily into higher employment. In these areas of the economy at least, sheer necessity must in time break down the colour barrier.[1]

## SOUTH WEST AFRICA

### The Country

South West Africa has an area of some 320,000 square miles and occupies the drier side of the continent from the Kalahari to the Atlantic Ocean. Most of the country is plateau land with an average altitude of 3,600 feet, varied by a number of small mountain ranges. The coastal belt is the desert called Namib. No permanent river flows through the territory, the only running streams being on the boundaries, the Orange River in the south and the Kunene and Okavango in the north. The rainfall is unreliable and droughts are of frequent occurrence. The zone of highest rainfall is the north-eastern corner, which is also the most densely populated part of the territory. The plateau round Windhoek, the capital, has extensive grasslands and is very good ranching country. The Caprivi Strip is a freakish tongue of land a hundred miles long by thirty wide running westwards from the north-eastern tip of the territory and separating Angola and a part of south-west Zambia from the Republic of Botswana. The Strip is generously watered by the Okavango, Kwando or Linyanti, and Zambezi Rivers, and is not infrequently flooded in places.

### German Colonization and After

In 1882 a German merchant named Franz Lüderitz purchased land round Angra Pequeña from the local chief. The British Government refused to take advantage of the opportunity offered to them by the German Chancellor Bismarck to act as the protect-

---

[1] As regards the Coloured people, a break occurred early in 1971 in the building trade.

ing power, with the result that in 1884 Bismarck himself, weary of protracted negotiations, assured Lüderitz and his associates of German protection. This led in due course to annexation by Germany of the settlements and the hinterland. In 1903 the Herero tribe rose against the Germans and the revolt was put down with such appalling ferocity that the tribe was reduced in numbers from eighty thousand to fifteen thousand. The Hottentots joined in the rebellion and it was not till 1908 that the authority of the Germans was re-established. Reforms in the German colonial system hardly had time to prove themselves before war broke out in 1914 and South West Africa was captured by South African forces. When the war ended the mandate to administer the territory on behalf of the League of Nations was conferred on South Africa. The mandated territory included the Caprivi Strip. Owing to the inaccessibility of the Strip and the consequent difficulty of controlling it from South West Africa, it was placed under the administration of the Union in 1939.

The Odendaal Commission (1962) recommended that the principle of separate development on the South African model should be extended to South West Africa, and this recommendation was accepted. But in spite of a vigorous and costly programme of development for the proposed homelands, it does not really seem that any of these except Ovamboland have the potential to become genuinely independent and self-supporting.

## The Question of Status

At the end of the Second World War, South Africa, alone of the states still administering mandates, declined to place South West Africa under United Nations trusteeship on the grounds that U.N.O. was not legal heir to the defunct League and that the latter had no power to transfer its functions to any other organization. Moreover, pointing to the close associations between the two countries, South Africa proposed that South West Africa be incorporated in the Union as a fifth province, supporting this proposal with the statement that the majority of the natives were in favour of it.

In spite of much international pressure, South Africa, while affirming her intention to administer South West Africa in the spirit of the mandate, has persisted in her attitude towards the United Nations and the question remains unresolved. The demand for incorporation has not been pressed but it is to be noted that the two countries have been brought much closer together politically by the grant to South West Africa of comparatively strong represen- tation (exclusively European of course) in the South African House of Assembly and Senate, and by a Citizenship Act (1949) which makes it possible for those ex-enemy aliens who were 'denaturalized' to apply once more for naturalization.

In 1958 a good offices committee of the United Nations, ap- pointed to consult with the Union Government on a possible basis for agreement, suggested that South West Africa might be parti- tioned, the north, which holds most of the native population, to be administered by the Union as an integral part of the Union under United Nations trusteeship, the rest of the territory to be annexed to the Union. The Union Government announced itself willing to consider this suggestion if invited to do so by the United Nations but at the next session the latter rejected partition as a solution. The South African attitude has often been the object of bitter inter- national criticism but there is no likelihood of any important change at present. In effect South West Africa is part of the Republic.

## The People

The Herero, almost exterminated by the Germans, are slowly regaining strength and in South West Africa have increased to 40,000. There are also well established colonies of Herero in Bot- swana, the descendants of people who took refuge there from the Germans. They occupy a position of some prestige and do not appear likely to return to South West Africa. The Herero are a people of striking appearance whose tall, lanky build and straight narrow features have been ascribed to a Hamitic strain.[1] The Ovambo, an important tribe numbering about 272,000, have their home in the north in the country bordering on Angola. They were never subdued by the Germans but are law-abiding, peaceful and conservative in their habits. The Nama, of whom there are about 40,000 and who live in the south of the territory, are Hottentots in origin but are now almost completely detribalized. The Bergdama or Damara, a little-known people who number 50,000–55,000, live in small settlements in the north and centre of the territory. It seems that they are true Negroes[2] though they speak the language of the Nama Hottentots by whom they were captured and enslaved long ago. Their customs have also been influenced by the neigh-

[1] Seligman, *Races of Africa*, pp. 170–1.
[2] Seligman, *Races of Africa*, p. 82.

bouring Bantu. The oddly styled Bastards, who do not appear to resent the name, are 'coloured' people, descendants of Europeans and Hottentots, who form a community of about 14,000 people centred on the town of Rehoboth. Finally there are something over thirteen thousand Bushmen. The Caprivi Strip contains a population of riverain people who employ themselves in agriculture and fishing.

The white population is about 96,000 and consists largely of farmers, miners, traders, professional men, together of course with a number of government officials and missionaries. Whites started to settle in this territory during the 19th century, even before the establishment of German authority. They are mostly of South African or German extraction. The official languages are Afrikaans and English, as in South Africa, but German is widely used in social and private life.

## Economy

Except in the north, agricultural conditions are poor owing to scanty rainfall, and most of the territory is devoted to stock raising both for dairying and for meat. In particular the breeding of karakul sheep for pelts is a flourishing industry. There has been a remarkable development in the fisheries of the Atlantic coast and these are now an important factor in the economy. In value of production the principal industry is mining. There are extensive deposits of alluvial diamonds of high quality from the mouth of the Orange River northwards to Conception Bay, a distance of 300 miles. Other minerals are copper, lead, vanadium, tin, manganese, beryl, lithium and various semi-precious stones.

South West Africa is connected to the South African railway system, and Windhoek has good air services. Walvis Bay and Lüderitz Bay (former Angra Pequeña) are good natural harbours.

The hydro-electric project on the Kunene River between South West Africa and Angola has a high place in development planning.

## The White Lady of the Brandberg

Among the many fine Bushman paintings in the caves of the Brandberg in the country north of Walvis Bay there is one that is of very special interest. This is 'The White Lady of the Brandberg'. It is a portrait of a young woman with attractive features and of slim build, a net of pearls round her hair, her hips and breasts adorned with ribbons and pearls. In her right hand she carries a cup and in her left a bow and four arrows. There are plumes in one armlet and she is wearing shoes. Her face and neck, and her body from well above the waist to her feet, are white. She gives a marvellous impression of youth and freshness and grace and not unnaturally has provoked much speculation and argument. Who was this White Lady? Was she a princess? Did she come from Egypt or North Africa? Or did she belong to some early race that is now extinct? A less romantic theory is that she was just a local woman whose face and body had been daubed with clay. Whoever she was, her portrait is the most important rock painting in Africa, and, with the exception of some in Spain, in the world.                                    (*Plate* 15)

## Lesotho, Botswana, Swaziland

Embedded in the Republic of South Africa are the three territories of Lesotho, Botswana and Swaziland. All three were once British dependencies administered by the British High Commissioner in South Africa[1] and hence known as the High Commission Territories. Under the British régime Botswana and Lesotho were known as the Bechuanaland Protectorate and Basutoland respectively. They changed their names to the present ones, which mean the same thing in the vernacular,[2] when they became independent in 1966.

Although politically distinct from South Africa, the three territories are ethnically and geographically part of the powerful Republic which partially or wholly surrounds them. Culturally they are also within the South African orbit and their economic connection with their giant neighbour is such as to amount to dependence.

### LESOTHO

*History*

The modern 'Basuto Nation' was founded about 1830 by a chief named Moshesh during the turmoil caused by the wars of the Zulu chief Shaka. Moshesh gathered round him the remnants of broken tribes and by wise statesmanship and clever diplomacy became the acknowledged leader of a large and expanding group of people who presently became known as Basotho, commonly and incorrectly Basuto. With the arrival of white people in his country Moshesh

---

[1] As British diplomatic representative he ceased to be High Commissioner on 31 May 1961 and became Ambassador to the new Republic.

[2] The prefixes Bo- and Le- convey the meaning of country, land (of).

came to the conclusion that the best guarantee of his people's future was British protection, and his policy was henceforward directed to this end. In 1868 Basutoland was declared British territory.

Moshesh died in 1870 and in the following year Basutoland was annexed to the Cape, a step taken without much consultation with the people. War between the Cape and Basutoland broke out in 1880 when the Cape Government tried to disarm the Basuto. The result was inconclusive and open war was followed by a period of great confusion. Finally the Cape asked the British Government to be relieved of the troublesome charge. The British Government, exceedingly tepid, eventually yielded and in 1884 the Basuto were once more taken over by the imperial authorities.

After this last annexation Basutoland led the uneventful but not unhappy existence of a British dependency. In the 1914–18 war several thousand Basuto volunteered for service in the African Labour Corps. In the 1939–45 war over twenty thousand enlisted in the Royal Pioneer Corps and saw service in North Africa, the Middle East and Italy, earning high praise for their endurance and devotion.

British rule lasted over eighty years. The form of government was traditional, the ruler being the paramount chief and under him a large number of lesser chiefs and headmen. Most of these, including of course the paramount himself, were descended from Moshesh. British power was represented by a resident commissioner and by a cadre of administrative officers, technical officers and police. The 'parliament' of Basutoland was the Basutoland Council, consisting of elected and nominated members, all Basuto. The Council's functions were purely advisory and in 1960, as a first step towards self-government, it was replaced by a legislature.

Independence was duly granted in 1966. Paramount chief Constantine Bereng became head of state under the name Moshoeshoe (Moshesh) II, with chief Leabua Jonathan, leader of the National Party, as prime minister. In January 1970, during the first election since independence, chief Leabua, alleging irregularities and violence on the part of the opposition, declared a state of emergency and suspended the constitution. This drastic action followed four years of strife between prime minister and head of state, the former accusing the King of meddling in politics and flirting with opposition politicians. The King withdrew into obscurity and chief Leabua proceeded to rule the country with the support of the National Party.

## The Country and the People

Lesotho is an island in South African territory, surrounded by the provinces of Natal, the Orange Free State and the Cape. It is a high mountainous country, and of the total area of 12,000 square miles, no less than two-thirds are at an altitude above sea-level of 6,000 ft. and more, rising to 11,000 ft. in the Drakensberg range. It is not without reason that it has been called 'the Switzerland of southern Africa'. Two of the largest rivers in South Africa, the Orange and the Tugela, have their source in Lesotho and the country is well watered by numerous streams that flow off the mountains. This country of mountains has no railway and most of the main roads are in the western lowlands. For the rest there are tracks and bridle paths which the people use to get from place to place.

The Basuto (or Basotho, as they should now properly be called) are a hardy, proud, independent people, like most mountaineers, with a well developed sense of national unity based on a common language and culture. They came early under the influence of Christian missionaries and a 1956 census recorded over 70% of the population as belonging to one or other of the Christian denominations.

## Economy

The economy of Lesotho is based on agriculture and livestock and the people are a race of small peasant farmers. Pressure on available land is strong. The African population was about 1 million in 1969, and the arable land only represents 12–13 per cent of the total area of the territory. The lowland areas are now full to saturation and population is spreading into the mountain areas, which until fairly recently were reserved for the grazing of stock. Since 1936 Administration and people have been fighting a gallant battle against soil erosion with the help of substantial grants from the British Government. The exports consist of wool and mohair, followed by wheat, sorghum and cattle. Lesotho has no industries to speak of, and has to import all consumer and capital goods, as well as some agricultural produce and livestock. Imports exceed exports in value, but this is offset by the 'export' of labour to the mines and industries of South Africa (about 60,000 go there to work every year), and by the consequent flow of money back to the territory. There is a small output of diamonds.

BOTSWANA

## The Country

The Republic of Botswana covers an area of 225,000 square miles, and extends from the Molopo River, a tributary of the Orange River, in the south, to the Chobe River, which joins the Zambezi, in the north. The eastern boundary is the Transvaal and Rhodesia, while on the western side the boundary is South West Africa. The territory is thus surrounded by South Africa or by South African-controlled countries except along the line where it adjoins Rhodesia.

Most of the territory consists of the Kgalagadi desert, the home of the Bushmen, not really a desert in the sense that the Sahara is one, but rather a steppe, where grass does grow when it rains, and where, if sweet underground water could be found—this is by no means improbable—human and animal life could easily be sustained.

The eastern side of Botswana is quite hilly, and in places comparatively fertile. It is in this relatively productive country that the majority of the population lives.

The remote north-western corner of Botswana is called Ngamiland. This is the delta of the Okavango River, which rises in Angola and after flowing into the territory in a fine broad stream, presently spreads out in a vast swamp cut by narrow channels through the reeds and papyrus. Apart from the Okavango system and its northern neighbour the Chobe and a few unimportant streams on the eastern side, there is no permanent running water in Botswana. Real forest is also very scarce and is represented almost exclusively by a belt along the southern bank of the Chobe River. There are great areas of *mopane* (Colophospermum Mopane) which might pass for forest if one were not too particular, but for the remainder Botswana consists largely either of treeless steppe or of thorny scrub.

## History

In 1817 the London Missionary Society established a station on the Kuruman River in southern Bechuanaland 140 miles south of the future British Protectorate. Under the direction of the great Robert Moffat the Kuruman mission took a leading position among the Protestant missions of South Africa. The mission's most famous son was David Livingstone, who spent the first years of his ministry in Bechuanaland. In 1836 the Great Trek brought the Boers to the

G

frontiers of Bechuanaland, which thereafter had to resist continuous pressure from land-hungry trekkers. In 1884–5 the British Government, hitherto hesitant but now urged on by various motives, the first of which was fear of German expansion from South West Africa, took over most of Bechuanaland, annexed the southern part as a colony under the name of British Bechuanaland and declared a protectorate over the country north of the Molopo River.[1] In 1895 British Bechuanaland was transferred to the Cape Colony and is now part of the Republic of South Africa, but the Protectorate, which had meanwhile been extended to the Zambezi, remained at the people's wish a direct responsibility of the British Government.

British rule took the form of indirect administration through the tribal authorities and it lasted until 1965. In that year the Protectorate was granted self-rule under an African government and in 1966 became an independent republic. The president is Seretse Khama, scion of a long line of chiefs, whose marriage to an English girl in 1948 (the famous 'Seretse affair') aroused world-wide interest and considerable controversy.

### The People

The African population is 650,000 and consists of Batswana (the modern form of Bechuana) and a number of subordinate tribes. The Batswana, though not unique in this respect, differ from many other African tribes in that they live in largish towns. Arable lands and pastures are often at great distances from the towns, and the Batswana spend a considerable part of the year away from home on their lands or at their cattle posts.

### The Economy

The main railway line from Cape Town runs up the eastern side of the country. Earth roads of varying quality radiate from it to the principal towns. Work started in 1970 on a road from Francistown to Kazungula, whence the Zambezi may be crossed by ferry into Zambia. There are aerodromes at the important centres.

The Batswana have long been accustomed to work in South African mines and industries, and large numbers of men are absent from Botswana at any one time. In their own country the Batswana are peasant farmers and their pursuits are cattle raising and agriculture,

---

[1] A protectorate was then a far more tenuous form of government than it later became.

with emphasis on the former. There are over 1½ million cattle in the territory. The abattoir and cold storage built by the Colonial Development Corporation and opened in 1954 deals with over 100,000 cattle a year. South Africa is easily the biggest buyer of carcases, taking half the total number. But the biggest buyer of boneless beef from Botswana is the United Kingdom. Agricultural exports are much smaller since in cereals Botswana is barely self-sufficient and is often compelled to import essential foodstuffs.

Botswana has long been known to possess large reserves of coal as well as lesser deposits of other minerals. During the last decade, however, there have been valuable discoveries of copper, nickel and diamonds in the northern areas. Exploitation of these minerals depends on the provision of power, water supplies, transport and communications. If and when this essential infrastructure is set up, the prospects of a thriving mining industry will be good.

SWAZILAND

*The People and their Government*

The Swazi belong to the Nguni branch of the Bantu family and are therefore akin to the Zulu and the Xosa. They number about 420,000 and their traditional government is that of a paramount chief acting with the help of two councils, one made up of chiefs and notables, the other a smaller one which advises him in personal and family matters.

After 65 years as a British protectorate Swaziland became an independent kingdom within the British Commonwealth in 1968. Parliament consists of a senate and a house of assembly. Both are part nominated by the King, part elected. The King is Sobhuza II, K.B.E., who as paramount chief had ruled the Swazi since 1921. Swaziland has a European population of about 10,000.

*The Country*

Swaziland has an area of 6,700 square miles and like Botswana is almost surrounded by South African territory, being bounded on the north, west and south by the Transvaal, and on the east by Tongaland in the province of Natal; but in the east it also has a common boundary with Portuguese East Africa, and the port of Lourenço Marques is easily accessible.

The country falls into three well-defined geographical divisions, roughly equal in size, which run from north to south and are known as the high-, middle-, and low- (or bush-) veld. It is on the

whole a well-watered country and where rainfall fails, as it sometimes does, it will no doubt in due course be supplemented by
irrigation from the several excellent rivers which the country is
fortunate enough to possess.

## History

The Swazi say that they originally lived in southern Tongaland,
and that they migrated about 150 years ago to the country west of
the Lebombo mountains, between the Pongola and Great Usutu
Rivers. About 1815 they were involved in a dispute with the
Ndwandwe, another Nguni group which was ultimately absorbed
by Shaka's Zulus. The Swazi fled to the site of present day Bremers-
dorp in the Eastern Transvaal under their chief Sobhuza or
Somhlolo. Here they prospered and expanded. Under Sobhuza and
his successor Mswazi they occupied the country right up to Bar-
berton in the north and extending towards Carolina and Ermelo in
the west. They also claim that the tribes living in the district now
called Lydenburg gave allegiance to the Swazi chief. These wide
dominions were later considerably reduced. In 1846 Mswazi ceded
whatever rights he had round Lydenburg to the Lydenburg Republic. Then the Pretoria Convention of 1881, which defined the
frontiers of the Transvaal, still further reduced the area over which
the Swazi formerly held sway. All these modifications were made
quite peaceably and the Swazi were never seriously disturbed by
war after their original flight to the north from their home in
Tongaland. They suffered occasional raids from the Zulus, which
they always survived, and the Zulu chief Dingaan, Shaka's mur-
derer and successor, was killed by the Swazi when he fled north
for safety after his defeat by the Boers and his own brother Mpande.
One Zulu raid took place in 1847, and in 1855 the Swazi ceded a
narrow strip of land to the Boers along the northern bank of the
Pongola River on purpose to put Europeans between the Zulus and
themselves.

Apart from these mild diversions the Swazi seem to have
weathered the nineteenth century fairly well. This may have been
due to the fact that they were themselves of fighting stock and knew
very well how to look after themselves. In addition they appear to
have accommodated themselves more easily to Europeans than
either the Basotho or the Batswana. They were for a long time
friends and allies of the Transvaalers, and they were also friends of
the British. The Swazi managed to preserve a comfortable balance

between the two until quite late in the century, though in the end they too became involved in the rivalry between Boer and Briton and in 1894 passed into the power of the South African Republic.

After the Boer War Swaziland was attached to the Commission of the Governor of the Transvaal and in 1906 was transferred to the High Commissioner for South Africa.

## Land

The land question is complicated by the reckless concessions given out by Mswazi's successor Mbandeni. This wretched chief sold away every conceivable right until the whole of the country had in fact been parcelled out to concessionaires. In 1907 one third was expropriated and became available for the Natives and since then other land has been bought by the government and the Paramount Chief with the result that about one half of Swaziland is now available for native occupation.

Land distribution in Swaziland is a patchwork affair and European and African areas are much intermingled. It has been suggested that this situation, while increasing the difficulty of governing the country, has the good effect of increasing understanding between the two races and has also influenced the African to adopt higher standards of housing and agriculture.

## Economy

Compared to Lesotho and Botswana, Swaziland has a fairly advanced economy and a varied one. Asbestos from the Havelock mine, one of the world's larger mines, gives the country a significant place among producers. In recent years asbestos has been overtaken by iron ore, which is now Swaziland's most valuable export. To carry the ore from the mine to the coast it was necessary to build a railway to the border of Mozambique. This railway also enables large coal deposits to be exploited. On the whole Swaziland enjoys a good rainfall and this makes it possible for softwoods to be grown commercially. These are now an important feature of the economy. Sugar is another leading export, cane being grown under irrigation from the waters of the Usutu and Komati Rivers. In spite of these developments the Swazi remain to a large extent subsistence farmers. They do, however, manage to supply themselves with staple foods and they keep considerable numbers of cattle. Cotton and rice are grown as cash crops. Although many Swazi go to South Africa in search of work, migrant labour is not such an important aspect of the economy as in Lesotho and Botswana.

*Prospects*

Lesotho, Botswana and Swaziland have always had a special place in the politics of southern Africa. South Africa long claimed that the High Commission Territories, as they were then, should be part of the Union, and the question of 'incorporation' hung over the future for many years. The South African case was based on geographical, economic and political grounds, some of which were very strong. Fortunately better counsels prevailed. The people themselves were resolutely opposed to incorporation, while Great Britain, though her attitude was at times equivocal, rightly came to the conclusion that she was under a strong moral obligation to protect these territories as long as protection was needed.

Under independent governments the three countries appear at present to be on satisfactory terms with South Africa. They enjoy the benefits arising from the existence of a rich, well equipped and well disposed neighbour. On the other hand it suits South Africa to have on her borders three reasonably stable states sufficiently realistic not to be excessively influenced by the attitudes of other countries further north. The only thing likely to disturb the position would be the growth in the territories of movements actively hostile to the Republic. South African reactions would be sharp and the result would be the loss of a relationship which it is in most people's interest to preserve.

Apart from politics, there is another important question to be answered. Have these countries by themselves potentially the means to provide their people with the fuller, richer life to which they have the right to aspire? In so far as internal resources are concerned, the answer in the case of Botswana and Swaziland is a qualified yes. Indeed one can foresee the time when, thanks to mineral discoveries, Botswana may achieve considerable freedom from the South African economic system, though one would expect strong links to remain. But Lesotho, overcrowded and living off emigrant labour and a precarious agricultural and pastoral economy, is a different proposition. Heavy dependence on outside sources seems certain for many years to come.

# CHAPTER TWO

# CENTRAL AFRICA

THIS region comprises Rhodesia, Zambia, Malawi (the former Federation of Rhodesia and Nyasaland) and the Portuguese colonies of Mozambique (Portuguese East Africa) and Angola. It stretches in a broad band across the continent and is bounded on the south by southern Africa and in the north by Tanzania and Congo/ Zaïre. It may be argued that the Portuguese colonies do not properly belong to Central Africa, but there are good reasons for including them. Angola lies roughly on the same latitude as the three inland territories; it has strong and fairly recent historical associations with them;[1] and it contains the upper basin of the Zambezi River, which is a dominant feature of the region. On the other side of the continent Portuguese East Africa is clearly the seaboard of Central Africa. It was for centuries the door in and out of Zambezia (if one may so call the country through which the great river flows), and it is the natural entrepôt for the trade of the central and eastern parts of the region, though political events since 1965 have made the position in this respect ambiguous.

## The Country

The region is flanked on either side by a coastal plain which rises more or less steeply through an intermediate zone of irregular terraces to the great plateau which forms the backbone of Africa. In Mozambique the littoral belt is widest in the south and narrows towards the north. The coastal climate is tropical, rainfall fairly abundant and vegetation luxuriant. The Mozambique plateau has a mean altitude of 3,500 feet and is rimmed on the west by mountains. The temperature is reduced by altitude and rainfall shows a decrease from the coast inland, increasing again in the highlands. Mozambique has several important rivers, including the mighty Zambezi which cuts the country in two, and the Limpopo which rises in the Transvaal and runs into the Indian Ocean north of Lourenço Marques. The natural vegetation is largely of the

[1] For instance, Livingstone's first journey; claims made by the Portuguese to possession of a broad belt across Africa which included these territories; the trend and direction of the Slave Trade.

savannah type but there is dense forest inland from Beira and fertile zones in the areas watered by the great rivers and in the uplands near the frontier of Tanzania. Malaria is endemic on the coast and in low-lying areas; there is tsetse fly in many places and it is believed to be spreading. The total area of the territory is about 298,000 square miles.

In Angola the coastal plain is thirty to one hundred miles wide and is really nothing but the northerly extension of the South West African desert. The rainfall is low and the coast is only saved from complete aridity by the relative humidity of the atmosphere. The plateau has an altitude of four thousand to seven thousand feet and is a rolling well-watered tableland falling away in the east to the Congo and Zambezi basins and in the south to the South West African desert. Large numbers of streams and rivers, the most important of which is the Kwango, flow northwards off the plateau into the Kasai, one of the largest of the Congo's affluents, which in its upper course forms for three hundred miles the boundary between Angola and the land of the Congo. Other rivers rising on the plateau are the Kwanza and the Kunene which both flow westwards to the Atlantic, the latter in its lower course forming the boundary between Angola and South West Africa. The vegetation of Angola is savannah of various kinds and there is some forest along the larger rivers in the north. The area of the territory is nearly half a million square miles.

Rhodesia, Zambia and Malawi all lie on the great African plateau. Rhodesia has an area of approximately 150,000 square miles and consists of a belt of highland at a general level of something over 3,500 feet running through the middle of the country from the south-west to the mountainous eastern border, enclosed by the lowlands of the Zambezi and Limpopo Rivers and of Mozambique on the north, south and east. Rainfall averages 32 inches in the year and is more reliable on the eastern side than on the west, and the south-west of the country tends to be dry. The natural vegetation is savannah but there are considerable areas of open forest, and in the Zambezi lowlands denser forests where valuable timber is found.

Zambia with an area of approximately 290,000 square miles is flat and undulating and lies between 3,000 and 4,000 feet, rising occasionally to 5,000 feet. There are individual mountain peaks of 8,000 feet. The area includes much of the watershed of the Zambezi and Congo Rivers. The rainfall varies between 50 inches in the north to 25 inches in the south and drought often occurs between

May and October. The vegetation is savannah merging into park-
land in areas of heavier rainfall. The climate is eminently bearable
except in the valleys of the Zambezi and Luangwa during the hot
and rainy seasons.

The key to the geography of Malawi is the Great Rift Valley,
which runs through the territory from end to end and forms the
trough in which lies Lake Malawi. Malawi proper consists of the
Lake itself and a narrow strip of land to the west of it. East and
west of the Rift the country is mountainous and precipitous. There
are high plateaux culminating south of the Lake in the mountain
masses of Zomba (7,000 feet) and Mlanje (10,000 feet) in the Shire
Highlands. At the other extreme, the Rift in the south is only 600
to 300 feet above sea-level. The Shire River flows from the south
end of the Lake and joins the Zambezi 250 miles from the Lake.
The climate varies with the altitude. On the Lake shore it is rather
hot and very humid and in the Shire Valley still hotter in some
months of the year. But in the highlands it is very pleasant and
healthy, and there are mists and cold nights, and fires are welcome
in the house. The rainy season lasts from November to April and the
rainfall varies from 30 to over 60 inches in the year. The total area
of Malawi is 46,000 square miles, including more than 9,000 square
miles of water.

*The People*

Portuguese East Africa was inhabited from the earliest times by
people who have long disappeared but who have left evidence of
their existence in the form of implements and rock paintings.
There are also ruins of the Zimbabwe type, indicating the presence
at one time of a race of superior culture which was without doubt
African. The population today is overwhelmingly Bantu, but
there still survive remnants of an older, possibly pre-Bantu race of
whom the Chopi are an example. This ancient race did not know
iron, and was overpowered and subdued by the invading Bantu
tribes.[1] These invaders were probably the ancestors of the Tonga
people who now predominate in the country south of the Sabi
River.[2] Exactly when the invasion took place is by no means sure,
but it was certainly in fairly remote times. After living undisturbed

[1] Henry Ph. Junod, 'Notes on the ethnological situation in Portuguese East
Africa on the south of the Zambesi' (*Bantu Studies*, Vol. X, No. 3).
[2] Not to be confused with a small group of Tonga who live round Inhambane.
These, like the Chopi, are survivors of earlier inhabitants. There are Tonga in the
northern part of Malawi and two groups in Zambia.

perhaps for several centuries, the Tonga themselves were invaded by Soshangane and his Nguni tribesmen, seeking an empire of their own. This they found in Gazaland, where they subdued the Tonga tribes in typical Zulu fashion, raiding, looting and incorporating the young men into their regiments. Many Tonga emigrated to the Transvaal, where they still are, usually as subjects of the local Sotho and Venda chiefs. After Soshangane's death his sons quarrelled over the succession and there was much fighting and insecurity. His grandson Ngungunyane was the last of the independent Nguni chiefs; after playing a part in Anglo-Portuguese rivalry he was subdued by the Portuguese in 1895.

The middle belt of the colony between the Sabi and Pungwe Rivers is occupied by a large tribe named Ndau which is connected with the people called Mashona who live on the eastern side of Rhodesia.[1] North of the Pungwe there is a mixture of tribes, many of whom also have connections with the Mashona.[2] In the northern part of the territory the virile Yao occupy the north-west corner while east of them the Makua, a large group with many sub-tribes, stretch down from the Rovuma to the Zambezi delta. The African population of Mozambique is about seven million, and in 1960 there were 97,000 Europeans (now probably 130,000), 19,000 Asians, and 31,000 people of mixed blood.

The people of Angola are Western Bantu who, though presenting a rather diverse ethnic appearance, have nevertheless coalesced so as to form large ethno-linguistic groups, remnants in some sort of the medieval kingdoms that once flourished here. The largest single group are the Ovimbundu who live on the plateau of central Angola. A powerful monarchy until subdued by the Portuguese at the turn of the present century, the Ovimbundu group is still important and influential. Other groups are the Bakongo south of the estuary of the Congo River, who have affinities with their northern neighbours in Congo/Zaïre; the Mbundu near Luanda and along the lower Kwanza valley; and the Chokwe, a vigorous people in north-eastern Angola, who originally came here from Katanga. In the arid country on the borders of South West Africa are to be found small non-Bantu communities of Hottentot and Bushman origin. The African population of Angola is between five and six million and there are about 250,000 Europeans.[3]

[1] Junod, op. cit.
[2] Junod, 'A contribution to the study of Ndau demography, totemism and history, (*Bantu Studies*, Vol. VIII, No. 1).
[3] For more about the people of Angola, see Wheeler and Pélissier, *Angola*.

We now leave the Portuguese possessions on the eastern and western sides of the continent and move inland to the three independent republics of the interior.

Archaeologists and historians have convincingly demonstrated that for a long time in the past the eastern side of central Africa was inhabited by a powerful people with a comparatively high standard of civilization. The ruins of Zimbabwe, a massive citadel built of many small blocks of granite skilfully laid without mortar, testify to a craftsmanship far superior to any that existed among the people living there in the nineteenth century. Buildings of a similar type, but simpler and smaller, are to be found in other parts of the region. As we have already noted, Zimbabwe is now generally recognized as the work of a native race.[1]                                  (*Plate* 14)

From the earliest times of Portuguese settlement there had been tales of a great king in the interior known as the Mwenemutapa. Indeed one Portuguese explorer, Antonio Fernandez, visited him at his capital north of the present site of Salisbury. Mwenemutapa was the dynastic name applied to successive rulers of a confederacy of tribes which at the time of the Portuguese arrival had already occupied central Africa from the Limpopo to the Zambezi for several centuries. This confederacy may well have included the original builders of Zimbabwe. One thing is certain, and that is that the old lords of the land mined for gold, for their workings are there for all to see. News of these workings filtered southwards and the chief attraction to European pioneers was the belief that the land that lay to the north of the Limpopo contained unlimited wealth in gold.

The principal African inhabitants of Rhodesia now are the Matabele in the west and the Mashona cluster in the east and south. The latter are sometimes called the Makaranga, but this name properly applies to only one group of the tribes in the Mashona cluster.[2] The Matabele are Nguni who seceded from Shaka's Zulu empire and then migrated under Boer pressure to the neighbourhood of modern Bulawayo. They were a warlike and bloodthirsty people, who established an empire of terror between the Zambezi and the Limpopo valleys and beyond. The Mashona were among the people whom they periodically raided for slaves and regarded as their subjects.

Like the Mashona and the people of the coastal plain, the tribes round Lake Malawi were also to experience the effects of Zulu

[1] pp. 13–14.
[2] F. W. T. Posselt, *A Survey of the Native Tribes of Southern Rhodesia*.

expansion. Yet another Nguni chieftain, Zwangendaba, in a migration that is surely one of the most remarkable in African history (there is yet another as remarkable, which will be described later), fought his way to the southern end of Lake Tanganyika. After the death of their leader his followers, who are now called Angoni,[1] split into several groups but all ultimately settled round and about Lake Malawi, where they had no difficulty in establishing themselves among the comparatively peaceful people of the Lake, with whom they intermarried, and many of whom they incorporated into their own system. About the middle of the nineteenth century the country was also invaded by Yao from Portuguese East Africa. Today the native population of Malawi consists, as to a little over three-quarters, of the original tribes and of people who have immigrated from Portuguese East Africa during the present century. The remainder, forming about 24 per cent of the whole, is made up of Yao and Angoni, the former rather the more numerous.[2]

Zambia has no less than seventy-three tribes speaking thirty different dialects falling into six main language groups. With few unimportant exceptions these tribes are descended from people who invaded the country, some from the direction of the Congo and some by a route east of Lake Tanganyika, not earlier than the beginning of the eighteenth century. Many of the tribes are small, many are disorganized, with little cohesion and without strong loyalties to any acknowledged authority. Tribal wars and the Slave Trade had already caused them to disintegrate before the coming of the Europeans. Some tribes have withstood these corrosive processes better than the others, for instance the Bemba in the north and the Barotse in the west. About 130 years ago Barotseland was invaded by a people of Sotho stock called Fokeng, who had been driven from the Orange River by tribal wars and arrived in the Zambezi valley after a journey fully comparable to that of Zwangendaba's Angoni. Under their chief Sebetwane, who became a friend of Livingstone, these Makololo, as they were called, prospered for a time in their new surroundings. They declined under his successors and in 1873, Sepopa, a chief of local ancestry, led a rebellion and annihilated all the male Makololo. The women passed to the conquerors, who also conserved the Sotho language which to this day is spoken in Barotseland.

[1] So spelt nowadays. It is obviously derived from the generic name Nguni.
[2] These figures are taken from Hailey, *Native Administration in the British African Territories*, Part II, pp. 24–25, quoting from the 1945 census. They are therefore twenty-five years old, and the situation may have changed.

The population of Rhodesia is something over 5 million. Malawi and Zambia fall short of that number with $4\frac{1}{2}$ million each, the figure for Malawi being slightly the larger. There are 230,000 Europeans in Rhodesia, 60,000–70,000 in Zambia and 7000 in Malawi.

## HISTORY

*Rhodesia*

In 1888 three emissaries of Cecil Rhodes, C. D. Rudd, J. R. Maguire and F. Thompson, extracted a mineral concession from Lobengula, chief of the Matabele. This was the Rudd Concession. The British South Africa Company, formed by Rhodes the following year with the Rudd Concession as its foundation stone, was granted a Royal Charter which gave the company the right to acquire very full powers of administration in an extensive 'field of operations'. In 1890 a band of pioneers entered Mashonaland and proceeded to make farms for themselves and to look for gold.

Inevitably there was friction with the Matabele, who looked upon the Mashona as their subjects and Mashonaland as within their territory. Lobengula himself, though he had never intended that the Rudd Concession should lead to outright occupation of land which he regarded as his, did his best to keep the peace. But hostilities broke out in 1893 when a raiding party of Matabele entered the settled area in order, so they said, to punish some delinquent Mashona. They were driven out with losses, and a force of pioneers, supported by the Bechuanaland Border Police, invaded Matabeleland. Lobengula's army was smashed in two battles, the chief himself fled and some weeks later died, all resistance collapsed, and the pioneers began to measure out farms and gold claims in Matabeleland. The Matabele, their spirit by no means crushed, rose in rebellion in 1896. The situation was complicated by a rising among the Mashona, hitherto believed to be timid and peace loving people. By negotiations with the chiefs, conducted with considerable courage, Rhodes persuaded the Matabele to lay down their arms. The Mashona rebellion dragged on far into 1897, when it came to an end with the capture or surrender of the leaders. Southern Rhodesia, uniting Matabeleland and Mashonaland, was constituted in 1898.

The history of Southern Rhodesia was one of constant, and lately, spectacular growth as a colony of settlement. In the early days of the century there was much discussion as to the country's future. There had grown considerable discontent with Company rule and the settlers now discussed alternative forms of government. The issues narrowed themselves to two: whether the territory should have its own government, or whether it should join the Union of South Africa. A referendum held in 1922 decided on the former, and in 1923 Southern Rhodesia became a British colony with responsible government. Southern Rhodesia made an outstanding contribution towards the British cause in the war of 1939–45. Rhodesians served on all fronts with all the services and took part in some of the fiercest battles of the war. The Colony also became an important part of the Empire Air Training scheme, and thousands of airmen were trained for the Royal Air Force at the Rhodesian training centres.

### Zambia and Malawi

The Portuguese, with their settlements on the east coast, had long regarded the Zambezi valley as properly theirs. On the other hand these claims were not supported by any solid or consistent attempts at settlement, and they were challenged by British missionaries and explorers long before the Scramble for Africa began. Livingstone landed at the mouth of the Zambezi in 1858 and discovered Lake Malawi in the following year. The Universities Mission to Central Africa, which came out to exploit this new field, began badly with the death of several of its members, including Bishop Mackenzie, and then retreated to Zanzibar in order to prepare a more gradual and better planned advance. Inspired by Livingstone's life and death the Free Church of Scotland founded the Livingstonia Mission in 1875 and in the following year the Church of Scotland established the mission at Blantyre. In 1878 the brothers Moir arrived to start the African Lakes Company, which was to work in close co-operation with the missionaries. In 1886 Portugal tried to counter these first British steps in Central Africa by making comprehensive treaties with France and Germany in which those powers recognized a Portuguese claim to all the territory between Portuguese East Africa and Angola. This would have had the effect of giving Portugal a broad belt right across Africa, thus barring the British advance from the south. The British Government protested and the claim came to nothing, but meanwhile, as Cecil Rhodes prepared to occupy Mashonaland, three most enterprising men, Harry Johnston, British Consul in Mozambique,

Alfred Sharpe and Joseph Thomson, negotiated treaties favourable
to the British with chiefs from Lake Malawi across to the Congo
Free State in the very territory claimed by the Portuguese, while
Lochner, a servant of the British South Africa Company, concluded
a treaty with the King of Barotseland. In 1890–91 the Scramble for
Africa resolved itself into a series of agreements between the
European powers. The agreement with Portugal assured Nyasaland
and Mashonaland to Great Britain. The convention also, incidentally,
put a stop to a spirited attempt by the British South Africa Company
to obtain possession of Gazaland, which was adjudged to be within
the Portuguese sphere. An agreement with Germany fixed the
boundary between the British sphere and German East Africa. In
1891 Malawi, as Nyasaland is now called, became a British protectorate, and the country to the west of it, now known as Zambia,
passed under the administration of the British South Africa
Company.

Once the international and constitutional position had been
settled, it became possible to deal with the Arab slave traders who
preyed on the weaker tribes round the north of Lake Malawi. The
African Lakes Company with the aid of European volunteers had
for some time waged war against the slavers, but with only moderate
success. Harry Johnston, now Commissioner for the British Protectorate, set himself to exterminate the pests with meagre forces
but with unlimited energy and this he practically succeeded in doing
by 1896 when ill health compelled him to go home. In addition he
set up the beginnings of an administration within the Protectorate,
concluded a land settlement and introduced a system of taxation.
It was a remarkable feat by a remarkable man.

From the end of the Slave Trade until quite recent times the
history of Malawi was a peaceful one. The situation at the beginning of the 1914–18 war was hazardous, owing to the common
border with German East Africa, but the immediate danger over,
the country made a notable contribution to the forces that fought
the East African campaign. It was during this war that John
Chilembwe, an African minister partly educated in the United
States, encouraged by the Germans, rose with his followers in
the Blantyre district and murdered several Europeans. Chilembwe
himself was killed and the rebellion fizzled out. During the 1939–
1945 war 30,000 men of Malawi, including a high proportion of the
small European population, served in the forces.

In the British South Africa Company's territory north of the

Zambezi it was not possible at first to do more than keep open communications and fight the Slave Trade. However, in 1899 and 1900 the territory was divided for the purpose of administration into two parts, North-western and North-eastern Rhodesia, but the two territories came together again in 1911 under the name of Northern Rhodesia. Meanwhile Europeans had entered the country and demanded representation. This they got in 1918 in the form of an Advisory Council. The question of amalgamation with Southern Rhodesia, and then, perhaps, with South Africa, was one that was frequently canvassed during the early years of European settlement. A large body of opinion in both countries declared itself against amalgamation of the Rhodesias, without which any closer connection between Northern Rhodesia and South Africa was hardly possible. Moreover European opinion in Northern Rhodesia was alarmed by expressions of Afrikaner nationalism, both in South Africa and among some of the settlers themselves, and also by the way the South African Government handled labour troubles among white workers. By the end of the First World War the Europeans were disenchanted with the Company itself and were actually looking to the Colonial Office to take the country over. In 1919 all the leading Europeans demanded that Northern Rhodesia should become a crown colony with proper unofficial representation. In 1924 Company rule was brought to an end, a Legislative Council was established, and Northern Rhodesia became an imperial protectorate.

## Federation

Although early suggestions for the amalgamation of the Rhodesias had not borne fruit, it remained true that there was a strong and growing community of interests between the three British territories. The question of closer association did not therefore die away but on the contrary became the subject of inquiry by a commission under Lord Bledisloe in 1938. The Commission reported against immediate amalgamation, and recommended instead the creation of an inter-territorial body to co-ordinate various common services. Nothing was done during the war years but in 1945 the Commission's recommendation was implemented by the establishment of the Central African Council, a consultative body with a permanent secretariat but, unlike its counterpart in East Africa, with no central legislative assembly. Pressure for a closer connection continued, and after long discussions the Federation of Rhodesia and Nyasaland was founded in 1953.

To the outsider the Federation was rather a puzzling affair. By no means all the Europeans concerned approved of it and many Africans capable of forming an opinion were actively against it. Against the undoubted advantages of unity as a source of economic strength and of power to resist the downward pull of South Africa must be set the disparate nature of the elements which it was proposed to unify: on the one hand a self-governing colony with a large European ruling class holding all the power and half the land; on the other two predominantly African protectorates, one rich, one poor, governed from London on traditional colonial lines. Adverse factors worked strongly against the Federation from the outset and it fell apart in 1963 after a short and troubled life. The three countries involved in it went their separate ways. Northern Rhodesia and Nyasaland became independent republics under the names of Zambia and Malawi respectively, and Southern Rhodesia, now the only Rhodesia, through its predominantly white representation, began to agitate for its own independence.

Meanwhile the power of the British Government to influence Rhodesian domestic affairs had dwindled to almost nothing. In 1961 the country acquired a new constitution, which, while containing some built-in safeguards against abuse by the Rhodesian whites of their position, left the British Government virtually powerless.

Between 1963 and 1965 protracted negotiations took place between Britain and Rhodesia on the issue of independence. No agreement was reached and on 11 November 1965, the anniversary of the armistice between the allies and Germany in 1918, Mr. Ian Smith, prime minister of Rhodesia, cut the Gordian knot by declaring his country independent unilaterally. A new constitution was promulgated abolishing all elements of subordination to Great Britain and arrogating the conduct of external affairs, hitherto Britain's responsibility. But the link with the Crown was retained, as were also many features of the 1961 constitution.

Mr. Smith's declaration let loose a storm. Denouncing the new régime as rebellious, the British Government imposed economic sanctions on Rhodesia including an oil embargo. At the same time Great Britain resisted a call by various African states to reduce Rhodesia to submission by force. (There was in any case no chance that the use of force would be supported by the British public). Saboteurs and guerillas, trained and armed in other countries

H

('freedom fighters' or 'terrorists' according to which side one is on), began to make attempts to enter Rhodesia from bases north of the Zambezi.

Anglo-Rhodesian relations were at a low ebb when in December 1966 talks were suddenly arranged between Mr. Smith and Mr. Harold Wilson, the British prime minister, aboard H.M.S. *Tiger*. Mr. Wilson's terms for a settlement were rejected by the Rhodesian Cabinet and Britain then requested the United Nations to impose mandatory sanctions on Rhodesia. This was done.

For more than a year after the *Tiger* talks there were no great developments in the situation, but a major crisis erupted in March 1968 round the execution in Rhodesia of three Africans convicted of murder and sentenced to death before independence. While renewed calls for the use of force against Rhodesia were rejected, the Security Council extended the scope of mandatory sanctions. Before the year was out, however, Mr. Wilson and Mr. Smith met again, this time on H.M.S. *Fearless*, but still without reaching agreement.

Meanwhile in Rhodesia a commission appointed to devise a new constitution had reported in April 1968. This constitution as finally adopted provided for a two-chamber government, consisting first of a national assembly with fifty members elected on a white voters' roll, eight on a black roll, and eight elected by chiefs, headmen and councils; secondly of a senate of ten white members, ten chiefs and three members nominated by the head of state. There is provision for an increase in the number of black M.P.s in proportion to the African contribution to income tax until the number equals that of the whites. This is a very distant goal.

The constitution proposals were approved by a referendum in June 1969. By the same referendum Mr. Smith obtained a mandate to declare a republic, which he did in March 1970.

Meanwhile neither sanctions nor the more direct activities of freedom fighters had proved at all effective. Guerilla forays into Rhodesia met with varying success but security forces helped by local villagers gradually gained the upper hand, killing or capturing numbers of infiltrators.

Similarly Rhodesia has succeeded in overcoming sanctions. The tobacco industry has suffered severely, but this has been partly offset by agricultural diversification. On the other hand there has been a significant expansion of local industry and a great intensification of mineral production. It must here be said that in resisting sanctions Rhodesia has been much helped by the sympathetic attitude of the South Africans and the Portuguese, as well as by the connivance of other nations.

But what of the other partners in the Federation, the new republics of Zambia and Malawi? Kenneth Kaunda, leader of the United National Independence Party (UNIP) and president of Zambia since 1964, has weathered several political storms but his position is still apparently firm. Dr. Hastings Banda, a leading opponent of the Federation, became president of Malawi when that country became a republic in 1966. The two countries have since pursued widely divergent policies. Dr. Kaunda has proved to be one of the most persistent critics of Rhodesia and South Africa. At some cost to his country he has joined as far as possible in enforcing sanctions against Rhodesia, and it is believed that Zambia has guerilla training camps within its borders and is a jumping-off place for terrorist incursions south of the Zambezi. In 1970 Dr. Kaunda was among the most vehement in condemnation of a suggestion that Great Britain might sell arms to South Africa. Politically and economically, Dr. Kaunda's aim is to break Zambia's ties with the white-ruled south and to form instead close associations with more radical East Africa.

Dr. Banda, on the other hand, accepts the dependence of Malawi on his more prosperous neighbours and is prepared to receive with both hands the good things that association with them will bring to his country. He has responded cordially to South Africa's 'outward policy' and he is on good terms with Rhodesia and Mozambique. His pragmatic attitude has incurred the anger of other independent African states but he is quite unmoved by criticism. He governs his republic in a brisk paternal way, laying special emphasis on morality and the virtue of hard work.

## Mozambique

The Portuguese have been a long time in their present East African colony, longer certainly than some of the Bantu tribes who now people the hinterland. When their empire included the whole of the East African coast, they had treated with the Mwenemutapa and traded for gold up the Zambezi. In 1531 a trading post had been established at Sena, about 100 miles up the river and another at Tete a few years later. In 1572 Francisco Barreto ascended the Zambezi with twenty-two ships and a thousand men, and when he, and most of his expedition with him, died of fever, his successor Homem again pushed inland, establishing a trading post as far up the Zambezi as Chicora and others on the Mazoe, and reached the

Manica gold field by way of the Revue. No permanent occupation of the interior was contemplated and the up-country tribes were as little affected by the coming of the Portuguese as they had been by the Arabs. Some attempt was made by Christian missions to proselytize the people of the interior. In 1560 the Jesuits undertook an expedition which got beyond Manica, but which was withdrawn in 1562 after the leader had been murdered. The Dominicans succeeded in establishing stations on the coast and up the Zambezi valley. The missionaries showed courage and endurance, but the impression that they made was negligible.

During the second half of the seventeenth century the Portuguese empire in East Africa wilted under the Arab assault and soon nothing was left but the settlements south of Cape Delgado which as the years passed sank deeper and deeper in squalor and decay, saved only from extinction by the active participation of the colonists (including high officials) in the Slave Trade.

At the time of Livingstone's Zambezi expedition in 1858 the Portuguese still claimed sovereignty of indefinite extent over the interior, but could do nothing to clothe those claims in substance. At any distance from the coast conditions were anarchic. Slave raiding by the Yao at the instigation of Portuguese and Arabs was endemic, and in the neighbourhood of Lake Malawi the country had been swept clean by a fierce tribe called the Mazitu. 'The borders of this land,' wrote Kirk, 'are deserts. All the people have been killed and it has been a dreadful slaughter, for the shores are covered with skulls, and where a foraging party has passed fresh bodies beginning to decompose lie scattered on the sand.'[1] Some years passed before anything was done to stop these horrors and to stifle the Slave Trade at this source. Apart from sponsoring Livingstone's expedition the British Government manifested no interest in the hinterland of Portuguese East Africa until about 1877, when Consul Frederick Elton from Mozambique travelled into the interior. Thereafter Central Africa became the scene of considerable tensions between the British and Portuguese which were only resolved in 1891 by the agreement which became the basis of all future Anglo-Portuguese relations in Africa.[2]

To develop the territories now recognized as theirs, the Portuguese, like the British in Rhodesia, chose the device of the chartered company. Two such companies, the Mozambique and the

[1] R. Coupland, *Kirk on the Zambesi*, p. 205.
[2] p. 99.

Nyasa, received charters to develop and also to administer the very large areas within their respective concessions. The Mozambique Company was to a great extent independent of the government, with a governor and a civil service of its own, the government retaining only the administration of justice, defence and foreign policy. The concession expired in 1941 and the company was wound up in the following year. The Nyasa Company came to an end in 1929. Yet a third company, the Zambezia, had rights in large areas, including some of the most fertile in the country, but did not possess the same administrative powers as the two chartered companies. Several years passed before the Portuguese succeeded in asserting their authority over the whole territory. It was not, in fact, until 1912 that Mataka, last of the chiefs still unsubdued, was forced to fly across the Rovuma into German territory, and the way was clear for the development of the interior.

*Angola*

Diego Cão discovered the Congo River in 1482 and erected a stone pillar at the river mouth. He sent an embassy of four of his men to the chief who lived some distance inland, and discovering on his return from his explorations further south that his envoys had been detained at the chief's town, seized four Africans and took them with him back to Portugal. The King of Portugal treated the four hostages as honoured guests, caused them to be instructed in the Christian faith, and himself acted as godfather when they were baptized. When therefore Diego Cão took them back to their home in 1484 or 1485 these messengers of goodwill paved the way for excellent relations with the Manicongo, or King of the Congo, as the chief was called, which led in 1490 to a Portuguese expedition with priests, skilled workers and a number of christianized Africans. This expedition had as its object the conversion of the chief to Christianity and the creation under him of a civilized state in friendly alliance with Portugal. It is sad, but hardly in the circumstances surprising, that this brave attempt to bring western civilization to Africa should have failed. It is, however, worth remembering as an enlightened experiment in race relations.

The next important Portuguese expedition to Angola was of quite a different kind. In 1574 Paulo Dias de Novais sailed from Lisbon armed with a *donataria* to a large area south of the Kwanza River. A *donataria* is a form of territorial proprietorship subject to certain development conditions and corresponds in some sort to the charters granted to British companies centuries later. Dias was not able to make any headway against native opposition, and when he died in 1589 hardly anything had been done to fulfil the conditions of the donation. When Portugal was joined with Spain under the Spanish Crown in 1581, the Dutch, in prosecution of their war against Spain, took Luanda and then Benguela. The Portuguese came back in 1648 and were kept busy for several years in reasserting their position in the country. When finally they succeeded in re-establishing themselves in the very small area in which they had a foothold it was not to initiate a vigorous programme of development. The attention of Portugal had long since been diverted from Angola to the glittering possibilities of Brazil, where untold wealth waited to be exploited by the exertions of sturdy blacks. In 1500 or thereabouts the raffish inhabitants of São Tomé had turned their island into a great slave centre, and Angola had become a hunting ground for rival factions of slavers early in the sixteenth century. The trade was so profitable and called for so little expenditure of money or energy on the part of those engaged in it that it soon replaced all the more exacting occupations. No further attempt was made to develop agriculture and mining and the possibilities of the country were entirely neglected. The rulers became corrupt, there were abuses in the public administration, the old missionary ideals decayed, and the country fell into a condition of stagnation from which, in spite of the efforts of individual governors, it did not really emerge until the twentieth century.

The Scramble for Africa left Portugal secure in the possession of Angola. She had consistently asked for considerably more, including the whole of the Congo River mouth, but these wider claims were opposed by Great Britain, whose particular concern in these parts was the suppression of the Slave Trade. In 1884 Great Britain and Portugal signed a treaty which in fact recognized Portuguese claims on the coast, including the river mouth and some distance inland, but provided for free navigation of the river, which was placed under an Anglo-Portuguese commission. This treaty roused a storm of protest and the Portuguese, recognizing that it would have to be abandoned, now turned to Germany and France and proposed an international conference. This proposal led to the Conference of Berlin of 1884–5.[1] Subsequent negotiations and agreements fixed the northern boundary of Angola at the southern bank of the Congo River and also gave the Portuguese the Kabinda

[1] p. 52.

enclave, which lies north, but not immediately north of the Congo River mouth.

## ECONOMY

### Zambia

The copper mining industry is the mainstay of the economy of Zambia. In 1969 the return from the sale of 853,000 short tons of copper and 2,333 tons of cobalt was over £400 million. The industry provided 97 per cent of domestic exports, 52 per cent of the net domestic product and 59 per cent of the total government revenue. The Nchanga mine, which by itself accounted for nearly a third of the production of the Copperbelt in 1969, is the second largest copper mine in the world. The mines employ nearly 5000 Europeans and 40,000–50,000 Africans.

Without copper Zambia would be a poor country. Cattle raising is restricted by tsetse fly and although a certain amount of commercial farming is done by Africans to supply a market for maize, groundnuts, tobacco and cotton, most African farming is of the subsistence type. Indeed it is estimated that a very limited number of European farmers are responsible for about a third of the total agricultural production. There is a promising inland fishing industry and there is a considerable potential in tourism. It might be said that after copper, Zambia's wild life is the country's best economic asset.

The government plays a prominent, indeed a dominant part in the economy. In 1969 the state acquired a 51 per cent share in the equity of the two big mining companies, Anglo-American and Roan Selection Trust. In November 1970 the president announced a similar measure for banks and other financial institutions. Control of the major industries is vested in ZIMCO (Zambia Industrial and Mining Corporation). The industries are run by three parastatal organizations, MINDECO, INDECO and FINDECO, concerned respectively with mining, industry and finance.

Although the Rhodesian and Zambian economies were in many ways complementary, an important aim of present Zambian policy is to cut loose from the Rhodesian system. A giant road transport scheme was launched to provide an alternative to the Rhodesian railway. An oil pipeline has been laid to Zambia from the coast of Tanzania. Local coal is being worked to reduce dependence on the Wankie colliery in Rhodesia. In the long run a railway (the Tanzam railway) is being built by Communist China to link the Tanzanian Central line with Kapiri Mposhi in Zambia.

Two-thirds of Zambia's power comes from the power station on the southern (Rhodesian) side of the Kariba dam. A similar station is to be built on the northern bank. This was an integral part of the original Kariba scheme. A hydro-electric station is also being established on the Kafue River within Zambia.

Zambia exports chiefly to Great Britain, Japan and West Germany. Although copper naturally forms the chief export commodity, substantial quantities of lead and zinc are also exported. Ironically enough, in spite of Zambia's ideological differences with the white-ruled south, trade with South Africa has increased by 150 per cent since independence.

Like all economies, that of Zambia has its difficulties. It is wholly one-sided, being entirely dependent on copper. There has been a rush of population to the towns. Agriculture is short of manpower and is backward. There is an unemployment problem, and those in employment, particularly the miners, tend to make inflationary wage demands. The attitude of the skilled European miners, without whom the industry could hardly function, is sometimes uncertain, and there is a danger that they might leave, as they could probably find work elsewhere. There are also the problems associated with the break with the Rhodesian system. However, the country is comparatively prosperous, and as long as copper retains its importance, it will continue to be so.

## Rhodesia

Southern Rhodesia did not turn out to be the land of Eldorado that the pioneers expected. There was no large continuous reef as on the Rand, and mining was in the hands of small men, running small mines. Asbestos overtook gold as an export and Southern Rhodesia became the leading world producer of the highest grade asbestos though third in total production. Other minerals that have since gained importance are chrome, nickel and iron. The great colliery at Wankie has a capacity of six million tons of coal a year. As gold mining ceased to expand, so the tobacco industry grew until the crop became the country's most paying export.

During the years after the Second World War the economy grew very fast. The number of whites increased from 80,000 to a quarter of a million, new developments sprang up like magic, and towns like Bulawayo and Salisbury expanded so as to become unrecognizable in a decade. This was the time of the Federation, the rise and fall of which has already been described. It was also the period of the Kariba dam and power plant on the Zambezi below the Victoria Falls, the largest dam and hydro-electric scheme in Africa at that time and one of the largest in the world.

The post-war years also saw a remarkable expansion of industry, both light and heavy. A wide range of consumer goods was produced, mostly in factories situated in Bulawayo and Salisbury. Half-way between these towns there is a large iron and steel plant at Redcliff near Que Que. The coal is brought down from Wankie some 300 miles away, but there are great reserves of iron ore near Que Que itself. At Gwelo there is a plant for treating the chrome ore of Selukwe and Kildonan. A recent development is a plant in the Sabi valley for exploiting rich phosphate deposits.

The first railway to serve Rhodesia was built by the British South Africa Company from Vryburg in the colony of British Bechuanaland through the Bechuanaland Protectorate. This railway reached Bulawayo in 1897. The line from Beira to Salisbury through Umtali was opened in 1899 and Salisbury and Bulawayo were joined by rail in 1902. From Bulawayo the line reached the Victoria Falls in 1904. From there it was continued across Northern Rhodesia to the Congo, where it arrived in 1909. In 1955 a new railway was opened between Southern Rhodesia and Lourenço Marques.

Rhodesia is the only country in the former Federation where extensive land alienation took place. About half the available land is occupied by Europeans, the other half being set aside for African occupation. The Land Apportionment Act of 1930 was supplemented by the Native Land Husbandry Act of 1951, which is designed to prevent the abuse of land and to improve African agriculture. These are admirable aims but the land division is obviously inequitable. This injustice has been perpetuated by the present régime in the Land Tenure Act of 1969.

As to the future of the Rhodesian economy it is difficult to speak with assurance. So far, as we have seen, the country has come safely through sanctions, partly through diversification, partly through increased production and partly through assistance given by other nations. Apart from sanctions there is another question which still affects the economy, especially the manufacturing section, though it is not a new one:[1] can expansion continue while the purchasing power of the majority remains so low? The future of manufactures must surely depend on a rise in the African standard of living so as to create a market for the goods which are being produced.

[1] It was raised 10 years ago in the first edition of this book, p. 98.

## Malawi

The economy of Malawi depends on agriculture, the principal export crops being tea and tobacco, followed *inter alia* by groundnuts, cotton, tung and coffee. The most important food crop is maize and enough is grown to provide a surplus for export. Pastoral activities are restricted by tsetse fly but there is a cattle population of about 500,000. Minerals are known to be present, especially bauxite, but little mining has taken place so far. The government is making considerable efforts to establish industries, and there are a number of development projects aimed mainly at the improvement of agriculture. Malawi has railway outlets to the ports of Mozambique.

Malawi receives substantial help from South Africa in the economic field. A trade agreement was concluded between the two countries in 1967. A South African loan is helping to finance the new state capital at Lilongwe, and South Africa also supplies several forms of technical and personal assistance.

Remittances from Malawians working abroad make an important contribution to the economy. In 1968 it was estimated that 250,000 to 350,000 men were employed in Rhodesia, Zambia and South Africa.

## Angola

Agriculture is still the backbone of Angola's economy, and accounts for 65 per cent of exports. Coffee is the main export, representing over 50 per cent of the total, followed by diamonds as the second export commodity. But oil prospecting in the coastal areas has been successful, and the traditional bases of the economy, coffee and diamonds, may soon be overtaken by oil. Iron ore is also an important and growing export. Other minerals such as copper and manganese deserve mention.

Most of the coffee is grown on plantations owned by Europeans, and Africans confine themselves mainly to subsistence farming, though native coffee production accounts for about a third of the total. Cattle raising is a fast-developing industry. Besides coffee, other crops are sugar, tobacco, palm oil, palm kernels and maize.

Fishing is an important economic activity. The fishing grounds off Benguela are exceedingly rich and 400,000 tons of fish are landed annually. The bulk of the catch is processed into oil and other fish products.

Angola has four railway lines. The most important is the Benguela line, which connects the port of Lobito with Dilolo on the borders of

Congo/Zaïre and so provides the Katanga mines with a vital outlet to the sea. The other lines run inland from the ports of Luanda, Mossamedes and Amboim.

Development plans include agricultural assistance and settlement, the improvement of public utilities and especially the utilization of the waters of the Kunene River for irrigation and the production of power. The projected power station will supply both sides of the Angola-South West Africa border and the cost of the scheme will be shared equally between the Portuguese and the South African governments. The whole scheme is expected to be completed by 1978.

## Mozambique

The principal exports of Mozambique are cotton, cashew nuts, tea, sugar and copra. Owing to the fall in world prices, sisal, formerly a large export, is now in a period of crisis. Bananas, pineapples, and citrus grow well and are exported to South Africa. Other crops are rice, maize and groundnuts. Stock raising is restricted by tsetse fly but there are about a million cattle in the territory.

The only mineral exploited so far on a large scale is coal. There is a small export of columbo-tantalite, which owing to a world scarcity of this mineral fetches a high price. Great quantities of ilmenite lie in the sands north of the Zambezi River, and a very large iron ore deposit has been found at Namapa in the north of the country. There have been recent discoveries of diamonds, asbestos and manganese, and there are promising indications of uranium. Other minerals are known to exist in varying quantities. There is prospecting for oil along the coast and natural gas has been discovered not far from Lourenço Marques.

A number of processing industries have grown up on a basis of local raw materials. The most important of these manufacturing enterprises are sugar milling, the distillation of power alcohol, the manufacture of cement and asbestos products, soap making, cotton ginning, flour milling and tobacco production. Special mention should be made of an oil refinery which is one of the pillars of the economy.

Mozambique has a number of good ports of which the most important are Beira and Lourenço Marques. The transit trade through these ports is a very rewarding feature of the economic life of the country. Two main railway systems, one based on each of these ports, link Mozambique with central and southern Africa and between them deal with traffic from the Transvaal, Swaziland, Rhodesia, Congo/Zaïre, Malawi and Zambia. A new line connects Malawi with the port of Nacala, thus providing Malawi with an alternative sea outlet to congested Beira. Nacala, which is a fine deep-water harbour, is being improved and extended.

Great hopes are pinned on the dam which is being built in the Cabora Bassa gorge above Tete on the Zambezi River. It was this gorge and its rapids that prevented David Livingstone from finding a navigable route into central Africa in 1858. When the whole scheme is complete the dam will generate considerably more electricity than either Aswan or Kariba, and will provide enough power to supply a large part of southern and central Africa. It will make the Zambezi navigable to an extent hitherto quite impossible, and it will permit the irrigation of $3\frac{1}{2}$ million acres of land in a part of Mozambique which has until now been restricted to subsistence farming.

In spite of its potential advantages to neighbouring countries, including independent African countries, the Cabora Bassa scheme has excited the hostility of anti-colonial elements, who see in it an instrument for perpetuating Portuguese rule which they are striving to destroy. There have been threats of sabotage and the scheme may be expected to become a target of guerilla activity.

### MADAGASCAR (MALAGASY REPUBLIC) AND THE COMORO ISLANDS

*Madagascar—Country and People*
The island of Madagascar is nearly one thousand miles long and 360 miles across at its greatest breadth. It is the fourth largest island in the world which is not also a continent. It lies opposite Portuguese East Africa, from which it is separated by the Mozambique Channel at an average distance of 250 miles. The physical appearance is not unlike that of the African continent of which it was a part in very remote times. That is to say, a plateau with an elevation of about 4,000 feet runs down the middle of the island and is flanked on either side by a coastal plain. The 'backbone' is much nearer to the east than to the west, with the result that the eastern plain is narrow and the rise to the plateau abrupt, whereas the western plain is fairly broad and in consequence the slope is more gradual. In the south the slope from the coastal plain to the plateau is also gradual. The east coast is almost a straight line and Tamatave, the principal harbour, is protected only by coral reefs. In the extreme north-east there is one very large indentation, the bay of Diego-

Suarez, which is one of the finest harbours in the world. There are several good estuaries on the west coast and a good harbour at Tulear. The capital of Madagascar is Antananarivo, situated on the plateau and splendidly sited on a rocky ridge which towers over the surrounding rice-fields.

The eastern side of the island is hot and wet and rain falls throughout the year. The rainiest period is from December to July, but it is never really dry, and nearly 4 inches fall in October, which is the driest month of the year. The east coast is also subject to cyclones. The west coast has well marked wet and dry seasons. The wet season, which is also hot, occurs between October and April; the dry cool season is from May to September. The plateau is fairly cool and drops to nearly freezing point in the dry season between May and September. During the rest of the year it is warm to temperate. The annual rainfall, most of which occurs between December and March, is 54 inches. There are no arid districts on the island except the southerly tip and the extreme south-west.

There are two substantial massifs on the plateau, both of volcanic origin, that of Tsaratanana (9,450 feet) in the north and that of Ankaratra (8,575 feet) in the centre of the island. The eastern side of the island, where the gradients are steep and rainfall constant, is cut by the gorges of perennial streams. On the more gently sloping western side, where the rains are seasonal, the smaller rivers only flow during the rainy season. The largest river on the island is the Betsiboka, which runs into the sea on the north-west coast. Other rivers on the west side are the Mania, the Mangoky and the Onilahy. The most important rivers flowing eastwards are the Mangoro and the Maningory. In the south the Mananara drains a substantial area. Madagascar has no really large lakes. The largest, Alaotra, is twenty-five miles long but in the remote past was considerably larger.

Vegetation follows the climatic zones. Hot and wet conditions on the eastern side have favoured the growth of evergreen forest, much of which unfortunately has been destroyed by fire or by clearance for agriculture. The plateau, with high winds and poor soil, is mainly grassland and savannah. The western side, with a seasonal rainfall, has deciduous forest. The vegetation in the dry south and south-west is sparse and semi-desertic. There are mangrove swamps in the estuaries of the western rivers.

That Madagascar became separated from the African continent in very remote ages is illustrated by the great differences between

the plant life of the island and that of the mainland. Equally significant is the fact that many African animals, such as the anthropoid
apes and the larger ungulates and carnivores, are absent from
Madagascar. On the other hand the island has many small animals
which are almost peculiar to it, and the fauna generally is marked by
a strong individuality which it owes to long isolation from other
zoological regions. There are no less than thirty-nine species of
lemur, some of them very highly specialized; a great number of
different chameleons; several animals belonging to the civets, the
largest of which, *Cryptoprocta ferox*, forms a genus and a family
to itself; and many birds, insects and fish. It is noteworthy that the
fauna has Asian rather than African affinities, giving support to the
theory that Madagascar, while once part of Africa, was also
physically connected with Asia.

Certainly the population is not African in origin. The Malagasy,
as they are collectively called, are in fact basically of Malayo-
Polynesian and Melanesian stock, resembling the people of the
Indian and Pacific archipelagos in appearance, customs and
especially in their language. There is an African admixture, particularly among the western tribes, and there are several Arab
colonies. There are also Indians and Chinese, and 54,000 French
by birth. The total population is 7 million.

The most important native people, as well as the most numerous
and advanced, are the Merina or Ambaniandro, commonly called
Hova,[1] whose homeland is Imerina on the plateau near Antananarivo. The Sakalava occupy most of the western side of the
island and the Betsimisaraka a considerable stretch along the eastern
seaboard. South of the Hova on the plateau are the Betsileo round
Fianarantsoa. Other important tribes are the Antaimoro, whose
chiefs are of Arab origin and who still use Arabic script, the
Antaisaka, the Antanosy and the Bara. The most backward tribes
of the island are the Mahafaly and the Antandroy in the extreme
south.

*History*

The first European to see Madagascar was a Portuguese sea
captain named Diego Diaz, who sighted the east coast on 10 August
1500. Because that day was the Feast of St. Lawrence, Diaz named

---

[1] Strictly speaking 'Hova' applies only to one class of Merina society, the middle
class or freemen. The nobles are Andriana and the slaves Andevo. Now the whole
tribe is called 'Hova'.

his discovery 'Isle of St. Lawrence'. During the seventeenth and eighteenth centuries the French tried to establish posts on the island but usually failed owing to resistance on the part of the natives. The island was in those days a notorious haunt for the pirates who infested the Indian Ocean. The people of the island were apparently divided into small tribes until quite modern times. The seventeenth century, however, witnessed the growth of the Sakalava kingdom which at its zenith occupied half the island. When this empire declined it was succeeded by that of the Merina under King Andrianampoinimerina and then under King Radama (1810–28), the latter a particularly able ruler who made Imerina a progressive and expansive kingdom. During his reign the London Missionary Society began work at Antananarivo, the language was reduced to writing, the Scriptures translated, and schools established. Radama's wife and successor Ranavalona I (1828–61) fiercely opposed foreign influences and undid much of the work of her predecessor, and her son Radama II was assassinated after a short and not very promising reign. However, the two succeeding monarchs, Queen Rasoherina (1863–68) and Queen Ranavalona II (1868–83), the latter married to an able prime minister, both proved to be competent rulers who reformed and reorganized the administration, encouraged Christianity and education, and established diplomatic relations with Britain, France and the United States, who all posted consuls to Madagascar.

In 1883 differences arose between the Malagasy and the French and the latter occupied Tamatave and Majunga. In 1885 a French protectorate was accepted by Queen Ranavalona III, but after a period of strained relations lasting some ten years a French expedition occupied Tamatave and in 1896 Madagascar was annexed to France. The royal power was abolished and in 1897 Ranavalona was sent into exile first to Réunion, then to Algiers. The task of pacifying the new colony and establishing French authority was entrusted to the humane, energetic and far-sighted Gallieni, who, with the possible exception of Lyautey—at one time one of his subordinates—was the most remarkable of the French administrators of the nineteenth and twentieth centuries.

In 1942 Madagascar was occupied by the British to forestall a possible Japanese occupation and in the following year handed to the Free French. In 1947 there was a serious rebellion which was only suppressed with difficulty. Like other French colonies Madagascar made very fast political advances in the following

decade and under the name Malagasy Republic is now an autonomous republic within the French community.

## Economy

The principal cereal crop is rice, which is cultivated in all parts
of the island except in the arid southern areas. It is the main food
crop and enough is normally grown to provide a surplus for export.
Another important agricultural product is cassava or manioc, from
which tapioca is derived. Maize, beans and sweet potatoes are
extensively grown as food crops.

Coffee is Madagascar's most important export, followed by rice
and then by vanilla, of which the island is the world's largest producer. Other exports are sugar, sisal, meat, cloves and tobacco.

On the plateau stock raising constitutes the backbone of the
economy. The cattle are of the Zebu type and are not of very high
quality. However, a cattle improvement scheme is in operation and
scientific breeding has begun. The cattle population is about ten
million and there are some 800,000 sheep and goats and half a
million pigs. Both tinned and fresh meat are exported, also a limited
number of hides and skins.

As to minerals, Madagascar is a world producer of graphite though
not in the front rank. Mica is also exported and shipments of chromium
began in 1969. Other minerals include gold and semi-precious
stones. Several companies are prospecting for oil.

Industry, hitherto confined to processing local products, is now
being extended to other fields. The most important development in
this respect is an oil refinery at Tamatave. Among other industrial
enterprises there are textile factories, a paper mill and vehicle assembly
plants.

Good roads connect the larger towns and there is a network of
earth roads passable in the dry weather. There are four railway
lines. The main line runs from Tamatave through Moramanga to
Antananarivo. From Moramanga there is a line to the great rice-
growing area round Lake Alaotra. Another runs south from Antananarivo to the town of Antsirabé, and Fianarantsoa, centre of the
Betsileo, is joined to the coast by a line to Manakara. Some of the
rivers, especially on the western side, are to some extent navigable
and on the east a chain of lagoons connected by canals, called the
Pangalanes, runs down the coast for about 400 miles and carries
traffic. There are air services to France from Antananarivo and there
is a good system of airways within the island.

32–34. VIEWS OF MOUNT KILIMANJARO. The highest mountain in Africa (19,340 feet), with a perpetual cap of snow, Kilimanjaro is on the frontier between Kenya and Tanzania, 170 miles from the coast and 210 miles south of the Equator. The view from the air (*above*) shows the Kibo and Mawenzi peaks on the right and left, with Mount Meru in the background to the south-west. The views from the trees (*right*) and a cross-roads (*below*) show the mountain as it appears in the distance

35. LAKE TANGANYIKA. A view from Kigoma of the 400-mile long lake in the western arm of the Rift Valley between Tanzania and Congo (Kinshasa)

36. GREAT RIFT VALLEY. A mail train climbs the valley from Kampala on the way to Nairobi; the mountain in the background is the extinct volcano Longonot

37. Falls on the Abbai. The Abbai or Blue Nile rises in Lake Tsana in Ethiopia and runs south, west and then north to its confluence with the White Nile at Khartoum

38. Cape Guardafui. A nineteenth-century print showing the steep headland at the north-east tip of the Horn of Africa

39. THE TREE OF PARTING. This tree in western Tanzania is near the place where Stanley and Livingstone parted in 1871, Stanley going to the coast and Livingstone to his death on his last expedition

40. LIONS IN KENYA. A lion and lioness happily lolling in the Nairobi National Park

41–42. GIRAFFE AND ELEPHANT IN EAST AFRICA. A reticulated giraffe in the Meru Game Reserve, Kenya (*above*), and a bull elephant in the acacia bush country of northern Tanzania (*below*)

43. CAIRO. A view of the minarets towering over the rooftops of the older eastern part of the city

44. MOMBASA HARBOUR. The old harbour of the main seaport of Kenya

45-46. EGYPTIAN ANTIQUITIES. The 200-foot Step Pyramid of Saqqara is the oldest known stone building in the world—it was constructed for King Zoser nearly 5,000 years ago (*above*); this relief from the Temple of Montu at Tôd, showing part of a procession with the bull-god Montu followed by his soul in the form of a bird, is only about 2,000 years old, but it is unmistakably in the tradition of the ancient Egyptian inscriptions (*below*)

47–48. ETHIOPIAN ARCHITECTURE. The old castle of Gondar, 30 miles north of Lake Tsana, which is not unlike medieval European castles of the same period (*above*); and one of the rock-monasteries of Lalibala, 100 miles east of Lake Tsana, which are the most remarkable examples of Ethiopian architecture (*below*)

49–51. PEOPLES OF EAST AFRICA AND THE HORN. Masai dancers in Tanzania (*above*); two Somali elders (*left*); mother and child, Uganda (*below*)

52. Dhow off Mombasa. The typical sea-vessel East Africa

53. A Fishing Fleet, Kisumu. Boats setting out from Kisumu on Lake Victoria, the largest inland sea in Africa and the third largest in the world (over 26,000 square miles), and also the main source of the Nile

54–55. Dagaa Fishing. The dagaa (*left*) is a small sardine-like fish considered a delicacy in East Africa which can be caught by lamplight during the night (*right*)

56. West Africa. A Fulani girl. The Fulani are a Hamitic people distributed throughout the region

57. CAMEROON. A
HEADMAN from the
northern hills

58. A MADAGASCAR
VILLAGE
surrounded by
rice fields

59–60. GUM ARABIC IN THE SUDAN. The acacia bark being tapped to collect the gum (*above*), and a Government gum auction in progress at El Obeid (*below*)

61. WATER STORAGE IN THE SUDAN. The hollow trunk of a baobab tree is used for keeping water

62. ASWAN DAM, EGYPT. Water gushes from this £300,000,000 dam, "Nasser's Pyramid", inaugurated 1971

63–64. AGRICULTURE IN THE SUDAN. Peasants ploughing their land (*above*); the cattle are of the Zebu (hump-backed) type. (*Below*) A peasant pauses by a canal on his way home with some millet

65–66. THE TSETSE FLY. A fly half an inch in length (*above*), and an immunized Ankole cow being used as a bait for flies in Uganda (*below*)

The economy of Madagascar is hampered by remoteness from the European and American markets and by the consequent high cost of transport. Two-thirds of the island's trade is with France. To find new markets the government has put out feelers to South Africa which have been well received.

\*      \*      \*      \*      \*

The Comoro islands lie in the Mozambique Channel 300 miles off the coast of Madagascar and 200 miles from the east coast of Africa. The group consists of four principal islands: Mayotte, Anjouan or Johanna, Moheli and Grand Comoro. The population of about 250,000 is of mixed Malagasy, Negro and Arab blood. The Arab influence is an old one and most of the people are Moslems.

The French took possession of Mayotte in 1843 and French protection was extended to the other three islands in 1886. In 1908 the group was attached to Madagascar for purposes of administration and was declared a French colony in 1912, this declaration being ratified in 1914. The islands now have the status of a French overseas territory.

The soil of the Comoros is fertile, food grows plentifully and exports include copra, coco fibre, sugar, vanilla, sisal, wild pepper and essential oils. There are only a limited number of cattle owing to the mountainous nature of the islands. It remains to add that the climate is very pleasant and that there are no poisonous snakes.[1]

---

[1] The authority for this excursion into herpetology is *La France de l'Océan Indien* (Terres Lointaines, Vol. VIII).

I

# CHAPTER THREE

# EAST AFRICA

THIS is the region comprising the republics of Kenya, Uganda, Tanzania, Rwanda and Burundi. Tanzania includes the islands of Zanzibar and Pemba, which once formed a British protectorate, then for a short time an independent country under a hereditary sultan.

The region is bounded on the north by Ethiopia and the Sudan, on the south by Zambia, Malawi and Mozambique, on the west by Congo/Zaïre and Lake Tanganyika and on the east by the Indian Ocean. The north-eastern tip of Kenya is separated from the sea by the southerly projection of the Somali Republic. The principal towns are Nairobi and Mombasa in Kenya; Kampala, Entebbe and Jinja in Uganda; Dar-es-Salaam, Tanga, Tabora and Zanzibar town in Tanzania; Kigali in Rwanda and Bujumbura in Burundi. The total area is 704,000 square miles and the population about 40 million.[1]

The coastal plain is rather narrow, varying in width from about ten to forty miles, and stretches from the Somali border in the north to Portuguese East Africa in the south. It is fringed with coral reefs through which there are occasional deep water inlets, but natural protected harbours suitable for large ocean-going vessels are few. The climate is warm and the atmosphere humid. The average rainfall is 45–47 inches in the central part, considerably less in the north and south. The rains fall in well-defined seasons, the long rains in April and May, the short, lighter rains in November and December. There are great mangrove swamps in the river deltas and these are backed by a thin cultivated palm belt which soon gives way to tree savannah and in places to bush considerably thicker than the savannah further inland.

---

[1] Distribution is as follows:

| | | sq.m. | | pop. | |
|---|---|---|---|---|---|
| Kenya | sq.m. | 224,960 | pop. | 11,000,000 | |
| Uganda | ,, | 93,981 | ,, | 9,000,000 | |
| Tanzania | ,, | 362,688 | ,, | 12,635,000 | (mainland) |
| | ,, | 1,020 | ,, | 365,000 | (Zanzibar) |
| Rwanda | ,, | 10,169 | ,, | 3,700,000 | |
| Burundi | ,, | 10,747 | ,, | 3,400,000 | |

Behind the coastal plain there is an extensive low plateau called the 'nyika', an area of poor light soils except on the banks of rivers, with a rainfall ranging from five inches to thirty inches, broken by occasional outcrops of high ground and ranges of hills. The 'nyika', which has been compared in shape to an hour-glass,[1] bulges in the north so as to form the inhospitable steppe of northern Kenya, and again in the south to include a large area in Tanzania north of the Rovuma River. The neck is about 100 miles wide inland from Tanga.

West of the 'nyika' the ground rises gradually to the great continental plateau which in East Africa lies between 4,000 and 10,000 feet. Through the plateau, roughly in a north-south direction, run the two arms of the Rift Valley. The eastern arm is a deep trough, in some places forty miles wide and 3,000 feet below the level of the surrounding country, its floor dotted with lakes and extinct volcanoes. The western arm contains Lakes Tanganyika, Kivu, Edward and Albert. Between the two arms is the depression which contains Lake Victoria and the drainage system of the Nile.

The plateau is dominated almost throughout its length by a number of mountain masses. Of these the most important are the Kenya ranges, the Ruwenzori range on the borders of Uganda and Congo/Zaïre,[2] and the mountains of northern and southern Tanzania. The highest individual mountains are Kilimanjaro (19,340 feet), Kenya (17,040 feet) and Mount Stanley in the Ruwenzori range (16,794 feet). All except the last are extinct volcanoes, and Kilimanjaro, which is also the highest mountain in Africa, has in its higher peak, Kibo, an almost perfect crater.          (*Plate* 100)

The climate of the plateau is exceedingly varied and depends much on altitude. The rainfall ranges from 100 inches in the northwest corner of Lake Victoria to 20 inches in central Tanzania. The higher parts have a cold bracing climate exceedingly congenial to Europeans. At lower altitudes, under say 5,000 feet, it can be very hot, but the atmosphere is not excessively humid, and the hot days give way to cold nights. Many a traveller in these parts has welcomed a good log fire at night.

Vegetation is as diverse as climate. Huge areas of the plateau, especially towards the south, consist of savannah, with low trees and shrubs which give the country a parklike appearance. Some of

---

[1] *East Africa Royal Commission 1953-1955 Report* (H.M.S.O., Cmd. 9457), p. 7.
[2] The Ruwenzori range is also part of the western rim of the Congo basin.

the dryer parts produce little more than thornbush and scrub, but the mountainous areas of high reliable rainfall still have large blocks of fine natural forest and formerly had much more. The high mountains have a vegetation of particular interest; characteristic features are the forests of tree groundsels and giant species of lobelia.

Two great rivers and several lesser ones run through the southerly part of the region. The Rovuma forms the boundary with Portuguese East Africa, and the Rufiji flows into the sea in a broad delta some eighty miles south of Dar-es-Salaam. Other rivers are the Ruvu and the Pangani, flowing into the Indian Ocean, and the Malagarasi, which feeds Lake Tanganyika. In the more northerly part the rivers are fewer and smaller. The Tana flows into the Indian Ocean not far south of Lamu on the Kenya coast. The Kagera between Tanzania and Uganda has an importance of its own: it is the chief feeder of Lake Victoria and may thus be said to be the beginning of the greatest, in length at least, of all African rivers, the Nile. There are, of course, innumerable lesser streams throughout the region, but they are almost entirely seasonal and only flow during and shortly after the rains.

The island of Zanzibar is in the Indian Ocean at a distance of twenty-two and a half miles from the mainland of Tanzania, with its dependency Pemba lying about twenty-five miles to the north-east. Two-thirds of Zanzibar consists of low-lying coral country, though there is one ridge rising to 390 feet above sea-level on the western side. On the other hand Pemba is for the most part rich, fertile country. Its highest point is 311 feet above sea-level. Climatic conditions are very much the same as on the coast of the mainland, except that the rainfall is heavier and the heat is often mitigated by a sea breeze. The heavier rainfall is responsible for a more luxuriant vegetation than is to be found on the mainland, and both islands were formerly covered with forest, but this has now been almost entirely cleared for agriculture.

East Africa is the home of innumerable wild animals, though certainly not as many as before. The growth of the population and its spread under more peaceful and prosperous conditions into areas hitherto uninhabited, economic development and more intensive cultivation, indiscriminate killing for meat or for valuable trophies, all these factors have brought about a reduction in the animal population and even when animals have survived they have retreated to more inaccessible areas. The East African governments

are concerned to ensure the survival of animals to the greatest extent
compatible with human needs and every effort is made to balance
the interests of the African with game preservation by appropriate
legislation and the creation of game reserves and national parks.

*Tsetse Fly*

East Africa, especially at the lower altitudes, has its fair share of
the pests that threaten animal and human health in one way or
another, but the most injurious and so far the most intractable is
probably the tsetse fly, which causes trypanosomiasis in humans and
in cattle. Ways and means have now been found of exterminating
the malarial mosquito, formerly the most dangerous enemy of man
in the tropics, but all efforts to exterminate the tsetse have proved
ineffective, and even the methods of control so far devised are
chancy, arduous and expensive. Happily the human form of trypanosomiasis is curable and can of course be avoided by keeping out
of a fly-infested area. But to cure animal trypanosamiasis in all the
animals that might contract it is too vast and expensive a proposition to be practicable in African conditions. The territory most
seriously affected is Tanzania, where about two-thirds of the mainland is infested with tsetse, which is steadily spreading. Kenya and
Uganda both have wide areas of infestation, but less than Tanzania.
The tsetse fly has far-reaching demographic and economic consequences. Infested country may not be uninhabitable but it certainly tends to cause concentration of people in the areas that
are less heavily infested. Huge areas are as it were sterilized against
human occupation. The presence of tsetse also makes the keeping
of cattle impossible. Thus the people living within the area are not
able to practice a balanced economy by a combination of agriculture and cattle-rearing.                    (*Plates* 65–66)

THE PEOPLE

*Europeans*

Europeans have lived in Kenya for nearly three generations and
in the course of time have created out of virgin country a civilized
landscape of remarkable beauty, with good houses and pretty
gardens, orderly plantations, well tended farms, and towns with a
good number of fine buildings. When independence came, large
numbers of farmers gradually left, leaving only the comparatively
few who were prepared to envisage a future under the new conditions. But there still remained a large European community in

Kenya (it was roughly 42,000 in 1968), representing a wide variety of
nationalities and interests.

In Tanzania too the settlers have dwindled but there are still many
Europeans of diverse nationalities in offices, banks, factories, and in
the various agencies of foreign aid. Uganda had about 9,000 Europeans
in 1968 and there are, or were then, a number of East Germans in
Zanzibar.

East Africa is no longer a country of settlement for Europeans.
That short-lived though colourful squirearchy on the Equator has
gone for ever. It was indeed a predestined casualty of the changes
that recent years have brought to Africa. Now this region is one in
which Europeans will serve for limited periods as members of some
international body, or as teachers and welfare workers, or as business
men and employees in local firms. Only the missionaries, whose
dedication is lifelong, will come to stay permanently.

## Asians

As early as the first century A.D. there was in existence a long-
established trade between East Africa and India. Well before the end
of the fifteenth century Indians had settled as bankers, moneylenders
and middlemen in all the larger coastal towns. However it was not
until the nineteenth century, when the continent was opened to the
outside world, that Asians spread into the interior and assumed a
commanding position in the commerce of the country.

The two principal divisions were Moslems and Hindus, but there
were also Sikhs, Goans, Sinhalese and others. These Asians in due
course acquired a monopoly of the petty trade; they predominated
as artisans and clerks; they controlled a high proportion of the import
and export trade; they developed the cotton ginning industry; and it
was they who were the pioneers of the sugar industry in Uganda.

The heyday of the Asian was the colonial period. Independence
brought a change. The new governments not unnaturally wanted
trade to be in African not Asian hands and took steps to make this
policy effective. This was a disaster for the Asian traders and many
began to move out, some trying to get into Britain, others going to
India. How far the process of Africanization will go, how fast, and
how successful it will be remains to be seen. Meanwhile the situation
of the East African Asian is not a happy one.

## Arabs

These former masters of the East African coast now live in somewhat diminished state. Their community was dealt a crushing blow

by the Zanzibar revolution of 1964 (p. 131) but they still evoke a certain respect among the Swahili of the mainland coast by virtue of their position in the world of Islam.

## Africans

The African population of East Africa consists largely of Bantu peoples, with enclaves of Hamites and Nilotes. It represents many different stages of culture, from the advanced and politically highly organized Baganda to the primitive Watindiga of Lake Eyasi, who are hardly a degree above the South African Bushmen. It includes people as different as the progressive Chagga of Kilimanjaro, who have readily adopted certain aspects of western life, and the aloof and dignified Masai, who cling tenaciously to their own ways. There are nomads, and semi-nomads, cattle people and people with no cattle, farmers and hunters, cultivators of coffee or cotton, and people who cultivate practically nothing at all. Similarly, there are tribes with well established constitutions, an official hierarchy, a respected, semi-sacrosanct chief. Others may not recognize any more complicated authority than the head of the family. In a study of this scope it is impossible to do more than to take a few examples at various points in the scale.

The Baganda are probably the most highly developed people in East Africa. They live in the former kingdom of Buganda, which is now part of the modern republic of Uganda.[1] In fact Buganda was formerly merely a part of the empire of Bunyoro, but at the time of the first European explorers it had risen to the dominant position in the region. The kingdom of Buganda was the end-product of Hamitic immigration which had placed an alien aristocracy, the Bahima, with an elaborate 'king ritual', on the lacustrine Bantu peoples.[2] As Bunyoro declined in strength, so did Buganda grow and the Europeans found it a compact, despotic state centralized on the king, or as he was called, the Kabaka, with a powerful and efficient hierarchy of chiefs appointed by him and holding office at his discretion.

During the colonial era the Kabaka presided over a well developed system of government and was assisted by ministers and by a council which in early days was entirely selected by him but later became more representative.

[1] Bu and U are different prefixes of the same noun class. Buganda and Uganda are therefore the same word in different languages, though geographically they now have different meanings.
[2] p. 10.

The Baganda are sophisticated, quick-witted, intelligent, colourful, with an instinct for commerce and a taste for politics. Basically they are farmers, many holding their land in a form of individual ownership, while others live on the larger holdings as protected tenants. There are also a large numbers of landless labourers, many of them immigrants who have become permanent residents.

In Rwanda and Burundi an aristocracy of Hamitic origin, the Watusi, occupy a position analogous to that of the Bahima in Uganda. They are traditionally believed to have come from the north-east some 500 years ago, bringing with them cattle which are distinguished by horns of extraordinary length. They have mingled less with the local Bantu arable farmers, the Bahutu, than the Bahima have done in Uganda and have retained their physical characteristics in notable measure. These are a long head, fine features and exceptionally tall build, many Watusi reaching a height of 6 feet 6 inches and 7 feet. As we shall see, their position in relation to the Bahutu has now undergone a drastic change.

As we move eastwards we come to the Chagga who live on the slopes of Mount Kilimanjaro, highly intelligent farmers who have for many years grown and marketed coffee of good quality, and who operate an intricate system of irrigation on the densely populated slopes of their great mountain.

The Kikuyu, or Agikuyu as they call themselves, are the biggest and most important tribe of Kenya. According to their own tradition they started as a tribe in the area of the present Fort Hall district, the exact place of origin being a large *Mukuruwe* (acacia) tree. Owing to pressure of an increasing population they moved southwards about the sixteenth century into Kiambu, then occupied by a tribe of hunters and honey collectors called Wandorobo. The Kikuyu bought land from the Wandorobo by very complicated processes in which religious rites played an essential part. A piece of land so bought was called a *githaka*, and there developed from this system of land acquisition a real landowning class, which is a rare thing in Africa. Each *githaka* also had its quota of tenants, and in the course of several centuries the Kiambu district became very well populated and prosperous. At about the same time as they came down into Kiambu the Kikuyu also moved up to the foothills of Mount Kenya.

At the end of the nineteenth century four major disasters ravaged this part of Africa. A great smallpox epidemic, a great rinderpest outbreak, a drought with consequent famine and a plague of locusts. Although these disasters were not confined to Kikuyuland they had here certain peculiar indirect effects which will be described later.

The social organization of the Kikuyu is exceedingly complex and cannot be given in detail here. It comprises two distinct aspects: on the one hand there is a patriarchal sub-clan system closely linked with land ownership; on the other an organization based on certain territorial units, the word for which means 'ridges'. Traditionally the Kikuyu have no chiefs in the sense that Europeans understand the word. Authority formerly resided in the councils of elders evolved from the twin aspects of their social system. Kikuyu chiefs in colonial times were largely the creation of the European administration.

The Kikuyu are in a sense the most active and progressive people in East Africa. They have certainly been the dominant element in African nationalism in Kenya.

The Luo came to their present home in north-western Kenya several centuries ago as part of a Nilotic invasion from the south-eastern Sudan. They now occupy the shore of Lake Victoria north and south of the Kavirondo Gulf and the undulating country behind it. Some outlying sections stretch southwards into Tanzania.

The Luo are mainly agriculturalists, but they also keep sheep and goats. Their country, though overcrowded in places, enjoys a good, well distributed rainfall. They are a strong, tough, persistent people and they are keenly interested in politics. They have produced bold, outspoken leaders who have played an important part in national affairs. Between the Luo and the Kikuyu there is an often bitter rivalry. Many observers think that this may have a fateful influence on the future of Kenya.

The Masai are Nilo-Hamitic pastoralists who live on the plains of Kenya and Tanzania. Tall, elegant, red-skinned, hair in a pigtail, spear in hand, they watch their cattle which, they say, God let down to them as a divine gift when He separated earth and sky. In addition to cattle they keep sheep, goats and pack donkeys. The most important feature of Masai society is the division into age sets. These are groups of coevals who have undergone initiation, which includes circumcision, during the same initiation period. The Masai have no chiefs, the centre of political authority being an age set of elders. But there is a religious head, the Laibon (*oloiboni*), who has no executive power but wields great influence.

Secure in their sense of superiority, the Masai stand aloof from the concerns of the rest of Africa around them. The time may come when they will forsake their traditions, abandon their national dress, take to agriculture and generally adopt the way of life of the Bantu peasant. If this should happen, we shall have to mourn the disappearance of another aristocracy.

Poles apart from the Kikuyu on the one hand and the Masai on the other are the Swahili. These are the African people of the coast and of Zanzibar, Bantu with a more or less strong admixture of Arab blood but more often of Arab culture. They are all, nominally at least, Moslems. Their language, an admirably flexible instrument of Bantu origin with many Arabic and other foreign words, is the *lingua franca* of East Africa and in parts of Congo/Zaïre. The Swahili are worldly, witty and polite. They have an ancient poetic tradition and theirs is the only truly East African literature. They are shrewd in matters of trade and commerce. The more sophisticated have about them a not unattractive decadence peculiar to the old Arab civilization of the coast.

There is thus no *type* of East African. Instead, there are a large number of different people at different stages of civilization and representative of different cultures, each following a way of life differing in some way from the others, all with different ambitions and aspirations, and with different material and mental equipment wherewith to attain them.

## History

The Scramble for Africa ended in the recognition by Germany of the British protectorate over Zanzibar and in the division of the mainland between Germany and Great Britain, Germany taking the southern part and Great Britain the northern. In their first attempts to colonize East Africa, both Germany and Great Britain relied on the device of a commercial company endowed with powers of administration. In 1884 the German explorer Karl Peters founded the Union for German Colonization, and the British Government, always anxious to avoid expense, were delighted to entrust the new territories to Sir William Mackinnon's Imperial British East Africa Company. The early years of European occupation were very turbulent. The German company met with bitter resistance from the Arabs and was quite unable to deal with an uprising led by one Bushiri and hence called the Bushiri Rebellion. So ineffective was the Company that the German Government took over and a protectorate was declared in 1891. Internal troubles continued, however, for many years and there were many tribal risings, all ruthlessly suppressed. The most serious was the so-called Maji Maji Rebellion, which occurred in 1905–6 and involved the whole of the south-eastern part of the territory.

In the British sphere missionaries had been at work in Uganda since 1877, first the Protestants and then the Roman Catholics, known respectively to the natives, quite accurately, as 'Waingereza' (English) and 'Wafaransa' (French). The Kabaka of Buganda, Mwanga, under Arab influence, caused Bishop Hannington to be murdered as he set foot in the country, and then instituted a savage persecution of the Christians, many of whom died martyrs' deaths in circumstances of great heroism. In this anarchic situation Captain Lugard, representative of the Imperial British East Africa Company, was hard put to it to keep any sort of order, and indeed fighting broke out from time to time until 1892.

The Company's means were quite inadequate to deal with a situation of this kind, and there was a serious danger that all British authority would be withdrawn. After much hesitation the British Government stepped in, relieved the Company of all its responsibilities west of Lake Naivasha and declared a protectorate over the kingdom of Buganda in 1894. Other parts were added later. In the following year the government bought the Company out of the remainder of the British sphere and the territory from Naivasha to the coast became the East Africa Protectorate and later, Kenya. In 1902 the Eastern Province of Uganda was added to it, to be followed by the Rudolph Province in 1926. In Uganda the brief era of peace that followed the declaration of 1894 was broken by a mutiny of Sudanese troops in 1897, which became a rebellion when Mwanga, declaring himself a Moslem, and Kabarega, chief of Bunyoro, joined in. Peace was not restored until 1899, when Mwanga and Kabarega were captured and removed to the Seychelles. In 1900 Sir Harry Johnston, Special Commissioner for the Protectorate, negotiated with regents on behalf of the infant Kabaka an agreement whereby Buganda, while ranking as a province of the Protectorate, retained extensive powers of self-administration and in which the Kabaka's high position was recognized.

The Maji Maji Rebellion came as a shock to public opinion in Germany where it was realized that incessant native troubles pointed to something seriously wrong in the administration of German East Africa. Colonial affairs, which had hitherto been the concern of a sub-department of the Chancellor's office, were transferred to a newly created ministry, and Bernard Dernburg, the first Colonial Secretary, began to introduce some very badly needed reforms. Dernburg was succeeded in 1911 by Wilhelm Solf, who did much to further the policy of his predecessor, but the intentions of these two well-meaning men were frustrated by the 1914–18 war. After a long campaign, in which the German commander von Lettow-Vorbeck manœuvred with much skill against heavy odds, German East Africa was taken by British and Belgian troops. After the war the greater part, renamed Tanganyika Territory, came to Great Britain as a mandate from the League of Nations. Ruanda and Urundi fell to Belgium under the same conditions. These mandates became U.N.O. trusteeships after the 1939–45 war.

Although Kenya, Uganda and Tanganyika were all three administered by Great Britain for a long time, the two former since the 1890s and the latter since 1918, their evolution differed considerably. Uganda was never anything but an African territory, owned and to an increasing extent administered by Africans. This characteristic is reflected in the history of Uganda under British rule. Despite excitements now and then this was an era of progress and increasing prosperity for the African. Kenya, on the other hand, soon became a colony of settlement with a strong and energetic resident European community. Although generalizations of this kind are dangerous, nevertheless it might be argued that the history of Kenya until the Second World War was largely concerned with the efforts of these Europeans to establish a home in Kenya and to assure conditions such as would in their opinion make their own community permanent and prosperous.

Tanganyika was largely an African territory and the emphasis was laid chiefly on African interests. There were islands of European settlement in the north and in the south, while the lead in economic matters was in the main taken by Europeans and Asians. But the energies of the British administration since its inception were almost exclusively devoted, directly or indirectly, to the economic and social advance of the African, while the training of the people to govern themselves was steadily kept in view, though the methods changed and the tempo increased considerably in later years.

In Ruanda-Urundi the Belgians followed very much the same policy as the British in Uganda. There was some non-native immigration, but the aim was to foster and improve indigenous institutions, and to preserve and develop the territory as an African country.

Of Zanzibar in its heyday it was said 'When you play the flute at Zanzibar, all Africa, as far as the Lakes, dances',[1] but with the establishment of European protectorates on the mainland the political importance of the island fell away. The slave market was closed in 1873 and the disappearance of the slave traffic was soon followed by a slump in the entrepôt trade in other goods as Europeans established ports on the mainland. Nevertheless the social and cultural influence of Zanzibar persisted, and it remained what it had always been, a meeting place of Asia and Africa.

With the Italians in Ethiopia and the Japanese in the Indian Ocean the 1939-45 war came very close to the East African territories, and all played an active and useful part in the war effort. Large numbers of Africans and, proportionately, of Europeans, served in the forces that took Ethiopia and subsequently moved on to other theatres of war, and those who remained at home concentrated on the production of food and materials so as to make the region as far as possible independent of imports from other countries. Large numbers of prisoners of war, internees, and refugees from central Europe spent the war years in East Africa, and the region also lay right along the lines of communication between North and South Africa.

The end of the war found East Africa, as a producer of primary materials in short supply, on the eve of a period of great prosperity, and bold plans were made for economic development. It is to this era that belongs the notorious Tanganyika Groundnut Scheme, an operation directed not by the Colonial Office but by the Ministry of Food, and by no means typical of the realistic and well integrated programmes that were also planned and carried out. This was the time too when it was realized that constitutional advance must be hastened to meet pressing demands from the Africans, and when self-government came to be regarded not as an ultimate aim but as a goal that must be reached in the near future.

In 1953 a speech by the Secretary of State for the Colonies roused fierce suspicions in Uganda that the country might be federated with the other East African territories against its will. Reassuring statements by the Colonial Office and the Governor went some way to allay public excitement but did not satisfy the Kabaka of Buganda, who argued that the reassurances were not so strong as others that had gone before, and went on to make new

[1] This is the version given by W. H. Ingrams in *Zanzibar, its history and its people*.

demands which, if accepted, would have nullified the British policy of developing Uganda, including the kingdom of Buganda, as a unitary state. After much discussion the Kabaka accepted the reassurances but refused to abandon the additional demands, whereupon the Governor withdrew British recognition of him and deported him forthwith to England. This step, designed to remove an obstacle to the policy of building a strong, independent, democratic, united Uganda, caused such a furore among the Baganda as to make it impossible to pursue any policy at all. Eventually both the Baganda and the British Government accepted the compromise proposals of a specially appointed constitutional committee, and the Kabaka was restored to his throne.

The matter did not end there. The issue was in essence a clash of opinion among Africans as to who should inherit the power which was then wielded by the British colonial authorities. The 'new men', radical nationalist politicians representative of an up and coming middle class, saw the future in terms of a unitary state in which they would be the rulers. The traditionalists, mainly centred on the Kabaka and his parliamentary assembly the Lukiko, conscious of the eclipse of the aristocracy in other parts of Africa, rejected the unitary state, in which they foresaw that traditional power would be weakened and destroyed. Instead they wanted a federation in which the kingdom of Buganda would be allowed to develop separately, with traditional authorities retaining their powers undiminished. The outcome of the conflict is described below.

Shortly after the Second World War there began in Kenya a movement called Mau Mau. It was confined almost exclusively to the Kikuyu and its origins appear to have lain in land shortage, various social and political grievances and more generally in a profound unease generated by the impact of an alien civilization. In due course the movement broke out in terrorism and murder on a grand scale. Though primarily xenophobic, Mau Mau killed many more Africans than Europeans. It was not finally suppressed until 1960, when the state of emergency officially came to an end.

*Independence*

The wind of change blew on East Africa as it did on the rest of the continent. In Tanganyika independence found its champion in Julius Nyerere, the son of a chief in the Lake Province, and founder of the Tanganyika African National Union. When limited self-government was introduced in 1960 TANU won 70 of the 71 seats in the legislature. Nyerere became prime minister in the following year when Tanganyika was granted full internal self-government. In December 1962 Tanganyika became a republic within the Commonwealth and Nyerere was elected president. The government was from the first closely linked with TANU (in fact almost indistinguishable from it) and Tanganyika was therefore a one-party state.

Zanzibar became fully independent under a government of which the Arab Sultan was the head. In January 1964 there was a revolution against the government, an unknown number of Arabs were massacred, the Sultan and many other Arabs fled (the Sultan himself eventually took refuge in England), and a revolutionary committee took power. In April of the same year Tanganyika was united with Zanzibar to form Tanzania. Nyerere remains president of the new state.

Since the revolutionary *coup* a curtain has descended on Zanzibar. Such information as does filter through gives the impression of a grisly little despotism infiltrated by Communist Chinese and East Germans and governed by the whims of the ruling Afro-Shirazi junta. On the other hand it is said that progress has been made in public health and education. What tune is now being played on the pipes in Zanzibar and whether the mainland is dancing to it are questions that cannot be confidently answered.

Hardly was Mau Mau done with in Kenya than this country also took its last steps to independence. A political party, the Kenya African National Union (KANU), was formed in 1960, and Jomo Kenyatta, a leading Nationalist, at that time still under detention for complicity in Mau Mau, was elected president of the party. A general election took place in 1961 and KANU gained a majority over its rival, the Kenya African Democratic Union (KADU). Kenyatta was released later in the same year, became a member of the Legislative Council in 1962 and prime minister of an independent Kenya in 1963. In 1964 he became president of the Republic of Kenya.

Independence came to Uganda in October 1962 and the Kabaka was sworn in as president exactly one year later. Milton Obote, leader of the Uganda People's Congress and a member of the Lango tribe,[1] became prime minister. President and prime minister lived in an uneasy relationship until 1966, when Obote suspended the constitution, dismissed the Kabaka from the presidency and assumed the title of head of state himself. The Kabaka managed to make his

---

[1] The Lango are a non-Bantu tribe in northern Uganda. With some reservations Seligman classifies them as Nilotic (*Races of Africa*, pp. 154-5).

way to England where he lived in obscurity until his death in 1969. Thus the struggle between the traditionalists and the new men ended in the victory of the latter.

Obote's triumph, however, was not of long duration. Early in 1971, while on his way back from a Commonwealth conference, he joined the ranks of African presidents thrown out by the army. The leader of the *coup*, General Amin, appears to enjoy considerable popular support.

The Belgian mandate of Ruanda-Urundi, formerly made up of two kingdoms, with a feudal régime in which the Watusi formed the governing class, emerged as separate independent states on 1 July 1962. Ruanda, now spelt Rwanda, became a republic, the King having already been deposed by rebellious subjects in 1959. The government was formed by the once subordinate Bahutu, who had driven the Watusi from the country in great numbers when the government fell. Many Watusi are reported to have been murdered since then.

Urundi, now Burundi, remained a monarchy. In 1965 an army mutiny was suppressed and was followed by a purge in which all the Bahutu politicians and officials were killed. At the end of 1966 the prime minister, a 24-year-old army officer named Michel Micombero, seized power and proclaimed Burundi a republic. At the same time the constitution and parliament were abolished. Micombero became president and rules through a cabinet of ministers and a party apparatus. The governors of the eight provinces are all army officers.

## Land

There is no subject on which Africans are more sensitive than land, which played a critical part in East African controversies, particularly in Kenya.

European settlers acquired land in the highlands by purchase from chiefs or from the Imperial British East Africa Company before the East Africa Protectorate was declared in 1895, but it was not until the turn of the century, when the cost of maintaining the Uganda railway through empty country made it imperative to find a source of revenue, that the British Government committed itself to a steady policy of European settlement. The climate of the highlands seemed to be well suited to Europeans and great areas moreover seemed to be unoccupied. The great pasture lands on the high plateau appeared to have no native tenants at all. We know now that this situation was only temporary and that a series of natural catastrophes had so scattered and reduced the human and cattle population as to create an impression of emptiness that was not normal. The entry of Europeans into Kenya thus coincided with a period of unusual depopulation. This coincidence, combined with ignorance of the nature of African land tenure, weakness in the face of settler demands, and indecision on the part of the British Government, led to alienation in a manner and on a scale which left the Africans of Kenya with an abiding grievance. This was not alleviated by subsequent demarcation of reserves to be 'set aside for the benefit of the Native tribes for ever', and was positively accentuated by the virtual exclusion of the highlands to any but white settlement. The belief that land shortage was due to the alienation of land to Europeans was one of the causes of Mau Mau.

In Uganda and to a great extent in Tanganyika, the land question was not complicated by a policy of European colonization. In Uganda all land outside towns and trading centres and in Buganda all land whatsoever was held in trust for the native population, while in Tanganyika the whole of the land, except that already alienated in German times, was held by the government to be administered for the common benefit of the people of the territory. In effect this meant that land could not be alienated to non-Africans unless it was not required for any foreseeable African use. In Zanzibar all waste and unoccupied land and all land occupied in accordance with local and tribal custom was vested in the Sultan. However, large estates came into the possession of Arabs under conditions equivalent to freehold, though not defined by law. In order to prevent Arab and African land from passing into alien hands, the attachment of this land or its produce was forbidden, and all alienation was made subject to the control of a board appointed by the British Resident.

### ECONOMY

The economy of East Africa as a whole presents a fairly buoyant appearance. The region is a major producer of several key crops for which the demand remains reasonably steady. The economy depends largely on agriculture and minerals play a lesser, though by no means insignificant, part. Over half of the total production is in the form of agriculture and livestock.

K

*Kenya*

The principal exports are coffee, tea, petroleum products, maize, meat products, pyrethrum, hides and skins, sisal and wattle bark. Minerals have not yet been extensively developed. Soda ash, salt and limestone are exported; gold and silver are mined in a small way, and the search for oil and other minerals continues.

After agriculture the second most important industry is tourism. Foreign visitors are attracted by Kenya's magnificent scenery, by the mountains, the forests, the coastline; by the city of Nairobi itself, with its hotels, shops and fine buildings; and most of all by the abundant game life in the reserves, in all its beauty and variety.

Considerable energy has been devoted to the establishment of heavy industry. Among existing plants are a steel-rolling mill, an oil refinery and a tyre factory. Several light industries have taken root. These are concerned, *inter alia*, with aluminium products, enamelware, textiles and the production of a number of consumer goods.

There are 7–8 million cattle in the country, besides innumerable sheep and goats. Great numbers of cattle are herded by nomadic or semi-nomadic pastoralists like the Boran or the Masai. Others are in the hands of sedentary farmers, including Europeans, who have created a thriving dairy industry.

The controversial land question has been resolutely tackled. As early as 1961–2, when Kenya was approaching independence, schemes for the transfer of mixed farming land from Europeans to Africans were put into operation. A large area was bought from Europeans to be turned into African smallholdings. It has been argued that smallholdings are not economic in the African context; but perhaps co-operatives may overcome the disadvantages of small-scale farming.

Opportunities for irrigation exist on the lower Tana River, where, it is thought, some 300,000 acres could be irrigated by means of storage reservoirs. It is intended to build several hydro-electric stations on the Tana as part of the national hydro-electric plan.

*Tanzania : the mainland*

Economic policy is based on President Nyerere's 'Arusha declaration' of 1967. This policy aims at public ownership of the leading sectors of the economy, fair distribution of resources to the whole population, and self-reliance on the part of the people. Much is expected of the *ujamaa* villages, compact communities organized on a socialist and co-operative basis.

Principal exports at present are cotton, coffee, diamonds and sisal. A second five-year plan was announced in 1969. The new plan faces the probability that no further expansion can be expected in old economic mainstays such as, for instance, sisal and coffee, and places emphasis instead on wheat, cotton, tea, oil seeds, flue-cured tobacco and cashew nuts. (Tanzania is already the world's second largest producer of cashew nuts.) Rice and sugar will be encouraged, so as to make the country self-sufficient in these crops. The mining industry will be expanded. Mainland Tanzania is already a leading producer of diamonds, and prospects for further development of the mineral industry seem fairly bright.

Government and people face an uphill task. The vast central area of Tanzania mainland is poor and dry and infested with tsetse. It is doubtful whether this area can in the foreseeable future provide more than subsistence agriculture. Even the great cultivation steppe between Tabora and Mwanza, which produces the bulk of the cotton crop, is overstocked and eroded. The most fertile land is on the periphery, in the northern and southern highlands, and perhaps in the hilly country a hundred miles or so inland from Dar-es-Salaam. Nevertheless the central plateau, unpromising as it may look, carries large numbers of cattle. A drastic improvement in pastoral methods could lead the stock-raising industry in this area to a bright future.

Some of Tanzania's rivers offer opportunities for irrigation. A large scheme to dam the Rufiji is being examined. Other possibilities are the Ruvu and the Pangani.

Fishing in the sea and on inland waters is an old craft in East Africa, and already makes a contribution to the economy as well as to the diet of the people. Finally, mainland Tanzania has wonderful opportunities for tourism, one of East Africa's fastest-growing industries.

## Zanzibar

It is difficult to get a clear picture of the economy of Tanzania's island appendage. Land previously owned by dispossessed Arabs has been distributed to the peasants. Cloves are still the chief export, followed by copra. All trade is in state hands, and the state holds a monopoly in salt, matches, tea and kerosene. The narrow basis of the economy and the character of the régime make the outlook uncertain.

## Uganda

Of the three anglophone East African countries, Uganda is the one that relies most heavily on agriculture, this sector being responsible for 85 per cent of exports. Coffee and cotton are the main crops, contributing some three-quarters of the total exports. The policy now is to diversify agriculture by expanding the tea and sugar industries. Tobacco is also gaining in importance.

The most productive farming area is that which lies along the western and northern shores of Lake Victoria. This is the former kingdom of Buganda, home of the most numerous and progressive people in the country. They grow coffee, cotton and maize as cash crops and plantains as their main food staple. They employ immigrants from western Uganda, Rwanda and Burundi as labourers. Other important farming areas are in the east towards Mount Elgon, and Kigezi in the south-west.

The principal mineral export is copper.

A hydro-electric plant at the Owen Falls now provides electricity to nearly all towns of any size and large quantities of electric energy are exported to Kenya. There has been considerable further investment in hydro-electricity and a new station is planned on the Murchison Falls. As in Kenya and Tanzania, tourism is a prolific source of revenue.

## Rwanda and Burundi

Both these countries are remote and without adequate means of communication with the outside world. They are overcrowded and overstocked, and pressure on available land is severe. This has caused a flow of labour to neighbouring countries, especially Uganda, where many migrants have settled permanently. Subsistence farming is the rule, and coffee is the only important cash crop, although cotton is grown in the dryer places and efforts are being made to increase the planting of tea and pyrethrum. Fishing on Lake Tanganyika is a developing industry. The local cattle, famous for their long horns, are commercially unsatisfactory despite their magnificent appearance, and there are too many of them. Minerals are exploited on a modest scale: tin, bastnaesite and wolframite are among the exports. Opportunities for electric power form one of the most hopeful features of the economy. One large hydro-electric plant has been built on the Ruzizi River and there are plenty of sites for more. The exploitation of natural gas from Lake Kivu is worthy of note.

## Transport

The main railway lines run, as might be expected, from the coast inland, with branches leading off in various directions. The Kenya and Uganda Railway, starting from Mombasa, was opened to Kisumu in 1901, to Kampala in 1926 and was extended to Kasese on the western border of Uganda in 1956. There are a number of branch lines in Kenya, while in Uganda a proposed extension of the north-western branch line will cross the Albert Nile by a bridge at Pakwach and go on to Arua, thus stimulating development in a remote corner of the country. The Tanzania system has two main lines, the Central and a northern. The latter runs inland from Tanga to Arusha, while the Central line crosses the whole breadth of the country from Dar-es-Salaam to Kigoma with an important branch from Tabora to Mwanza. Two minor branches run southwards. The two main lines are connected by a link from Ruvu on the Central line to Mnyusi on the northern. The northern line in turn is joined to the Kenya system by a branch from Kahe to Voi. Work has now begun on the railway which Communist China has undertaken to build through Tanzania to Zambia.

There are regular steamer services on the great lakes of the interior.

The principal ports on the East African coast are Kilindini on the island of Mombasa, Tanga and Dar-es-Salaam. Kilindini is the gateway to and from Kenya and Uganda and is also able to tap the traffic of the northern highlands of Tanganyika by the railway link that passes through Voi. The port of Dar-es-Salaam has developed greatly in recent years to deal with the growing trade of the country. Tanga is overshadowed by its northern and southern neighbours. These mainland ports have robbed Zanzibar of much of its former importance.

Most roads in East Africa are of earth and the quality varies. The best roads are said to be found in Uganda. Earth roads are of course very much at the mercy of the weather and many become quite impassable in the rainy season. However, of late years considerable improvements have been made and long stretches on the more important routes have been bituminized.

Air transport was freely used long before the Second World War and in recent years there has been a considerable development in air services. East Africa has several international airports and there are few places of any importance that have not got landing facilities of some kind.

*Questions without answers*

To those who try to read the future of any African country, the question is always, what will happen when the leaders who came to power on a wave of nationalist enthusiasm leave the scene to make way for others?

In Kenya President Kenyatta has reached the age when most men are ready to retire, content in the belief that their life's work is done. The bitter power struggles against left wing elements during the last ten years, complicated by rivalries within his own party, are no good augury for the future.

In the field of foreign affairs the Kenya sky looks clear, except perhaps for one small cloud. The northern frontier area has always been regarded by the Somali, not without reason, as properly theirs. The dispute has been papered over for the time being, but the claim may be renewed later.

General Amin, who has replaced President Obote in Uganda, is a decidedly less flamboyant, more predictable character than his predecessor. He also seems to be more sympathetic towards the Baganda community, and it would not therefore be surprising if that gifted people, after a period of eclipse, were to regain something of their former importance.

Since the army mutiny of 1964 President Nyerere of Tanzania has succeeded in establishing himself apparently immovably in the saddle. To the outside observer the threat to stability in Tanzania might arise from the president's emotional radicalism. This has allowed him, in co-operation with President Kaunda of Zambia, to encourage the penetration of his country by thousands of Communist Chinese. They are building the railway between Tanzania and Zambia, they are training guerillas, and they may even hold posts in some branches of the civil service. The thoughts of Chairman Mao have been translated into Swahili and are no doubt widely read by young people, and there are Chinese readers for school children. By securing Zanzibar the Chinese have obtained a good base for operations on the mainland. The president evidently believes that the Chinese will not meddle in politics and will pack and go when the railway is finished. It is to be hoped that he is right.

Mention of guerillas raises another point. It is no secret that Tanzania is used extensively to train men to liberate Mozambique, Rhodesia and even South West Africa and South Africa from white rule. In Mozambique the guerillas have met with some success, though the harassed Portuguese, faced with similar difficulties in Angola and Portuguese Guinea, claim that they are holding their own. But there is little hope of successful subversive action in Rhodesia at present and even less in South West Africa and South Africa. Most of the guerillas will end up prematurely dead or in prison and it is difficult to believe that those who are recruiting them and sending them out do not know it. There have been reports of substantial casualties.

More relevant is the presence of large bodies of irregular troops within Tanzania itself. Many of them are foreigners and they are trained by foreigners. Some have been induced to join by promises that have no chance of fulfilment. It is not difficult to imagine how, through boredom, frustration, defeat, or at the prompting of enemies external or internal, they might become a danger to the country that is harbouring them.

For lack of information it is almost impossible to write about Zanzibar. One must assume that the redistribution of land and the improvement in social services have been popular. But there are reports that the lawlessness of the ruling junta causes widespread discontent and that cumbersome state trading has brought about commodity shortages. In the longer term there is the question whether the union of Zanzibar and the mainland has in it the seeds of permanency. To President Nyerere the vagaries of Zanzibar's rulers must be an embarrassment, but since he was instrumental in forming the union he is hardly likely to want to dissolve it. Later presidents may have no such scruples, and it would be no great surprise if at some time in the future the two parts of Tanzania were to separate and become different countries once more.

Finally there is a question affecting all nations that face the Indian Ocean: it is that of Russian naval expansion and its likely effect on politics in that area. But since this is a matter of world strategy one can do no more than mention it here.

The East African economy seems healthy enough, depending as it does largely on agricultural products for which there is a steady demand. Moreover, while a great part of the population is restricted mainly to subsistence farming, conditions over the greater part of the area are not unfavourable, the population by and large is fairly evenly spaced, and crop failures usually amount to no more than local food shortages.

As to trade and commerce it remains to be seen whether the somewhat stringent treatment of the Asians will be a disadvantage. It is to be hoped that Africans will progressively take their place. The Asians were exceptionally astute middlemen, and the difficulty of replacing them effectively should not be underestimated.

It is unlikely that we have seen the end of mineral discoveries. In Rwanda and Burundi especially, but also in Kenya and Uganda, minerals are still a weak aspect of the economy, and developments in this sector would be welcome.

The question of foreign aid will be dealt with in another part of the book.

In sum, the difficulties that lie before East Africa are basically political. In Kenya and Uganda they are mainly internal struggles more or less acute between aspirants to power. In Tanzania the stake might be nothing less than independence itself in the face of communist pressure.

# CHAPTER FOUR

# THE HORN OF AFRICA

## SOMALILAND

JUTTING straight up from the sea at the junction of the Gulf of Aden and the Indian Ocean, towering above a little bay in which huddles a poor fishing village, dangerous to navigators because of winds and currents, stands Cape Guardafui, a notable landmark for travellers, for it is the extreme north-easterly tip of Africa. It is also the apex of Somaliland. (*Plate* 38)

*History*

The British connection with Somaliland began early in the nineteenth century when the East India Company sought a safe harbour for their ships on the southern shores of the Gulf of Aden. In 1874–5 the Khedive of Egypt claimed jurisdiction over most of the Somali coast and Egyptian forces occupied the main ports; but when the Khedival garrisons were withdrawn in 1884, the British occupied Zeila, Berbera and Bulhar, partly because these places were on the route to the east. From 1899 the British occupation of Somaliland was punctuated by campaigns against Mohamed bin Abdulla, the so-called 'Mad Mullah', who recruited a large number of fanatical followers and dominated the interior for twenty years. During this time British administration was practically confined to the coast, and it was not until 1920, when the Mullah was defeated and driven out, later to die in Ethiopia, that it was possible to begin to govern the country normally. In the years between the world wars some progress was made in introducing modern administration among an independent and very suspicious people. The human population grew in numbers, livestock increased, and trade developed in a limited way. In 1940 British Somaliland was overrun by the Italians but was reconquered in the following year.

In 1889, by treaties with Somali sultans and by agreements with Great Britain, Zanzibar and Ethiopia, the coast east of British Somaliland fell to the Italians. Three years later the Sultan of Zanzibar leased the Benadir ports to Italy and sold them to her in

1905. Italy then obtained the adjacent hinterland from the Emperor Menelik of Ethiopia in 1908 and Jubaland by cession from Great Britain in 1924. In 1941 British Imperial troops operating from East Africa speedily conquered Italian Somaliland, which was occupied by the British until the end of the war.

French Somaliland lies west of the British Protectorate. France had acquired the two towns of Ambabo and Obok in 1856 but did not take formal possession until 1883. In the following years she acquired the whole of the gulf of Tajura by treaty with the local Somali sultans. The seat of government was transferred from Obok to Jibuti in 1896.

At the end of the Second World War the British proposed that most of the country inhabited by the Somali should be brought under a single administration under either British or international trusteeship. For remote and irrelevant political reasons other nations turned this proposal down. Instead, former Italian Somaliland, renamed Somalia, was placed under Italian trusteeship with a promise of independence in 1960. At the same time the British Government encouraged political and economic progress in the Protectorate. Schools were accepted by the Somali for the first time, European medicine began to be appreciated, and later, councils were formed which stimulated among the Somali a wish to play a more responsible part in their own government. As independence for Somalia drew near, the Protectorate people became increasingly anxious to achieve self-government at the same time, so that the two territories might unite in a single nation. The British Government agreed to withdraw its protection and in 1960 Somalia and the former British Protectorate came together to form the independent Somali Republic. French Somaliland remained an overseas territory of France under the name 'Territory of the Afar and the Issa' (*Territoire Français des Afars et des Issas*).

## The Haud

The territorial question is complicated by an unfortunate legacy of history. In 1897 Great Britain made a treaty with Ethiopia delineating the boundary between Ethiopia and British Somaliland. It was then realized that the boundary cut across certain grazing grounds called the Haud, which had been used by the Somali since time immemorial, and letters designed to safeguard the use of the area to the Somali were accordingly annexed to the treaty. The Somali remained in ignorance of these arrangements until their frontier with Ethiopia was demarcated by a commission in 1931–35. Even then they were cushioned against the worst effects of the Treaty by the Italian conquest of Abyssinia, following which the Haud was administered as part of Italian Somaliland and was thus still available to the Somali. This situation continued under the British military administrations set up temporarily to govern the Italian colonies conquered during the Second World War. But in 1954, at the request of the Ethiopian Government, the Haud was returned to Ethiopian sovereignty. The Anglo-Ethiopian Agreement of 1954 confirmed the treaty of 1897, reaffirmed the right of the Protectorate Somali to use the grazing areas, and also provided a special measure of British protection to the tribes when they were in Ethiopia.

A somewhat similar territorial situation exists further south. The Italo-Ethiopian treaties of 1897 and 1908, which drew a boundary between Ethiopia and Italian Somaliland, left the province of Ogaden on the Ethiopian side of the line. This was an area that had long been claimed, and periodically invaded and infiltrated by Ethiopia, although the inhabitants were predominantly Somali nomads opposed to Ethiopian control. Like the Haud, the Ogaden was regularly visited for the grazing by British-protected clansmen.

After the liberation of Ethiopia by the British during the Second World War, the Ogaden was governed for several years by a British military administration. Ethiopian sovereignty over the area had been recognized by the Anglo-Ethiopian treaties of 1942 and 1944, and when the British plan for a unified Somaliland, which would have included the Ogaden, collapsed, the province was transferred to Ethiopia.

*The Country*

Somaliland forms a triangle with uneven sides, with its apex at Cape Guardafui. The northern side of the triangle runs for a distance of 600 miles along the southern shore of the Gulf of Aden, and the eastern side is twice as long and extends from Cape Guardafui southwards to the frontier of Kenya. The depth inland is 200–250 miles and the total area is something over 270,000 square miles. The country is on the whole arid and inhospitable, the north more so than the south, and the coast more so than the middle plateau and the highlands. Lack of water is the dominant feature of the region, and characteristically this is more marked in the north, where the watercourses are usually dry and only flow during, or immediately after rain. Only in the south are there two rivers with a perennial flow. These are the Webi Shebelle and the Juba. Of these only the Juba reaches the sea, as the Webi Shebeli dies away in sands and swamps inland. For the rest the people depend for water on scattered well systems, which are closer together in the south than in the north.

From this description it may well be imagined that the vegetation is generally sparse, in many places consisting as it does of thin scrub and short grass when there has been rain. However, trees and grass grow well towards the Ethiopian highlands and the middle plateau is covered by fairly thick bush and high grass.

## The People

Racially the Somali are Eastern Hamites, their closest connections being with the Hamitic (also called Cushitic) people of the Ethiopian lowlands and Eritrea. They are tall and handsome, their colour ranging from light brown to black. By nature they are warlike and tough, true sons of the hard, harsh land in which they live. They are devout Moslems of the Sunni school of the Faith. The Somali language, which with dialectal differences is the common medium of communication throughout Somaliland from the Red Sea to the Tana River in Kenya, is exceptionally rich in oral literature.

Politically the Somali are divided into four main groups: the Dir, the Isaq, the Darod, and the Hawiye. The first two live mainly in the north, the Darod in the north-east and south, the Hawiye in the east and south-west.

Although there are clan chiefs and sultans, these usually have little power and the effective conduct of affairs is in the hands of elders. In the absence of hierarchical authority, the political and social framework is provided by a complicated patrilineal system, sometimes close, sometimes wide, according to the matter at issue. Holy men, who teach the young, solemnize marriages, adjudicate in matrimonial matters and generally supervise the religious life of the tribe, are held in high esteem.

The Somali recognize a lesser group called Sab, whose home is mainly in the neighbourhood of the Shebelle and Juba Rivers. Unlike the Somali proper, who are predominantly pastoral nomads, the Sab have a leaning towards agriculture. They also fulfil certain tasks that the Somali consider degrading, such as leather working, smithing, and hunting.

The Somali's way of life is dictated by the conditions under which he lives. Grazing is sparse and water scanty. He must therefore always be on the move with his flocks to make the best of whatever pasturage may be available. The nomadic cycle may be affected by war, disease, natural barriers and several other circumstances, but the factors of grass and water are the dominant ones.

Not all Somali remain for ever in Somaliland. There is a large community in Aden, and they are found scattered about East Africa, often as cattle traders. There are colonies of them in several ports in the British Isles, and Somali sailors are found all over the world.

The spread of western education has naturally led to the growth of an urban intelligentsia of politicians, officials, business men, teachers, army officers, and other representatives of the professional and middle classes. Although these people live a life that is the reverse of nomadic, many of them retain their traditional ties with kinsmen in the interior.

Foreign communities include Arabs, Indians, Pakistanis and Europeans. Some of the Europeans are permanent settlers farming land in the south of the Republic.

The population of the Republic is about 3 million and that of the French territory 125,000. There are a million Somali in Ethiopia and 200,000 or more in Kenya.

*Economy*

The economy of the country is dependent on livestock and the most important form of livestock is the camel. This animal provides milk when it is alive and meat and a hide when it is dead. It also furnishes the means of transport at present essential to the people's way of life. In addition to camels there are cattle, particularly in the south, and great numbers of sheep and goats all over the country. Somali sheep are famous for their skins and their meat is of good quality. The goats are tough and durable and well adapted to the harsh conditions under which they live. The skins of sheep and goats form a valuable export.

Iron ore, uranium, thorium and rare earth minerals have been found but are not yet exploited. Prospecting for mineral oil has not so far been successful. Light industry is represented by a few factories for processing local products.

The remaining economic resources of Somaliland are slight. Various gums and resins are collected in the north-eastern part of the country, fibre is processed from aloe and fishing is an important local industry. The Italians, during their short occupation of

Somalia, promoted the cultivation of cotton, bananas, sugar cane, durra and maize, but taking it all in all, agriculture is an uphill task except in some especially favoured areas.

From the Red Sea port of Berbera there is a brisk export of cattle, camels, small stock, hides and skins. Kismayu on the Indian Ocean is a smaller port with a valuable export of bananas.

## After independence

The main problem of independence has been that of integrating the northern and southern parts of the Republic, one formerly British, the other Italian. In spite of difficulties arising from distance, lack of communications, different administrative traditions, divergent economic interests, not to mention an abortive military *coup* in 1961, matters seemed to be running in the required direction until 1969. In October of that year the president was assassinated (the motive was apparently not strictly political) and a week later a group of army officers, alleging maladministration and corruption in high places, seized power and proceeded to rule the country through a revolutionary council.

Ten years of independence have seen a strong growth of Russian influence in the Republic. This is shown especially in the close ties between Russia and the armed forces. There is, however, no evidence that foreign agencies played any part in the military *coup* of 1969.

## Somali expansionism

A common culture and tradition, allied to fierce pride and contempt for other nations, has bred in the Somali a strong national consciousness that transcends territorial boundaries. The Somali see in the unification of British and Italian Somaliland only a step towards a fully unified Somaliland which would include the French territory, the Haud, the Ogaden, and the northern part of Kenya, anywhere in fact where Somali in significant numbers are to be found. This view is entirely unacceptable to France, Ethiopia and Kenya, who are not in the least likely willingly to concede any of their territory. It also runs counter to the current concept of nationality in other ex-colonies, where, for lack of cultural unity, nation building is done by trying to unify heterogeneous elements within unalterable boundaries. These new countries have no sympathy with the Pan-Somali ideal, which they condemn as secessionism and in principle a potential threat to the stability of their own governments. Nevertheless the Somali will not easily abandon their passionate desire for a physical unity co-extensive with their culture and traditions. There may be here a possible source of future conflict.

## ETHIOPIA

Modern Ethiopia is a mountainous massif separating the Nile basin from the Horn of Africa, with lower plateaux falling away to the plains of Somaliland and to the dry northern borderlands of Kenya. The mountains are of volcanic origin and the highest is above 15,000 feet, while the tableland is scored by deep valleys and chasms. The Rift Valley divides the plateau of Ethiopia proper from the eastern plateau of the Somali and the Galla, forming a trough which is occupied by a chain of lakes down to Lake Rudolf, and then runs on into East Africa. The capital of Ethiopia is Addis Ababa, lying at 8,000 feet above sea-level in the heart of the highlands.

The massif of Ethiopia falls into three zones.[1] The first is the *Quolla*, which extends to an altitude of 5,000 to 6,000 feet and comprises the lower slopes and the valley bottoms. Next is the *Woyna Dega* ('highlands of the vine') an intermediate zone up to about 8,000 feet and the most densely populated of all. The highest zone is the *Dega*, open grass highlands extending from 8,000 to 13,000 or 14,000 feet. Temperatures vary according to altitude, but speaking generally the Ethiopian massif is the coolest area in north-east Africa although the deep valleys are very hot. The country south-east of the Rift has a somewhat similar climate but is rather hotter, while the low interior plateau bordering on the Somali littoral is very hot and dry indeed.

Most of the rivers of the massif flow westwards into the great tributaries of the Nile. Of these the most important is the Blue Nile, which has a natural reservoir, Lake Tana, in the heart of the Ethiopian mountains. The most important eastward-flowing river is the Hawash.

### History

Some time towards the beginning of the first millennium B.C., Semites from southern Arabia, offshoots of the Sabaean civilization which flourished there before Islam, crossed the Red Sea and proceeded to colonize parts of the Horn of Africa. The people whom

---

[1] The authorities vary as to the altitudes of the zones. Those quoted here are from Beaver & Stamp, *Africa*, pp. 184–5.

they found there were Eastern Hamites who were already in full occupation, having driven their Negro predecessors out to the western confines of modern Ethiopia. The Sabaeans established themselves on the plateau and there perpetuated the superior civilization that they had brought with them from Arabia, thus profoundly influencing the culture and language of the local Hamites with whom they mingled. The fruit of Semitic colonization was the kingdom of Aksum in northern Ethiopia, which reached the zenith of its power and achievement in the fourth century A.D.

In order to remove ambiguities of nomenclature it must here be said that Ethiopia was originally the name bestowed by the Greeks on the vast unknown country south of Egypt, the land of Cush of the Ancient Egyptians and later the Roman Nubia. It was only later that it was applied to Aksum and then to the rest of the plateau, being officially adopted as the name of the whole empire in 1941. The alternative 'Abyssinia' is derived from Habashat, an Arab tribe which lived on the opposite coast of the Red Sea.

Christianity came to Ethiopia in the fourth century and by the seventh the Bible had been translated into Ethiopic or Ge'ez, a Semitic language akin to Hebrew and Arabic but more closely related to Sabaean.[1] Ge'ez ceased to be commonly spoken centuries ago and has only survived as the literary and liturgical language. Ethiopian Christianity is monophysite (acknowledging only one nature in the person of Christ) and is closely connected with the Coptic church in Egypt.

From about the eighth century the rising tide of Islam cut Ethiopia off from the outside world, leaving it as a Christian island in a Moslem sea. The glory of Aksum faded and the focus of political power shifted to the south, to Amhara, Lasta and finally Shoa. Semitic language and culture were carried to the central and southern parts of the Ethiopian plateau, and while Islamization of the lowlands proceeded apace, Christianity spread in the highlands. Although Greeks from Egypt had traded down the Red Sea coast in the days of the Ptolemies and Greek influence had spread inland to Aksum, the first western Europeans to reach this remote and mysterious country were the Portuguese, attracted by tales of the fabulous Christian monarch Prester John. They rendered notable service in helping the Ethiopians to repel the Moslems who invaded the country in the sixteenth century, but attempts by Jesuit mission-

[1] The name comes from Agaziyan, like the Habashat an Arab tribe living on the Red Sea coast opposite Ethiopia.

aries to convert Ethiopians to the Roman faith ended in failure. Hardly were the Moslems repelled than a new danger arose, threatening Moslem and Christian alike, and which neither, weakened by war, was in a state to resist. This was the invasion of the country by the Galla, who overran the southern and eastern parts of the plateau, leaving to the Ethiopians only the northern highlands, the area of the old kingdom of Aksum. There followed a period of great confusion. The nominal ruler of the country, while retaining his ancient title of *Negusa nagast*, king of kings, had little real power over largely independent local chieftains. Indeed the period from 1769 to 1855 is called by Ethiopians *mesafint* ('Judges') for it was like the era of the Old Testament when 'there was no king in Israel: every man did that which was right in his own eyes'.[1] European visitors to Ethiopia from the end of the seventeenth century onwards included the French physician Poncet (1699), James Bruce (1769–72), the mission of Lord Valencia and Henry Salt (1805), and later Henry Salt alone (1809), and the French brothers d'Abbadie (1838–48) who collected a great deal of material in various fields of study. In 1854 Richard Burton made his difficult and dangerous journey to Harar.

In 1855 a petty nobleman named Kassa seized power and was crowned king of kings under the name of Theodore. He was very able and in a short time united the country, suppressed the turbulent nobles, revived the spirit of the people and renewed their religious fervour and patriotism. Unhappily his ability and intelligence were allied to a violence of character bordering on madness and this eventually alienated his people and contributed powerfully to his downfall. In 1864, for reasons largely dictated by his own neurotic suspicions, he threw into prison not only a British party including the consul, but also the envoys sent to procure the captives' release. More conciliatory means failing, a British army under Sir Robert Napier was sent to free the prisoners. Theodore's town of Magdala was stormed and taken on 13 April 1868 and the Negus committed suicide, having earlier released the British captives.

After four years of civil war a northern nobleman also named Kassa had himself crowned *Negusa nagast* under the name of John, his accession marking the return of the crown to the home of the kingdom of Aksum. John was a fanatically devout son of the church and a good warrior who crushed two Egyptian attempts to invade the country and then fell in action in 1889 against the Mahdists of

[1] Ullendorff, *The Ethiopians*, p. 82.

L

the Sudan. He was succeeded by Menelik, king of Shoa, who found himself confronted by a threat far more dangerous than that of the Egyptians or the Mahdists. In 1882 the Italians obtained a foothold in Assab and began to spread inland. They were soon busy consolidating themselves in Eritrea and by 1890 were well established round Asmara in the most northerly part of the Ethiopian plateau. One of Menelik's first actions on becoming emperor was to negotiate the treaty of Uchali with the Italians, but this was regarded by the latter as giving them the right to control Ethiopian foreign policy, an interpretation with which Menelik naturally could not agree. In 1895 the Italians advanced into Ethiopia and occupied Adwa.[1] In the next year Menelik fell upon them with a great army and routed them, inflicting heavy losses. Nevertheless, in the peace treaty that was then concluded, Eritrea remained in Italian hands.

The victory of Adwa caused the powers of Europe to take serious notice of Menelik, and several of them sent diplomatic representatives to Ethiopia. Menelik, free from external threats, now resumed the process which he had begun before his accession, that of absorbing the Galla country into his empire. He died in 1913, to be followed by a regency and then by Lej Yasu, an unsatisfactory young man who was deposed by the great nobles in 1916. Zauditu, daughter of Menelik, was then proclaimed empress, and Ras Tafari, son of Menelik's cousin Makonnen, was made regent and heir to the throne. War followed when Lej Yasu's father raised an army to help his son. The revolt was defeated and Lej Yasu, who was not captured until 1921, died a prisoner in chains in 1935. In 1928 Ras Tafari assumed the title of Negus and in 1930, on the death of Zauditu, he was crowned as the Emperor Hailé Selassié. He had already given evidence of his diplomatic skill when in 1923 he negotiated the admission of Ethiopia to the League of Nations. In 1936 an incident at the obscure frontier village of Wal Wal led to war with Italy and the conquest of Ethiopia by the Italians. Hailé Selassié fled into exile first in Palestine, then in England, but was restored to his throne in 1941 on the liberation of Ethiopia by British imperial forces.

Since the end of the last war, Ethiopia has been enlarged by the addition of a new province, that of Eritrea. This is the old Italian colony of that name, an artificial unit formed by the Italians during

[1] Also spelt Adowa, Aduwa, Adua. The spelling adopted here is that used by Ullendorff in *The Ethiopians*.

the Scramble for Africa and retained by them after their defeat by the Emperor Menelik at Adwa. Eritrea is a triangle with its hypotenuse running north-west for about 670 miles from the French Territory of the Afar and the Issa to the Sudan. The northern part of the territory is simply an extension of the Ethiopian plateau which falls away on the west to the Sudan plain and on the east to the coastal plain of the Red Sea. This plain runs the whole length of the territory and varies in width from ten to fifty miles except at the Gulf of Zula where the hills reach nearly to the sea. South of these hills there is a very dry and torrid zone inhabited by the Danakil, another name for Afar, who also live in parts of Ethiopia proper. The total area of the province is about 45,000 square miles.

The Italian administration came to an end in 1941 when the colony was captured by the British, and it was then governed for some years by a British military administration, which managed very well under difficulties. In 1952, by a decision of the United Nations, Eritrea was federated as an autonomous unit under the sovereignty of the Ethiopian Crown. In 1962 it was incorporated as a province of Ethiopia.

## The People

Apart from the Negroes who occupy the southern and western borderlands, the population of Ethiopia is basically Hamitic and may be divided into two groups. First the Ethiopians proper, Coptic Christians who live on the central highlands plateau, strongly semiticized by ancient admixtures from Arabia and speaking a Semitic language. Secondly, Hamites comparatively free from Semitic influence, mainly Moslem by religion, the majority speaking Hamitic languages, who live in the much larger area below the central plateau. That is a much simplified picture of a highly complicated situation. Neither group is pure and each has absorbed so much alien blood from the other, or from the Negroes, as to make clearcut definitions misleading. One interesting community which fits into none of these groups is that of the Falasha, formerly thought to be black Jews, but whom Ullendorff believes are descended from those elements in the kingdom of Aksum who resisted conversion to Christianity.[1] There is no certainty as to the size of the population, but a reasonable estimate at the end of 1970 would be 26 million.

The official language of Ethiopia is Amharic from the province

[1] Ullendorff, *The Ethiopians*, p. 111.

of Amhara, which has for centuries been the language of the court
and of most of the people of the central highlands. It represents the
southern development of Ge'ez, so strongly influenced by Hamitic
elements as to cause some people to deny that it is Semitic at all.[1]
The language most nearly akin to Ge'ez is Tigrinya, spoken in the
country corresponding to the kingdom of Aksum. Tigré is a form of
Tigrinya spoken in the northern lowlands. Almost all Tigré
speakers are Moslems.[2]

Christianity is the principal source and inspiration of Ethiopian
literature. Apart from devotional works, which are often transla-
tions from Arabic or Greek, historiography is the principal branch
of the older literature. There are a number of medieval chronicles
and also historical romances, of which the best known is the *Kebra
Nagast* ('Glory of the kings'). This patriotic compilation includes
the legend of the Queen of Sheba, how she visited Solomon and
bore him a son Menelik, founder of the royal line of Ethiopia.
The use of Amharic instead of Ge'ez as the language of literature
received a strong impulse from the Emperor Theodore, and a great
number of books in that language have been produced in recent
years.

Ethiopian art is expressed in painting and in ornamental writing.
As in literature, the inspiration is religious. The style is influenced
by several *genres*, of which the Byzantine is the strongest. Architecture is primarily ecclesiastic. The most remarkable examples,
though they are by no means typical, are the rock-hewn churches of
Lalibala.

*Economy*

The Ethiopian massif is on the whole a well-favoured land for
agriculture and produces a wide variety of crops. The principal
cultivated product of the *Quolla* is coffee, and there are also great
forests of wild coffee in this zone. The rich valley bottoms grow
rice, cotton, and sugar cane and there are also rubber trees, bananas
and other kinds of tropical flora. The *Woyna Dega* is the most
productive of the three zones. The soil is fertile and there are good
pasture lands. Cereals, the vine, the olive and tobacco are among the
products of this zone, and horses, cattle, donkeys, mules and sheep
are reared in great numbers. The *Dega* tends in places to be rather

---

[1] Werner, *Language Families of Africa*, p. 133.

[2] Ullendorff illustrates the relationship of these languages by supposing that
Ge'ez corresponds to Latin. In which case Tigrinya would correspond to Italian,
Tigré to Spanish and Amharic to French.

bleak and barren but it is good country for livestock, and temperate cereals are grown up to 12,000 feet. The lowlands surrounding the massif suffer from poor rainfall and thin soils and remain therefore a pastoral region with hardy fat-tailed sheep as the chief product.

So the influence of land surface and climatic conditions determine the choice of the inhabitants between an agricultural and a pastoral life. The people of the well-watered and fertile highlands are settled village-dwellers and and agriculturalists, and those of the more arid lowlands are nomadic or semi-nomadic pastoralists.

Although the greater part of the population depends on farming, productivity is low. Neither the agriculturalists nor the pastoralists rise much above subsistence level. It should be added that Ethiopia, like so many African countries, suffers much from soil erosion.

Little is known about the minerals of Ethiopia and they make no serious contribution to the economy. There is gold, platinum, iron ore and copper and there is a substantial deposit of phosphates south of Massawa near the coast. Prospecting for mineral oil is in progress but has not so far been successful. It is generally believed, however, that the mineral potential of Ethiopia is by no means negligible.

Coffee accounts for half the exports of the country. Other exports include hides and skins, oil seeds, fruit and vegetables. Industrial activity is increasing and there are plans for the further development of hydro-electricity.

Ethiopia has two sea ports, Massawa and Assab, but remains very dependent on Jibuti. The railway from Addis Ababa to Jibuti is in Franco-Ethiopian ownership. There is another railway that runs from Massawa to Asmara and thence to Agordat. There are some good roads but not enough of them. Ethiopian Airlines not only maintains an internal network but does much to make the country accessible to the outside world.

*Revolt in Eritrea*

The decision of the United Nations to associate the whole of Eritrea with Ethiopia was neither just nor wise, and, as was apparent to those who had any knowledge of these matters at that time,[1] contained within itself the seeds of disaster. The danger lies in the racial and religious composition of the people affected by that wayward arbitrament. The Christian, Tigrinya-speaking interior highlands are by religion, culture and history Ethiopian and until the arrival of the Italians were part of the empire of Ethiopia. They also

[1] Of whom the author was one.

constitute the most fertile and populous part of Eritrea. The
Ethiopian connection with the plains is much more tenuous and it
is doubtful whether the Negus ever exercised any continuous or
effective authority over the vast Moslem lowlands. Indeed Ethiopia
for many centuries had great difficulty in maintaining her maritime
outlets, and was only able to do so by uneasy arrangements with the
coastal Moslems. Such unity as there ever was between highlands
and lowlands was created by the Italians when they fused the two
into one colony, at the same time separating the whole from Ethiopia.

It was predictable that the 'autonomous' unit would not long retain
its autonomy. It was also highly probable that the lowland Moslems,
who number half the population of Eritrea, would react vigorously
against incorporation, as indeed they have. The country is in a state
of considerable unrest, and rebel activities are assisted by sympathetic Moslem Powers. Ancient historical connections, the danger
that concessions might encourage secessionism in other minorities,
the importance of Massawa as a sea outlet, must all persuade Ethiopia
to stand firm. On the other hand the Eritrean rebels seem to be both
determined and elusive. The trouble therefore appears likely to
continue for a long time. Meanwhile the support given to the movement from outside has caused friction between Ethiopia and other
countries, especially the Sudan.

### The Outlook

Upon his restoration the Emperor Hailé Selassié bent all his
considerable energies to the advancement of his backward country.
He set himself a programme of constitutional reform which is
designed to transform the empire into a properly organized modern
state. Significant progress has been made; but although Ethiopia
now has a bicameral parliament and a ministerial system, the lack of
trained Ethiopians causes a great burden of work to fall on the
Emperor. His reign has not been free from internal commotion. He
survived an attempted military *coup* in 1960, and in recent years he
has had to face dangerous opposition from young Radicals. In
addition to his domestic preoccupations, the Emperor has played his
part on the international stage, where he is a respected figure. In the
African context he has been particularly active in inter-territorial
affairs, notably in the Organization of African Unity. It is disturbing
that he should be the single integrating factor in a country with so
many potentialities for disunion. Unfortunately for Ethiopia, the
Emperor is no longer young.

CHAPTER FIVE

# THE NILE VALLEY[1]

MEASURED from its most remote source, the Kagera River, a feeder of Lake Victoria which rises in Burundi, the Nile has a length of more than 4,000 miles and is thus the longest river in the world. Leaving Lake Victoria by the Owen Falls near Jinja in Uganda it passes through Lake Kioga, is reinforced by the waters that drain Lake Albert, and then flows northwards into the Sudan across an almost level plain, its course at first much impeded by floating vegetation called 'sudd'. In Lake No it is joined by the Bahr el Ghazal, which is also choked by sudd, and then by the Sobat, a much more tumultuous river which brings down the waters of south-western Ethiopia. During the earliest stage of its journey it is called the Bahr el Jebel. After meeting the Bahr el Ghazal it becomes the White Nile until it reaches Khartoum, where it receives its most important eastern tributary, the Blue Nile. Thereafter it is simply called Nile for the remainder of its course. Two hundred miles below Khartoum the Atbara River flows in, like the Blue Nile from Ethiopia. For the rest of its journey, that is from the Atbara confluence to the sea, a distance of about 1,700 miles, the great river receives no other tributaries and practically no rainfall. Between Khartoum and Aswan there are six so-called cataracts, each a series of rapids representing a descent of the river to a lower level. The Nile enters Egypt a little to the north of the second cataract, which is above Wadi Halfa.

From the air the Nile and the belt of cultivation on either side of it appear like a thin silver-green thread running through an interminable desert on either side. Although the total area of Egypt is nearly 400,000 square miles, the settled and cultivated part is comparatively tiny, being little more than a band seven hundred miles long and only ten to fifteen miles wide along the banks of the Nile. In the Delta the inhabitable area becomes broader, but it is still small. The basic condition for cultivation and settlement is the

[1] In this chapter the name 'Sudan' denotes only the Republic of the Sudan, formerly a condominium of Egypt and Great Britain and called the Anglo-Egyptian Sudan.

seasonal flooding of the Nile between July and December. This phenomenon is due largely to the Blue Nile; for whereas the White Nile at Khartoum is a river of almost constant volume, the Blue Nile, rising in the mountains of Ethiopia, is periodically swollen by monsoon rains and melting snow. During the low water season the slower, steadier White Nile contributes 80 per cent of the water available to Egypt, but during the flood season nearly 70 per cent of the water comes from the Blue Nile and 17 per cent from the Atbara. The floods bring down enormous quantities of silt from the mountains of Ethiopia, thus providing the people of the lower Nile Valley with a rich alluvial soil annually renewed. So the Nile waters have created from what would otherwise be a desert a prosperous country and the mother of a very ancient civilization.    (*Plate* 37)

Egypt, like North Africa, has her back to continental Africa, and except for her excursions into the Sudan and towards Ethiopia, has been until recently almost exclusively associated with the Mediterranean and with Asia. The population, which numbered about 33 million in 1969, is basically Hamitic, and the peasantry has kept the original strain remarkably pure. The urban middle and upper classes, however, are exceedingly mixed and include many foreign elements. In addition to the settled peasantry and town-dwellers, there are nomadic Arabs in the deserts bordering on the riverine strip.

The greater part of the population is Moslem and Egypt occupies a key position in the Moslem world, forming, as it were, a bridge between eastern and western Islam. The University of Al Azhar in Cairo, home of a great body of Islamic scholarship, enjoys great prestige and influence. The Copts, who number something under three million, are the most important non-Moslem community, being members of one of the oldest Christian churches in the world, descendants of those Egyptians who became Christians in the fourth century. Their head is the Coptic patriarch of Alexandria, and they are especially numerous round Assyut in Middle Egypt, and in the famous oasis of Faiyum.

The Sudan has an area of a million square miles and a population of 15 million people. It stretches from Uganda and Congo/Zaïre in the south to Egypt in the north, and is flanked on the east by Ethiopia and the Red Sea and on the west by the Republic of Chad and the Central African Republic. It consists of a succession of belts of country running from east to west, starting in the north with the desert that borders on Egypt, progressing southwards to a band of grassy steppe which merges into savannah, and ending in the great marshy basin of the south. The people are exceedingly varied in origin though, as will be seen below, their cultural divisions are simpler. In the north, predominantly Berberine or Nubian peoples live along the river banks and follow a way of life not unlike that of the Egyptians. The desert supports nomadic Arabs in the west and nomadic Hamites belonging to the Beja tribes in the east. In the steppe and savannah belts there is a diverse population of nomadic Arabs, sedentary people of mixed Arab and Negro blood, and numbers of Nilotes of different tribes. Finally the deep south is the home of the great Nilotic tribes such as the Shilluk, Dinka and Nuer, and some other tribes of non-Nilotic origin.

Broadly speaking the Sudan may be divided into two great zones, the North and the South, one very different from the other but each having certain characteristics that give it some sort of homogeneity. The North, with a population of about eleven million, is Moslem, Arabic-speaking, somewhat under Egyptian cultural if not political influence. The people of the few large urban agglomerations and of the Nile bank villages are advanced, vocal and very politically minded. In contrast the South, with about four million people, is primitive, pagan where it has not been christianized, with political organizations at present spreading little further than the tribe, and speaking tribal languages. In order to advance their claim to control the Sudan, Egyptians in the past often used the phrase 'Unity of the Nile Valley'. Like many such slogans, this is somewhat misleading. Although Egypt and the Sudan have a common interest in the waters of the Nile and are bound by old cultural and religious ties, the points of difference are also strong, and must not be overlooked in any appraisal of the relations between the two countries.

*History*

When we last looked at the history of the Sudan it was as witnesses of Gordon's death at Khartoum and the subjection of the Sudanese to yet another régime of oppression.[1] In 1896 the British Government resolved on reoccupation. There were several motives for this decision: one was to free the Sudanese from the tyranny of the Khalifa Abdulla and to extirpate the Slave Trade; another was to put an end to provocative attacks by the Khalifa's bands on the southern frontiers of Egypt; a third to anticipate other nations,

[1] p. 50.

especially the French, who were casting eyes on the Sudan. National pride also no doubt played some part in the decision. The British public had felt very keenly the disgrace of Gordon's death, and it had always been assumed that the shame of 1885 would one day be avenged.

The invasion of the Sudan fell into two phases. The first was a brisk and inexpensive operation which led to the capture of Dongola. The British commander, Sir Herbert Kitchener, then succeeded in persuading the British Government to authorize a further advance in order that the power of the Khalifa might be destroyed entirely. This proved to be a far more difficult campaign than the first and involved immense problems of supply and transport which were, however, all successfully solved in the end. On 2 September 1898 the Khalifa's army was totally defeated at the battle of Omdurman opposite Khartoum, and the Khalifa himself was killed in a last battle in Kordofan on 24 November. Charging with the Lancers at Omdurman was the young Winston Churchill. By an agreement signed in 1899 the Sudan became a condominium of Great Britain and Egypt. Although the joint sovereignty of Egypt was specifically recognized, in fact she became no more than a sleeping partner. The intention of the agreement was obviously to ensure the predominance of Great Britain in the best interests of everyone concerned. In effect Great Britain assumed a trusteeship of the Sudan, with the result that after many generations of misgovernment and anarchy that country at last received a just and stable administration.[1]

We left Baring in Egypt,[2] where he and a handful of able British administrators between 1890 and 1896 performed the miracle of transforming a backward, oppressed and bankrupt country into a viable modern state. Finance was put on a firm footing, social services were established, the local administration was made reasonably honest and the army was reformed. All these measures were taken ostensibly in the name of the Khedive,[3] for although Egypt was at this time virtually a protectorate of Great Britain, she was still in theory part of the Turkish Empire. When Turkey joined the enemies of Great Britain in the 1914–18 war, the British position became anomalous. Moreover the Khedive, Abbas Hilmi,

[1] At the time of the agreement and for some time after, Egypt had no civil service able to fill the higher posts of government.
[2] p. 49.
[3] Title of the Viceroy of Egypt, accorded to Ismail Pasha by the Turkish Government in 1867.

was openly on the Turkish side. The pretence of Turkish sovereignty was therefore abolished, Egypt was formally declared a British protectorate, and the Khedive was deposed, being replaced by his uncle, Husain Kamil, with the title of Sultan of Egypt. The Egyptian Government threw itself quite wholeheartedly into the war on the British side, and the people bore with patience the dis-advantages and hardships that a state of war entailed.

Meanwhile the position of Egypt as a Mediterranean crossroads had tended to make Egyptians very conscious of their position of subordination. Thus it came about that in spite of the undoubted advantages brought by the British, especially to the peasants, Egyptian nationalism, which in the form of impatience of foreign control had existed since the earliest days of the occupation, began to make itself increasingly felt. Stimulated by Turkish intrigues, Moslem religious fervour and an inflammatory press, it had created much anti-European feeling among the masses well before the war. In 1918, under the leadership of Saad Zaghlul Pasha, it became vociferously insistent in its demands for Egyptian independence. Zaghlul was tactlessly treated by the British Government in London, inconclusive negotiations did nothing to allay popular discontent, there were widespread disorders, Zaghlul and a number of his associates were deported, until finally, in 1921, the British Government unilaterally terminated the Protectorate, reserving for itself however security of communications, defence, protection of foreigners and minorities, and the Sudan. At the same time Sultan Fuad, who had succeeded Husain Kamil, was proclaimed King and became a hereditary ruler, parliamentary government was estab-lished, and Saad Zaghlul returned from exile, soon to become prime minister. He lost no time in opening a campaign for the complete withdrawal of the British and for the incorporation of the Sudan in Egypt. To these demands the attitude of the British was clear. They were ready to give way on matters affecting domestic and internal affairs, but they insisted on their need to guard the Suez Canal, and they would not compromise on the Sudan. Matters were therefore at a deadlock when Zaghlul died in 1924, to be succeeded as leader of his party, the Wafd, by Mustafa Nahas Pasha. A tragic manifestation of nationalist feeling was the murder in the same year in the streets of Cairo of Sir Lee Stack, Commander in Chief and Governor-General of the Sudan. Attempts in 1927 and again in 1930 to conclude a treaty between Great Britain and Egypt came to nothing, but in 1936 agreement was finally reached and a treaty was

signed which provided for co-operation in time of war and the
gradual withdrawal of British troops. The treaty was to have a
duration of twenty years and it avoided the question of the Sudan.
The British High Commissioner was withdrawn from Egypt and the
two countries exchanged ambassadors. In 1937, at the instance of
Great Britain, Egypt became a member of the League of Nations,
and in the same year was helped by Britain to get rid of the
'capitulations', the system of extra-territorial jurisdiction which had
survived from the days of dependence.

During the 1939–45 war Egypt faithfully honoured her treaty
obligations and was an indispensable base for Allied operations in
the Middle East. After the Yalta Conference she herself declared
war on the Axis. When the war in Europe came to an end the
demand for the evacuation of British troops became violently insistent and to this was added a clamour for the transfer of the Sudan
to Egypt. The British Government agreed, perhaps rather tardily,
to withdraw troops and evacuation to the Canal Zone began in
due course; but on the question of the Sudan they remained
adamant, being strengthened in this determination by the prepara-
tions that were then being made for the Sudanese to become self-
governing and hence eligible to decide the matter for themselves.

On the night of 14–15 May 1948, simultaneously with the
termination of the British mandate for Palestine, Egyptian forces
entered Palestine, allegedly to restore order and to put an end to
'massacres perpetrated by terrorist Zionist gangs'. Whatever the
reasons, the intervention was unsuccessful and the Egyptians had
the worst of some rather desultory fighting before an armistice was
patched up in the following year.

The internal situation was far from peaceful. The Palace and
successive governments were frequently at loggerheads, and there
was much popular discontent, which the government usually
sought to divert from itself by parading Anglo-Egyptian differences.
The ill-success of Egyptian arms in the Palestine campaign and
political setbacks in the Sudan supplied material with which the
Moslem Brotherhood, a religious, nationalist and terrorist organization under Sheikh Hasan el Banna, used to attack the weakness
and corruption of the government. The Prime Minister, Nokrashy
Pasha, was assassinated by a member of the Brotherhood at the end
of 1948 and two months later Sheikh Hasan el Banna was himself
assassinated. Thereafter a series of crises ended in 1952 in a military
*coup d'état*, the establishment of a government headed by General

Mohamed Neguib, the enforced abdication of King Farouk who was succeeded by an infant son, and in 1953 in the declaration of Egypt as a republic. The new régime aimed at the eradication of corruption, the abolition of feudalism, land reform, a better distribution of wealth and an improvement in the standard of living of the masses. In 1954 another *coup* removed General Neguib, and his chief lieutenant, Colonel Gamal Abdul Nasser, became president and virtual dictator of Egypt. Nasser attained the zenith of his influence when, after nationalizing the Suez Canal, he defied an Anglo-French invasion. The invasion failed, partly because of international pressure and partly because a large body of British public opinion was against it. Nasser succeeded in gaining the sympathy of other nations as a victim while presenting himself to his people as the victor. This diplomatic triumph was followed in 1958 by the union of Egypt and Syria as the United Arab Republic. Thereafter Nasser's international position declined, though he continued to enjoy immense popularity among the Egyptian masses. Syria seceded from the Union in 1961. The Egyptian leader's prestige in the Arab world received a further setback from his country's long and in the main unsuccessful involvement in the Yemeni civil war. Finally Egypt's military reputation received an almost mortal blow from the crushing defeat sustained in the five-day war with Israel in 1967. When Nasser died suddenly in 1970 Egypt and Israel were still bitterly at odds, and the question was one of deep international concern.

The history of the Sudan during the first half of the 20th century was an altogether quieter business than that of Egypt. Generally it was a time of peace and progress. After the Second World War the British administration made way for self-governing institutions and the Sudan became an independent republic in 1956.

The carefully devised constitution bequeathed by the British did not last long. A group of army officers ousted the government in 1958. Then in 1964 riots and disturbances restored a civilian government. Finally in 1969 a group of younger and more radical officers seized power.

The years of independence have been a time of tribulation for the Christian and pagan peoples of the southern Sudan. As independence came nearer, old memories were revived, and fears of rule by the Moslem north were strongly expressed. These fears were quickly realized and tragedy followed. Facts are difficult to find but it seems clear that the south is in a state of continuous revolt. Military reprisals

have been harsh, and many thousands of refugees have flocked into
Ethiopia and northern Uganda. The rebels refuse to negotiate except
on a basis of complete independence, which the Khartoum government is certain to refuse. It is said that the new military government
is more imaginative, less repressive than its predecessors. Even so,
there is little hope of an early amicable settlement.

## Economy

Egypt is essentially an agricultural country and agriculture in
Egypt depends on irrigation from the waters of the Nile. There
are three methods of irrigation in use. The first and simplest consists of raising the water directly from the river or canal either by
*shaduf*, a lever with a bucket at one end and a weight at the other;
or by a wheel with buckets slung round it, worked by a buffalo or
a camel; or again by a kind of Archimedes screw worked by manpower. These archaic yet effective methods are still used when the
water is too low for flow irrigation, but many people now use
modern pumps.

Basin irrigation is also very ancient. In this method cuts are made
in the river bank so that at time of flood the rising water flows out
on to the neighbouring fields which are arranged in a series of
basins separated by embankments. The water remains on the land
for several weeks, deposits its silt, and then runs back into the
falling river, whereupon seed is planted in the muddy basins.

Basin irrigation, though an improvement on older methods, still
only allowed one crop a year. The next step was perennial irrigation.
This is effected first by barrages which enable the water at time of
flood to flow off into high level canals; secondly by reservoirs for
storing water for release during the period when the Nile is low.
By these means it is now possible to harvest two, or even three
crops a year from the same plot of land. To the several existing
reservoirs has now been added the mighty Aswan High Dam, $4\frac{1}{2}$
miles south of the old Aswan Dam which was completed in 1903 and
subsequently twice raised in height. The High Dam is a vast construction $2\frac{1}{2}$ miles long, 120 yards high, and two-thirds of a mile
thick at the base. It was built with substantial technical and financial
aid from Russia. The dam will have the effect of creating a lake
300 miles long (Lake Nasser), stretching many miles back into the
Sudan. Well over a million acres will be added to the cultivable area
of Egypt, another three-quarters of a million acres will be converted
from basin to perennial irrigation and the country's hydro-electric

power will be doubled. But it is suggested that the dam will ruin the agriculture of lower Egypt by holding up the silt on which soil fertility depends. Other more indirect environmental disasters are also predicted.

Another project is the New Valley, aimed at the development of part of the Western Desert by means of underground water.

In spite of fertile soil and abundant water the Egyptian peasant has a hard struggle to live. His food crops are corn of different kinds, rice, vegetables, and clover for fodder. The commercial crop is pre-eminently cotton, which is easily the most important agricultural export. The chief reason for the peasant's grinding poverty is over-population. The density in the closely settled strip along the Nile is 1,900 to the square mile and it is still increasing. An extensive land reform, involving the re-distribution of great estates into the hands of the peasants, has no doubt done something to improve the position. But pressure on cultivable land is severe; large numbers of individual holdings are less than one acre in size; and many peasants are without any land at all.

There is no serious livestock industry. The peasants raise great numbers of domestic fowls, sheep and goats, and they keep camels and buffaloes for draught purposes. Buffaloes also supply milk for making butter.

Egypt's promising oil industry received a setback in 1967 when the coastal oilfields on the Gulf of Suez were lost to the Israelis. Recent discoveries in the Western Desert, however, will go some way to compensate for this loss. Egypt also has reserves of iron ore, phosphates, manganese, bauxite and lesser minerals.

Egypt has a growing industrial economy in which the production of cotton, linen, silk and leather goods, the manufacture of cement and fertilizers, and oil refining play leading parts. The rail and road system is adequate and the Nile navigable throughout its course in Egypt. The Suez Canal has been closed since the war with Israel in 1967, and there is at present (1971) no knowing when it will be opened again, if ever.

The people of the Sudan have a more spacious if less complicated economy than the Egyptians. Between Wadi Halfa and Khartoum the villagers on the Nile banks practice irrigation and keep small stock. In the deserts on either side of them live camel-owning nomads. The central zone possesses vast grazing grounds and the people's wealth lies in camels and sheep in the northerly parts and cattle in the southerly. Close to the Nile there are mixed farmers

who practise irrigation but also receive seasonal rains. The Nilotic
tribes of the extreme south are also mixed farmers in the sense that
they grow subsistence crops. But with some exceptions their chief
interest lies in their cattle, which not only represent their wealth
but are also invested with quasi-mystical attributes and play an
enormously important part in the social and religious life of the
individual and of the tribe.

The Sudan is the world's chief source of gum arabic, which is
obtained from two different species of small acacia tree and is collected by the peasants as a supplementary source of revenue. The
most important crop grown for export is cotton. A small quantity
of American is grown in some places as a rain crop, but the emphasis
is strongly on the Egyptian long staple type, grown on irrigated
land. The greatest area of production is that of Gezira on the Blue
Nile, previously a flat clay plain with a precarious rainfall on which
the peasants kept some small stock and grew uncertain crops of
millets. After a long period of experiment and on the completion
of the Sennar Dam in 1925 this area was put under irrigation and
the Gezira Scheme became a highly successful partnership between
the government, who built the dam and maintained the canals,
two commercial companies who managed the Scheme, and some
thirty thousand Sudanese tenants who produced the cotton.
Profits were divided between the three parties. In 1950 the companies' concessions expired and they were replaced by a public
utility, the Sudan Gezira Board. The total area of the Scheme is
now two million acres, of which one quarter is under cotton and
part of the remainder under food and fodder crops for the tenants'
own use, while the rest lies fallow. This imaginative and well administered scheme is of great benefit to the African participants,
whose standard of living has been raised from poverty to a level that
is high in comparison with that of other peasants in much of Africa
and in most of the Middle East. Gezira methods have been applied
to several other areas in the Sudan and have influenced a number of
projects in other parts of Africa.                (*Plates* 59–60)

Minerals play but a small part in the Sudanese economy, although
a number are known to exist. Considerable quantities of salt are
exported annually and there is a modest export of other minerals,
including manganese, iron ore and chrome.

Reasonable communications in the northern Sudan make most
places of importance fairly accessible. The main railway line runs
from Wadi Halfa southwards to Khartoum, then up the Blue Nile

to Sennar, with an extension to Roseires. The Red Sea port of Port Sudan is linked to the main line by two branches, one from Sennar northwards through Kassala, the other crossing the desert eastwards from Atbara. There are two westerly projections: from Sennar the main line strikes westwards to el Obeid, and a 400-mile extension runs from er Rahad (43 miles short of el Obeid) to Nyala in the far west; in the north a line takes off north of Abu Hamed and runs to Karima below the fourth cataract. Another extension takes off from the Sennar-Nyala line and runs southwards to Wau. Plans for the future envisage extensions from Nyala to the frontier of Chad and from Wau to Juba.

Although communications in the south are generally poor, the Nile provides a highway of 2,400 miles from the Egyptian frontier almost to Uganda. In the northern part navigation is interrupted by the cataracts, but south of Khartoum shallow draft steamers ply freely up and down the White Nile as far as Juba, whence road services operate to Uganda and Congo/Zaïre.

Air services, internal and international, are well developed, and Khartoum is an important airport lying on the main air routes of Africa.

M

CHAPTER SIX

# MEDITERRANEAN AFRICA

THIS region comprises all the countries along the North African coast, from the western border of Egypt to the Atlantic coast of Morocco, and the Sahara desert behind them. Mauritania and Spanish Sahara are also included in it, since they have far closer associations with North Africa than with anywhere else.

Morocco, Algeria and Tunisia, the three countries forming the great north-western quadrilateral of Africa, collectively named the Atlas lands for reasons that will shortly be made clear, were formerly known to Europeans as the Barbary States, and to Arab geographers as the Gezira al Maghreb, or Western Isle, because they were isolated by ocean, sea and desert. This isolation is more apparent to a land people like the Arabs than it is to others. To the seafarers of Asia Minor and Europe, North Africa offered no problem of isolation at all, and the Mediterranean has from the earliest times permitted travel from one shore to another of peoples, their cultures, their trade, their armies. From the historical and human standpoints, as well as the physical, north-western Africa is closely associated with southern Europe and has many claims to be regarded more as the southern shore of the Mediterranean than as part of the north coast of Africa.

Libya, which consists of the two ancient provinces of Tripolitania and Cyrenaica, lies east of the Atlas lands between Tunisia and Egypt. In antiquity it served as a road along the North African coast: Phoenician and Greek sailors used Libyan harbours; Greeks and Romans had settlements there. Like the rest of Mediterranean Africa, Libya has been subject to outside influences since very early times.

Mauritania was understood by the ancients to mean the north-western angle of the African continent, but the term was revived by the French in 1904 to describe that part of the Sahara lying between Morocco and the lower Senegal River with a front on the Atlantic between Cape Blanco and St. Louis.

Spanish Sahara stretches for about 450 miles along the Atlantic coast south of Morocco to Cape Blanco. Ifni, the former Spanish enclave in Morocco, is now incorporated in that state, but Spain still retains the towns of Ceuta and Melilla on the Mediterranean coast of Morocco.

The northern part of the region, that is all that part which lies between the Sahara and the Mediterranean sea, falls into two zones. Libya is largely an arid plateau of moderate altitude relieved only by occasional oases and the fertile well watered highlands of western Cyrenaica called by the Arabs Jebel Akhdar (Green Mountain). The overwhelming impression is one of great aridity and emptiness, of rocks and sand and stunted vegetation, of flatness and monotony. The 'Western Isle', on the other hand, is distinguished by a series of lofty mountain ranges known as the Atlas system, running more or less parallel to the coast from Morocco in the south-west to Tunisia in the north-east. These ranges are most extensive in Morocco, where the High (Great or Snowy) Atlas reaches a height of 14,000 feet. South of the High Atlas is the somewhat lower Anti-Atlas, while running eastwards to Tunisia are two other ranges, the Tell Atlas and the Saharan Atlas, the latter of course the more southerly. These rarely reach 6,000 feet and are separated by a high plateau diversified by saline depressions called *shotts*. A branch of the Tell Atlas named the Rif Mountains runs westwards along the coast to the Straits of Gibraltar.

The North African coastal plain is a more or less fertile belt running the whole length of the region from Morocco to Egypt. It varies considerably in breadth and in some places, for instance round the Gulf of Sirte in Libya, where the desert comes down to the sea, vanishes altogether. It is broadest in Morocco where great plains run right up to the mountains from the Atlantic coast. In Tripolitania a sandy steppe called the Jefara lies between the comparatively narrow settled strip of cultivation and the hills that rise to the Libyan plateau.

### The Sahara

The Sahara is the world's greatest desert and occupies three million square miles, which is between a quarter and a third of the whole continent of Africa. Not all of this great expanse is desert in the usually accepted sense. There are considerable areas of scrub and steppe where some sort of vegetation just manages to exist, while on the indeterminate margins a poor grassland supports thin nomadic populations.

There are three kinds of surface. First the 'erg', sandy wastes

composed largely of drifting dunes. The largest unrelieved area of
'erg' is probably the Libyan desert. The 'hamada' is stony desert
with outcrops of bare rocks. The 'reg' or 'areg' is pebbly or
gravelly desert. This is the type preferred by caravans since movement there is easier, and vegetation and subterranean water more
abundant.

A high ridge widening to a plateau crosses the central Sahara
from east-south-east to west-north-west. The most prominent
features of this ridge are the mountain masses of Ahaggar and
Tibesti, rising in places to 9,000 feet and 10,000 feet respectively.
Much of the high ground is volcanic and many of the peaks are
extinct volcanoes. The western side of the Sahara, which includes
Mauritania, is flat and monotonous and only in one or two places
does the altitude exceed 1,500 feet.

Oases occur when underground water is sufficiently near the
surface to be reached by vegetation. This underground water can
be tapped by wells, and is usually very fresh and pure in contrast to
the brackish surface water when that can be found. An oasis is
therefore a patch of vegetation in the desert based on a number of
wells, usually supporting a settled population. The most important
resource of the Saharan oases is the date palm, which flourishes
under such conditions, but most inhabited oases have arable land
that can be cultivated by the inhabitants. Many of the oases are considerable settlements, or groups of settlements, such as the Fezzan,
Tuat and Kufra. Others, such as Jaghbub, are small and poor.

Finally, it goes without saying that the Sahara is in general
extremely hot, and during the summer the southern interior districts may be the hottest places in the world. The temperature falls
in winter and there is sometimes frost at night.

That man was able, before the days of the internal combustion
engine, not only to live in the desert but to master it and to use it,
was due to his possession of the camel. This unprepossessing but
useful animal is believed to have been introduced into Egypt in the
sixth century B.C. and camel transport was used by Alexander the
Great on his expedition to Siwa. It was some time before the camel
spread westwards into North Africa, but when it did the effect was
revolutionary.[1] The adoption of camel transport by their armies
enabled the Romans to subdue the hitherto recalcitrant southern
tribes;[2] the camel played a large part in the conquest by Berbers and

[1] See Bovill, *The Golden Trade of the Moors*, pp. 41–43 *et passim*.
[2] p. 26.

Arabs of the northern Negro lands and in the founding of the empires of the Sudan;[1] finally it was the camel that made possible the great development of trans-Saharan trade between North and West Africa.[2]

## The People

The general substratum of the Mediterranean African population, as we have already noted,[3] is Hamitic and belongs to that group of Northern Hamites called Berbers. Although they have to a surprising extent managed to keep their original stock pure, Berbers have adopted the religion and with it many of the customs of their Arab conquerors. The Berber element is overwhelmingly predominant in the far west and is still strong in the north-west, especially in the hills behind the coastal zone. Eastwards across Libya the Arab strain becomes stronger and civilization notably more Semitic. The people of Cyrenaica, for instance, are of pure Arab stock, descendants of the eleventh century invaders. In general the Berbers tend to be sedentary agriculturalists, whereas Arabs are nomad pastoralists. This contrast is reflected in the political organization of the two races. The Berbers, living in settled village communities, lean towards a democratic form of government based on popular assemblies. The Arabs, exposed to the hazards of desert life and needing strong leadership at times of emergency, tend to be under the despotic control of sheikhs. This pattern is not invariable: under favourable conditions Arabs can become town-dwellers and there are many Berbers who have been forced by their environment to adopt a nomadic way of life.

The dominant people of the Sahara are Moors in the west, Tuareg in the centre, and Tibu in the east. The word Moor comes from the Greek *mauros*, black, which may even be of Punic origin, and in ancient history was used to describe the natives of that comparatively restricted area named after them Mauritania. It later came to be applied generally to the people of north-west Africa of mixed Berber and Arab origin.[4] The Moors of modern Mauritania are properly Shanaqta and the Arabic name for their country is Shinqit.

The Tuareg are a tall, fair-skinned, slender people whose geographic centre is the Ahaggar plateau of the Sahara. Their best

[1] pp. 30–31.
[2] pp. 29–30.
[3] pp. 9, 24.
[4] It is a tricky word and is used in several other senses besides these.

known characteristic is that they wear a veil and hence are known as 'the people of the veil'. They speak a language called Tamahaqq and their alphabet, called Tifinagh, may be derived from the ancient Libyan script. Both the Moors and the Tuareg are Berbers, but many of the latter live in the southerly parts of the Sahara and have become changed in habits and appearance by contact with Negroes.

The Tibu are dark and speak a Sudanic language but are nevertheless not Negroes but probably an old Saharan race. Indeed they are stated to be the direct descendants of the ancient Garamantes who gave so much trouble to the Romans. The greater number now live in the Tibesti massif, from which they take their name, which means 'rock people', but they are also to be found scattered over a vast area of the eastern Sahara. Until ousted by the Senussi they occupied the oasis of Kufra. They were nominally converted to Islam in the eighteenth century but many still observe heathen rites.[1]

The Senussi who supplanted the Tibu at Kufra are members of one of the best known of those Islamic 'orders' which are an important part of North African politico-religious life.[2] The Senussi order was founded in 1843 by Sayyed Mohamed Ali el Senussi and spread very quickly, embracing all the Arab inhabitants of Cyrenaica and many people in the eastern parts of Tripolitania. Cyrenaica was soon dotted with the lodges (*zawiyat*) of the order, half-schools, half-seminaries, unifying the independent tribes of Cyrenaica under the founder and his successors.

Besides the Arabs and the Berbers there are other long-established communities in North Africa. A brief reference has already been made to the Jews. This community has various origins: immigration, traditionally dating as far back as the first diaspora; the conversion of Berber tribes in Roman times; the influx of Jewish refugees from Spain. The oddest Jewish settlement is the troglodytic village at Garian in the hills behind Tripoli. The dwellings consist of sunken shafts in the side of which rooms are excavated. There is an entrance tunnel with its mouth some way from the shaft. The bottom of the shaft is the farmyard and drainage pool. The advantages of this dwelling are that it is cheap,

---

[1] Seligman, *Races of Africa*, pp. 134–5. For Garamantes, see p. 26.
[2] The word 'order' is not strictly appropriate for the Senussi but it is not easy to think of a better one. The founder's aim was to lead people back to the original purity and spirituality of Islam. He did not purport to found a sect or cult but to point a 'way' (*tariq*).

defensible, and protected from heat and cold. The dwellers in these caves speak Arabic and are outwardly indistinguishable from their Arab and Berber neighbours, some of whom also live in caves.

The total population of the region is about 38½ million, of whom 80 per cent are divided between Morocco and Algeria.[1]

HISTORY

*Mediterranean Africa under Turkish rule*

In the flush of the reconquest of Spain the Spaniards and Portuguese carried the war into Africa and by the beginning of the sixteenth century had possessed themselves of a number of towns along the North African coast. The North African states replied by waging war at sea against any Christian nation that did not make special arrangements with them, usually involving payment of money. In Morocco the war was mainly carried on by Moslem refugees from Spain, some of whom at one time actually set up a veritable corsair republic at Rabat and Salé. The central and eastern states called on the Turks for help, and these, having expelled the Spaniards, established a Turkish régime with themselves as rulers in the three 'regencies' of Algiers, Tunisia and Tripolitania. The most powerful of the 'regencies' was Algiers, which became as it were the headquarters of the Barbary corsairs so dreaded by Christian seamen in the Mediterranean.

From the sixteenth to the nineteenth century Libya, Tunisia and Algeria remained part of the great Turkish Empire that stretched from Iraq to the eastern frontier of Morocco. At first governors were appointed who were directly responsible to Constantinople. Gradually all three regencies acquired a considerable degree of autonomy. Although the Sultan's suzerainty continued to be acknowledged, in fact his power became little more than nominal. Early in the eighteenth century the Karamanli family became hereditary and virtually independent rulers of Tripoli, the founder of the dynasty, Ahmed, having murdered all his rivals at a banquet.[2] At about the same time a Cretan Moslem, Husain Bey, founded the Husainid dynasty in Tunis. The first Turkish rulers in Algiers were the brothers Barbarossa, called in by the inhabitants to help them eject the Spaniards. The Barbarossa were

[1] The figures are roughly as follows: Morocco 16 million, Algeria 14 million, Tunisia 5 million, Libya 2 million, Mauritania 1·2 million, Spanish possessions 225,000.
[2] The story was told to the author with much zest and a wealth of detail by a descendant of Ahmed at the very place where the massacre occurred.

followed by a succession of pashas, aghas and deys who took little interest in the government of the interior and of whom many died violent deaths. In Cyrenaica the Sultan's authority was not acknowledged until 1640 when Mohamed Sakesli, an able ruler in Tripoli, appointed one of his men to be Bey of Benghazi.[1] The country continued in a state of anarchy until the rise of the Senussi order introduced some sense of unity and cohesiveness among the wild Arab tribesmen. The Turks, however, frowned upon the Senussi, and the founder's son, who had succeeded him as leader, withdrew to the oasis of Kufra to avoid them. By that time all the Arabs of Cyrenaica were adherents of the order.

The chief interest of the regencies was privateering, and this pursuit was the main source of their revenue. As time wore on, however, the scope of the corsairs was greatly curtailed by increased European naval construction and by the eighteenth century privateering had declined considerably.

In 1801 the United States refused to pay to Yusuf Karamanli of Tripoli, with whom they had negotiated a treaty, increased 'protection money' for the passage of their ships, whereupon Yusuf declared war by cutting down the flag pole of the American consulate. This war lasted until 1805 and is commemorated in the famous marching song of the American Marines. Thereafter Yusuf's activities became greatly restricted by growing European strength in the Mediterranean, and he was compelled to abdicate in 1834. The Turkish Government solved the question of succession by carrying off the whole Karamanli family and appointing a governor responsible to Constantinople.

### European intervention

The immediate pretext for the French invasion of Algiers in 1830 was a blow from a flywhisk inflicted on the French consul by the Dey but the major grievance was the Dey's threat to the continuance of the privileged trading position of the French. Behind it there was also the need to bolster the uncertain régime of King Charles X of France with a military success. During the next fifty years French rule was extended over the whole of Algeria and in 1881 the French declared a protectorate over Tunisia. Turkish rule survived in Libya until 1911 when war broke out between Turkey and Italy. The Italians invaded Tripoli and landed troops at several

---

[1] Although *bey* and *dey* differ etymologically, they both mean 'governor' in this context.

points along the coast. In 1912 the Sultan of Turkey renounced his sovereignty over Libya, granting to the Libyans 'full autonomy'. This did not mean very much, for by the beginning of the 1914–18 war the Italians had occupied the country.

European connections with Rio de Oro, the southern part of Spanish Sahara, go back to the fifteenth century, and it was the scene of some Portuguese activity in the early days. It was not however until 1884 that the Spanish Government formally staked a claim to a protectorate over a large area between Cape Bogador and Cape Blanco. Occupation of the remainder of this area, and of Ifni, was not accomplished until 1934.

In 1903 the emirs of Trarza and of Brakna north of the Senegal River in its lower course were persuaded to put their countries under the direct supervision of French officers. In the following year these areas were constituted as the territory of Mauritania which was later considerably expanded and became part of the Federation of French West Africa.

While the rest of north-west Africa fell first under Turkish and then under French domination, Morocco managed to retain its independence. The cities of Melilla and Ceuta had passed to Spain in the fifteenth and sixteenth centuries but the rest of the country was held together by occasional strong and energetic rulers who also contrived to ward off foreign intervention. When, as often happened, an able ruler was followed by weaker ones, the country fell into anarchy. A particular weakness was the difficulty of succession. The death of a ruler was almost always followed by fighting among his relations, with consequent confusion throughout the country. In the days of independence Morocco was a land of contrasts. There were splendid towns like Fez and Marrakesh, set in beautiful surroundings, with fine houses, mosques and markets, inhabited by dignified, cultured, hospitable people skilled in the art of living. On the other hand the government was despotic and often cruel, politics corrupt, and there were practically no public or social services. Morocco lay in a most important geographical and strategic position and at the beginning of the twentieth century was not surprisingly involved in a number of dangerous diplomatic crises. International rivalries ended in France being given a free hand to pacify and organize the country which she proceeded to do forthwith. In 1912 France and Spain divided Morocco between them, the French establishing a protectorate over the larger part, while a smaller zone in the north fell to Spain.

*French and Italian rule—nationalism—independence*

In Algeria the French, and in Libya the Italians purposefully set out to create 'colonies of settlement'. The Italians, newly arrived in Libya, were driven back to the coast by local revolts during the 1914–18 war, and the Senussi of Cyrenaica, as allies of the Turks, attacked the British in Egypt. But with the end of the war, and especially with the rise of the Fascist régime, the Italians took forceful measures to crush opposition and by 1932, at the cost of much suffering on the part of the population, 'pacification' was complete. Numbers of Italian peasants were then imported from the over-populated districts of Italy and planted both in Tripolitania and Cyrenaica under a scheme that envisaged ultimate large-scale peasant proprietorship. The Second World War broke out before the scheme could have a chance to prove itself.

During the debates that followed the war on the future of the Italian colonies, Libya was governed by two British military administrations, one in each province. These administrations gave Libya the best government that the country had had since the Romans and withdrew in an atmosphere of goodwill at the end of 1951, when the United Kingdom of Libya came into being. The King was Sayyed Mohamed Idris, the venerated head of the Senussi.

In 1969 the aged King, who was abroad at the time, was deposed by a group of army officers led by Colonel Muammar el Gaddafi, and the country became a republic. The new Libyan government is committed to radical Arab nationalism and is aligned with Egypt and with Egyptian foreign policies, especially on the Palestine issue.

The French, smarting from their defeat by the Germans in 1871, sought to salve their wounded pride by vigorous overseas development, looking to Algeria to provide territorial compensation for the loss of Alsace-Lorraine. Colonization was planned on a massive scale and was assisted by wholesale expropriation of native lands. This process was not accomplished without considerable resistance on the part of the Algerians and there were several insurrections, all suppressed with the utmost rigour. Politically Algeria became a French possession and both northern Algeria and Algerian Sahara ranked as part of France. Algerian Moslems shed their blood freely for France as soldiers in the French army. Nevertheless Algeria was not a country in which there was equality between the races. The effect of colonization was to create an Algerian people of European origin about a million strong, who occupied a position of considerable power and privilege. When General de Gaulle became president of France, the government adopted a more liberal attitude towards indigenous Algerians, but events were to demonstrate how far the more reactionary Europeans, the so-called *Ultras*, were prepared to go to resist change and reform.

After a period of quiescence at the turn of the century nationalist resistance to the French was renewed about 1920 and increased in intensity down the years. The last rising began in 1954 and assumed the character of a long war between a comparatively small nationalist army supported by the mass of the population, and large French forces. It required all the strength and authority of General de Gaulle to break down the intransigence of his compatriots and to bring hostilities to an end. After prolonged negotiations Algeria became a sovereign independent state in 1962. The head of the provisional government was Mohamed ben Bella, who was constitutionally elected president in 1963. He was deposed in 1965 by Colonel Houari Boumedienne, who thereupon assumed full powers as president of the Council of the Revolution. After independence large numbers of French colonists left, and by the middle 'sixties there were only 70,000 still in the country.

Although Tunisia was nominally a protectorate the country was in fact almost directly governed by a strong French administration, with a resident-general at its head. This administration, acting in the name of the Bey of Tunis, made laws, executed important public works, strictly controlled the native authorities and was all powerful. European settlement was encouraged and in 1956 there were over a quarter of a million Europeans in the country, of whom about three-quarters were French and most of the rest Italians. Resistance to French colonization among Tunisians began in the early days of the present century, and steadily spread in spite of efforts on the part of the French at different times to suppress, divert or canalize it. In 1934 the Neo-Destour party was formed having self-government as its object. After the 1939–45 war agitation by the nationalists became general throughout the country and acts of terrorism began to take place against the police and against Tunisians loyal to the French. The situation improved in 1954 when the French Prime Minister Mendès-France solemnly declared before the Bey at Carthage that France recognized Tunisia's right to autonomy and proposed that negotiations be opened immediately. A Tunisian government was formed largely from Neo-Destour members, and after prolonged discussions agreement was reached with France as to the conditions of Tunisian autonomy. These did not please everybody, and a number of nationalist extremists started a campaign against the more moderate leadership of Habib Bourguiba, head of the Neo-Destour. This campaign was defeated, but the promise to Morocco in 1955 of complete independence made it difficult for the French Government, when pressed by Tunisian leaders, to withhold it from Tunisia. In 1956 Bourguiba became head of the first independent government of Tunisia, and in the following year the monarchy was abolished and a republic proclaimed. The title of President of the new republic was conferred on Bourguiba.

The first French Resident-General in Morocco was Marshal Lyautey, a man of quite exceptional stature. This aristocratic soldier-administrator was very sympathetic to the Moroccan way of life and was endowed with an extraordinary capacity for dealing with people. His policy, similar in some ways to British 'indirect rule', was to preserve Moroccan institutions while at the same time adapting them to the needs of the modern world. When he left in 1926 the old French vice of close direct administration crept in, and the French Government tended increasingly to supplant the authority of the Sultan. Moroccan nationalism began as a reaction against the pervasive tendencies of French administration. Towards the end of the Second World War it developed into a demand for the abrogation of the protectorate treaty and for the independence of Morocco. The Sultan, Sidi Mohamed ibn Yusuf, took a leading part in voicing these aspirations and thus became the head of Moroccan nationalism. The nationalists were opposed by the great provincial nobility who in 1953 procured the deposition and exile of the Sultan and his replacement by an older member of his family. The new Sultan failed entirely to secure popular recognition, disorders broke out, the most influential member of the nobility rallied to Sidi Mohamed, and in 1955 the French had no alternative but to recall the exiled monarch and to meet the public demand for independence. Transfer of power took place in 1956 and Morocco recovered her ancient sovereignty. In 1958 the Sultan announced that the government would be a constitutional monarchy with a national assembly elected by universal suffrage. It is still too early to say how far these intentions will become a reality.

That part of Morocco which became the Spanish zone was a poverty-stricken, mountainous area with an old reputation for restlessness and recalcitrance. The Spanish occupation met with violent opposition, first from a picaresque adventurer named Raisuni and then from the more formidable Mohamed Abdelkrim. Many years were consumed in these struggles and it was not until 1928 that all opposition was overcome. The Spaniards then set about organizing the zone in a businesslike manner but the fall of the monarchy in Spain and the establishment of the Spanish Republic were followed by a period of confusion in Morocco which continued until the Spanish nationalist rising of 1936. The Franco régime was distinctly more liberal towards Moroccan nationalism than its republican predecessor and showed a certain sympathy with the increasing desire of Moroccans for national independence. When in 1956 the French zone regained independence Spain at once agreed to the reintegration of the northern zone with the rest of Morocco and the two zones came together as a united and independent kingdom.

## TANGIER

This ancient city, placed at the western entrance of the Straits of Gibraltar, was founded by Phoenician sailors and later formed part of the empire of Carthage. Occupied successively by Romans, Arabs, Portuguese and even British, it passed finally into Moroccan possession in the latter part of the seventeenth century. Large numbers of European merchants established themselves in this busy port which presently became the seat of several legations around which grew a considerable European colony. With the acquiescence of the Moroccan authorities the Europeans set up certain municipal sanitary institutions. These, together with an important diplomatic corps, gave to the city a special character which was generally accepted, and which in 1923 was specifically recognized by an agreement between Britain, France and Spain called the 'Statute of Tangier'. This placed the city under an international government in which the Sultan (which in fact meant the French) was represented by an officer responsible for the administration of the Moroccan population. In 1940 Spain, taking advantage of the fall of France, occupied Tangier but the international régime was re-established after the war by the victorious powers. When Spain and France recognized the independence of Morocco in 1956 the Statute of Tangier was abolished by international agreement and the zone reintegrated with the rest of Morocco.

## Spanish Sahara and Mauritania

In contrast to her attitude towards Morocco, Spain has so far resisted nationalist pressures in Spanish Sahara. In 1967 a U.N. resolution called for a referendum to ascertain the wishes of the local population as to their future. Spain maintains that this resolution has been implemented by the establishment of an assembly of chiefs and heads of families; that Spanish Sahara is a province of Spain; that the inhabitants have chosen to follow Spain and are Spaniards. Both Mauritania and Morocco claim the territory which, although barren and sparsely inhabited, has large reserves of phosphates (see *Economy* below).

Mauritania, formerly part of French West Africa, became independent at the end of 1960. Morocco claims the territory on racial and historical grounds but there is no good reason to suppose that the Mauritanians would willingly part with their independence.

### Economy

The economy of North Africa has been revolutionized by the discovery of oil and natural gas in the Sahara. Algeria, Libya and to a less extent Tunisia are all producers now. Indeed Libya is the biggest supplier of oil to western Europe. The oil is piped from the desert to Bejaia and Arzew in Algeria, La Skirra in Tunisia, Tobruk in Cyrenaica and to several ports in the gulf of Sirte. Natural gas is also piped to Mediterranean ports and is then exported to Europe in liquid form, mainly to Britain.

Mineral oil represents 99 per cent of the exports of Libya, but in other North African countries mineral resources are more diverse, and some are of considerable importance. To name but a few, Algeria has iron ore and phosphates, Tunisia phosphates, iron ore and lead, while Morocco, whose oil output is at present comparatively small, has not only very large phosphate deposits but also iron ore, lead, zinc, cobalt and manganese. There are massive deposits of phosphates in Spanish Sahara, and Mauritania has large quantities of high grade iron ore, also copper and salt.

Saharan oil is not without its problems. The difficulties of production in wild desert country need no emphasis, although these have in some cases been ingeniously overcome. The distance of the wells from the sea is to some extent offset by the proximity of the ports to western Europe. Another, less immediate problem is the possibility in the future of political trouble. State boundaries were drawn at a

time when the Sahara was thought to be no more than a profitless
waste. Some nations have therefore inherited more of it than others.
With the discovery of oil Saharan boundaries have taken on a new
significance and this may give rise to international disputes.

Apart from minerals the principal economic resource of North
Africa is agriculture, followed by stock raising. Until recently two
contrasting forms of agriculture existed side by side. One was
advanced, mechanized, used fertilizers and crop rotation, and was
that practised by the European colonists. The other was that practised
by the Arabs: archaic, simple though not necessarily primitive,
employing few mechanical aids, little if any crop rotation and practically no fertilizers.

With the coming of independence, the departure of the French and
the nationalization of much of the land which belonged to former
colonists, agriculture is now mainly in the hands of Arabs and itself
falls into two categories: that practised by the people of the fertile
coastal strips, static and sometimes assisted by irrigation of a simple
kind; and the shifting cultivation of the arid interior, usually associated with stock raising.

The crops are cereals, vegetables, tobacco and fruit including
olives, citrus, figs, apricots and dates; and the nomads grow somewhat precarious supplies of barley and not much else. The agricultural outlook is not very inspiring, especially when it is remembered
that in Algeria, for instance, the French colonists, now departed,
grew more than half the domestic crop. However, two crops call for
special mention: the vine and the olive. Although many vineyards
were abandoned when the colonists left, wine is still an important
export from Algeria and it also figures among the exports of Morocco
and Tunisia. The olive is Tunisia's economic crop, placing that
country among the world's leading producers of olive oil.

On the whole the North African peasant has not enough land on
which to live, though efforts are being made to enable him to make
the best of what he has. Water conservation has now made irrigation
possible, terraces have been constructed to combat soil erosion and
there has been a redistribution of land, including former colonists'
land. There have been several schemes for resettlement and modern
agricultural practices are encouraged. But tradition is tenacious and
it is difficult to arouse enthusiasm for reform in these conservative
farmers.

The rearing of stock is the most important occupation away from
the cultivated areas, and nomadic pastoralism is the way of life of

the interior. Sheep and goats predominate and are to be found almost everywhere. Cattle are raised in fairly large numbers wherever there are adequate water supplies. In the south towards the desert the most important domestic animal is the camel.

The other agricultural resources of North Africa are the forests. These have suffered from injudicious cutting and failure to replant but the forest areas are still quite extensive, especially in Tunisia and Algeria, and consist largely of cork trees and oak. Throughout the region there are great stretches of esparto grass which is exported for the manufacture of paper. There are very valuable fishing grounds off the coast of Morocco, and the seas off Tunisia and Libya are also well stocked with fish.

The manufacturing industries in North Africa have made considerable strides since the Second World War. They are chiefly concerned with the processing of primary products. Wine making, olive oil pressing, flour milling, fish and vegetable canning, the manufacture of chemicals, fertilizers and cement, the processing of minerals may be mentioned among the more important, but there are several others, covering a wide range. North African industry suffers from several handicaps, perhaps the greatest being restricted markets. However, we may look forward to a certain expansion in the production of goods for local consumption.

The French and the Italians endowed North Africa with a good road system, particularly in the coastal areas, and the most remarkable is the great road through Libya from Tripoli to the frontier of Egypt, well known to those who fought with the 8th Army in the 1939–45 war. A somewhat intricate railway system provides continuous communication from Morocco to Tunisia with lines branching north to the ports and south to the desert. The French showed considerable activity in modernizing the trans-Saharan trade routes, which count among the oldest in the world. Motor roads equipped with rest houses, refuelling stations and a telegraph system link North and West Africa, and the motor lorry has to a great extent replaced the camel caravan.

The interior of North Africa has few great towns except Fez, Marrakesh and Meknes in Morocco and Constantine in Algeria. Fez is the most famous, having long enjoyed great prestige in the Moslem world as the Mecca of the West. Marrakesh is a great market both for the mountain people of the Atlas and for the nomads of the Sahara who come to exchange hides and dates for cereals and European goods. Along the coast of North Africa there is a string of

67. TOUGGOURT OASIS. The reservoir and palms at this oasis in eastern Algeria.

68. DESERT RECLAMATION. The dunes at the Judeida Nursery in Tripolitania, Libya. The technique, which was developed by the Italians before 1914, is to lay down a network of marram grass squares to stop the sand moving, and then to plant a tree in each square. Gradually the sand turns to soil and the desert blossoms again

69–70. Classical Ruins in Libya. The theatre auditorium at Leptis Magna (*above*), and a general view of Cyrene (*below*)

71–73. Art in North and West Africa. A mosaic showing games in a Roman arena discovered at Gurgi near Tripoli in Libya (*above*); tombs of Touggourt kings in the desert of eastern Algeria (*bottom, left*); and a fine bronze from southern Nigeria of a hunter returning from the chase (*bottom, right*)

74–75. Berber Towns. A casbah surrounded by palms near Ouarzazate south of the Atlas Mountains in Morocco (*above*), and the old town of Jefren in Libya (*below*)

76–77. PEOPLE OF LIBYA. A Berber woman of Ghadames, where Libya, Tunisia and Algeria meet in the desert (*above*), and an Arab family of Derna (*below*)

78–79. THE SEARCH FOR OIL IN ALGERIA. The supply staging-post at the village of El Golea in southern Algeria (*above*); labourers making mud bricks and civil engineers checking levels for the mess-buildings at Azzene (*below*)

80. MOROCCAN ORANGERY. An irrigated orangery at the foot of the Kansera Dam on the Oued Beth

81. RICE-DRYING IN SIERRA LEONE. Rice being raked to ensure even drying

82. FREETOWN. The capital of Sierra Leone, which was founded in 1788 as a refuge for freed slaves

83. ISLAND OF GOREE. The oldest French settlement in West Africa

84–85. NIGERIAN TOWNS. The walled Hausa city of Kano, which is an old caravanserai (*left*); and the Yoruba city of Ibadan, which is the largest town in Nigeria (*below*)

86. JOS MARKET. Traders in the market at Jos in northern Nigeria; in the background is a stack of yams, one of the staple foods of the area

87. UNIVERSITY OF GHANA. A student at the University of Ghana on Legon Hill a few miles outside the Ghanaian capital

88–90. Cocoa in West Africa. Harvesting cocoa pods and cutting them open to extract the beans in Ghana (*above*); sorting cocoa beans in Nigeria (*below*)

91. WAGENIA FISHERMEN. These fishermen in the Congo rapids near Kisangani use osier traps operated by liana ropes

92. BALOIE POTTERS. Samples of their work in Congo (Zaïre)

93. TIMBER ON THE IVORY COAST. Logs piled on the river-bank to be floated down-stream to the coast

94–96. PEOPLE OF GUINEA. A Fulani woman of Guinea with a traditional hair-style; a Bissagos man of Portuguese Guinea about to do a snake-dance; an African boy of Guinea holding pineapples

97. PYGMY OF WAMBA. A pure-blooded pygmy or Negrillo. These people inhabit the dense rain forest of Equatorial Africa and live by hunting and trapping. Their average height is less than five feet

98–99. WATUSI DANCERS. Here some girls are doing the "dance of the crowned cranes", which is based on the graceful courtship dance of these birds

100. RUWENZORI MOUNTAINS. The "Mountains of the Moon" between Congo (Zaïre) and Uganda. The tree-groundsels are the first large plants below the glaciers at 15,000 feet

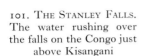

101. THE STANLEY FALLS. The water rushing over the falls on the Congo just above Kisangani

busy ports, beginning in the west with Casablanca, followed by the former international port of Tangier, then by Algiers, Oran, Annaba, Tunis, Tripoli, Benghazi, to name but a few.

Comment on the economic situation of North Africa must necessarily be in some measure conjectural. The physical drawbacks are formidable. There is a shortage of water, noticeable soil erosion and considerable pressure in places on available agricultural land from an increasing population. There is also the question of political stability, though the situation in this respect is certainly less confused that it was ten years ago. Taking it all in all, it seems safe to predict that the mineral wealth of the region, especially in oil, is a factor that will survive most vicissitudes. To this extent the future may be regarded with confidence.

N

CHAPTER SEVEN

# WEST AFRICA

THIS region consists of the area enclosed on the north and east
by an imaginary line drawn due east from the Senegal River
mouth to the western frontier of the Republic of the Sudan, thence
south-west to the Cameroon boundary; and on the west and south
by the Atlantic Ocean. It therefore includes all the lower part of the
great western bulge of Africa between the Atlantic Ocean and the
Nile Valley. Politically the region includes Portuguese Guinea; the
francophone republics Senegal, Niger, Mali, Guinea, Ivory Coast,
Upper Volta, Togo and Dahomey; and the anglophone Gambia,
Sierra Leone, Liberia, Ghana and Nigeria. To these is added Chad,
which has historic associations with Equatorial Africa, but at the
same time possesses so many characteristics in common with the
other sub-Saharan countries of West Africa that it must, for our
purposes, be treated as part of that region. The Cameroon Republic,[1]
on the other hand, is generally closer to Equatorial than to West
Africa and finds a place in the next chapter. The area of West Africa
is about $2\frac{1}{2}$ million square miles and the population about 114
million.

## The Country

The region reproduces the usual African picture of a coastal
plain rising more or less gradually to an inland plateau. This
plateau is lower than in most parts of Africa and lies mainly at an
elevation of 1,500 feet above the level of the sea. Rising above it,
however, there are several lofty massifs, of which the most important
are the Futa Jallon in Guinea, where the Niger, Senegal and Gambia
Rivers rise, the Bauchi plateau in Nigeria, the Tibesti range in
Chad, and the highland areas of Cameroon which terminate sea-
wards in the volcanic peak of the Cameroon Mountain.

The coastline runs from the mouth of the Senegal River in a
general south-easterly direction until it reaches the western end of
Liberia, whence it turns due east to Lagos at the bottom of the

[1] Hereafter referred to as 'Cameroon' for short.

Bight of Benin, from there south-east again to Cameroon. The coast is generally low lying and masked by sand-bars throughout a long stretch of its length. Cliffs are rare, Cape Verde and the neighbourhood of Abidjan being notable exceptions. The shore is either sandy and in places beaten by a heavy surf, or swampy and intersected by innumerable tidal channels. There arc also enormous areas of mangrove forest, especially in the river deltas and creeks. Along a considerable length of the coast a chain of navigable lagoons stretches behind the sand-bars. There are very few good natural harbours. Dakar, focusing a heavy three-way movement of trade between Europe, Africa and the Western Hemisphere, and a vital point in world strategy, is one, Bathurst at the mouth of the Gambia River another, and Freetown, like Dakar protected by a headland, a third. In addition to these a number of river estuaries offer shelter to shipping and access for some distance to the interior, but the ubiquitous sand-bars prevent their use by large ships.

West Africa has five major river systems, the Senegal, the Gambia, the Niger, the Volta, and that of Lake Chad. The Senegal, 950 miles long, rises in the Futa Jallon and runs into the sea at St. Louis. It is navigable for 215 miles from its mouth all the year round, and for short periods to Kayes, about 562 miles. The mouth is blocked by shifting sands. The Gambia has a wide estuary and is navigable for about 250 miles. The navigable stretches correspond to the eponymous former British colony, a mere narrow strip of land on either side of the river. The Niger also rises in the Futa Jallon and curves in an immense arc first north-east then southwards, entering the sea in the Bight of Biafra. It is navigable from its mouth for 450 miles in the rainy season, and there are long navigable stretches in the upper reaches. The chief tributary of the Niger is the Benue. The Volta is formed by the Black and White Voltas, and flows into the Bight of Benin. Lake Chad is really a large drainage basin with two important feeders, the Shari and the Wobe Rivers. The lake itself has a maximum depth of twenty feet and an area of 10,000 square miles in the dry season and 50,000 square miles in the wet.

## Climate

The climate of West Africa formerly had a most vicious reputation, and Europeans frequently succumbed to it. Modern medicine has gone far to protect human beings against its effects, particularly in preventing the insect- and water-borne diseases which are the indirect effect of the heat and humidity. Temperatures are consistently high, but the variations inland, where there are occasional night frosts, are considerably higher than on the coast, where the average temperature is 79° and the annual range only 6°. Rainfall varies both in quantity and incidence throughout the region. The wettest zones are the south-west, where Freetown, for instance, has an annual fall of 175 inches, and the south-east, where the Niger Delta receives more than 100 inches. The coastal zone of Ghana and Togo is comparatively dry, getting only 30 to 40 inches in the year. Inland, rainfall decreases progressively almost everywhere northwards from the coast, and there is a long dry season characterized by the dry and dusty Harmattan wind which blows off the Sahara.

## Vegetation

The vegetational zones reflect the east to west trend of the climatic belts, from luxuriance and profusion on the coast to bareness and poverty in the remote hinterland. Behind the coastal swamps there is a zone of equatorial rain forest which stretches from Sierra Leone to beyond Cameroon, interrupted only by the drier coastland of Ghana and Togo, and extending inland between one and two hundred miles. The forest gradually thins out into savannah of various grades and this gives way to grassland which presents a parched appearance throughout most of the year. These dry steppes eventually merge into the sandy waste of the Sahara.

## Fauna

The fauna of West Africa is not so varied and abundant as that of East Africa. The dense tropical forest is the home of the great anthropoid apes. Chimpanzees of different species are to be found in several parts of West Africa, and the gorilla inhabits the forest from Cameroon down to the Congo River in Equatoria.[1] One animal peculiar to the region is the pygmy hippopotamus.

## The People

Although true Negroes are the dominant race of the region, and stretch fairly continuously south from Senegal to Cameroon and beyond, West Africa presents a scene of great diversity. In spite of their many common characteristics, true Negroes still exhibit

[1] These apes are also to be found in the forested mountains of west and south-west Uganda in the East African region.

a wide range of differences, whether it be in their domestic life, their religion, or in their social and constitutional practices. Thus we find societies ranging from simple peasants living in hilltop villages to highly organized societies in very large towns; and cultures varying from that of primitive pagans to that of a sophisticated westernized intelligentsia. In several places the old forest kingdoms still survive but in diminished state. The introduction of European rule stopped the wars on which their power was based, and the more recent emergence of charismatic political personalities has detracted from their former glamour.

The largest community of true Negroes in West Africa are the Hausa, who are not of single stock or anything like it. They are a people evolved from a large number of diverse elements who have this in common, that they speak a language fundamentally Hamitic called Hausa. The Hausa are found in colonies and groups all over West Africa and as far away as Tripoli and Bombay. Their largest concentration, however, is in northern Nigeria, where they number 12 million[1] and where they appear to have settled in the very remote past. Even then they were organized in states, each named after its capital, a walled town in which the people could take refuge in time of war. The Hausa came under Islamic influence in the fourteenth century, and although religion did not strike very deep it no doubt contributed powerfully towards the development of their policy, which was extremely sound. Each state was governed by a king with an establishment of administrative officials and a trained judiciary. There was also a well organized fiscal system. In spite of these excellent arrangements, the Hausa states did not play any great part in the West African political scene. They were small, quarrelsome, and frequently exposed to the attacks of stronger neighbours. Their religion, never strong, degenerated still further (in the eighteenth century the rulers were actually pagans) and it was precisely this decay that prompted Othman dan Fodio to launch the *jihad* that made the Fulani masters of most of Hausaland.[2]

In build the Hausas are of medium height, thickset, and possessing great strength and endurance. Their skin is black, but they have rather thinner features than other true Negroes. They are industrious farmers, shrewd traders and fearless travellers. They are splendid fighters, and their services as soldiers in the Nigerian

---

[1] Estimates vary. Another figure is 20 million.
[2] pp. 31, 189.

forces in two wars were oustanding. The Hausa language has become the *lingua franca* over a very wide area.

The other large tribes of true Negroes of Nigeria are the Yoruba and the Ibo. Like the Hausa, these are hardly homogeneous communities but rather linguistic groups deriving from a great variety of ancestral stocks, and the word 'tribe' is therefore not appropriate. It is possible that the Yoruba were not originally pure Negroes and they may have originated from Upper Egypt like the Fulani. However that may be, their civilization was already an ancient one about a thousand years ago, when the people of Ife within the southern bend of the Niger were conquered by migrants of Hamitic stock from the east or the north. The focus of political power in due course shifted to Oyo which became the centre of an empire embracing not only Yorubaland proper but also considerable areas on either side of it. It was an empire based on military aggression, its wealth in great part derived from the sale of slaves. It disintegrated because the subject-peoples resented the manner in which all the wealth of the country always found its way to Oyo and nowhere else. The northern part of the empire fell before the assault of the Fulani while the southern part dissolved in civil wars. Even when the empire had broken up, slaving continued from the original nuclei, Oyo and Ife, and did not end until it was checked and finally abolished by British rule. The Yoruba group constitutes the dominant people of western Nigeria, and numbers over 11 million. They are a vigorous and intelligent people, highly urbanized and prosperous, who have adapted themselves with ease to modern conditions, while retaining their pride in their own history and institutions.

The Ibo, of whom there are rather over 9 million, are eastern Nigeria's counterparts (perhaps one should say the rivals) of the Yoruba. They live in the country which rises gently from the coast and are predominantly subsistence farmers, cultivating yams and cassava. Their main cash crop is palm kernels. They are noted for their very democratic and individualist outlook, and for their resistance to central direction and to complex forms of political organization. They like to live in small village communities separated by an expanse of bush, and large market towns such as Onitsha are exceptional.

As we move westwards the first large homogeneous people we meet are the Akan of Ghana and the Ivory Coast, ethnically a single people, though divided linguistically between Fanti- and Twi-speaking groups. Fanti is spoken along the coast and some distance inland. The Twi group spreads over the central part of the country and includes the Ashanti. Like the rest of the Akan peoples, the Ashanti probably came to their present home from the savannah country in the north and north-west, and having conquered the people then living in the forest land, founded a number of states which during the seventeenth and eighteenth centuries became the Ashanti Federation. It was during the emergence of the Federation that the Golden Stool became in the eyes of the Ashanti the visible symbol of their nationhood. According to tradition the Stool came down from Heaven and rested on the knees of Osei Tutu, chief of Kumasi, whose successors, as keepers of the Stool, are regarded with special veneration as leaders of the nation. When in 1900 a British governor, quite misunderstanding the significance of the Stool, demanded that it be handed over to him, the Ashanti were so outraged that they took to arms. The Ashanti are hardy, proud, strongly attached to their traditions and loyal to their institutions. Their skill and bravery in warfare, together with a great gift of organization, powers of combination and a sense of discipline, made them probably the most formidable people whom any European power encountered in West Africa. In later, more peaceful days they have proved themselves to be go-ahead farmers, and Ashanti now plays an increasing part in the economic life of Ghana.

The Ewe-speaking people of south-eastern Ghana and Togo deserve mention if only because they have made occasional appearances on the international scene with a demand that they should be united under one government. They provide a good example of the often capricious nature of colonial boundaries. In their case, as in many others, European treaty makers took no account of indigenous racial and political groupings.

The Kru are really natives of Liberia, but they are to be found distributed in communities round most of the ports of the coast. They are the sailors of West Africa and provide the crews for many of the ships that ply in West African waters.

A group of tribes called Mandingo are the most numerous and important negroid people in the western Sudan.[1] They were the founders of the medieval empire of Mali and are even now spread over an enormous area inland from the coast between the Senegal River and northern Sierra Leone. Their greatest concentration is in the basins of the upper Niger and upper Senegal and in the

[1] p. 30 fn.

northern part of the Futa Jallon plateau. Between 1882 and 1898, under a leader named Samory, they put up a spirited resistance to the French. They are now the great middlemen of that part of West Africa and their language is widely used as a *lingua franca*. In appearance they are tall and lean, and in some cases have high cheekbones and narrow eyes which are taken to indicate some Hamitic blood.

The Songhai are the modern representatives of the empire which destroyed Mali at the end of the fifteenth century. They now stretch from the neighbourhood of Timbuktu southwards across the great bend of the Niger. The Songhai often exhibit strong Hamitic traits, betraying intermixture with the Hamites of the Sahara.

The upper basin of the Volta River is the home of the Mossi, who can claim descent from some of the people who made up the Mossi-Dagomba states from the thirteenth or fourteenth centuries onwards.

The Mende inhabit an area of about 12,000 square miles in the centre and south-west of Sierra Leone and are the largest and most important tribe of that territory. The Temne, their neighbours, originally came from the upper Niger country and settled along the Sierra Leone River and the Port Lokko creek. It was from them that the British obtained the land on which to place the liberated slaves who were the original colonists. The Wollofs or Jollofs are a tall, black, statuesque people of martial traditions, the great majority of whom live in Senegal.

The Hamites are represented in West Africa by the Fulani, often called Peuls, Fula, Fellata or by their own word Fulbe. They are found throughout the region, from Senegal in the west to Darfur in the east. They are thought to have come originally from Upper Egypt and to have migrated westwards to the Atlantic Coast. They are distinctive in appearance, having fine features, a slim and tall physique, and light coloured skin. In character they are reserved and withdrawn, and they have a reputation for 'slimness'.[1] There were about six million in 1957 and this number has no doubt increased since then. They are disseminated among the Negro population, but their main concentrations are in Futa Jallon in Guinea, Massina in Mali and Adamawa in Nigeria.[2] Some are nomadic pastoralists, others sedentary farmers, and others both agri-

---

[1] An untranslatable South African expression implying smoothness, speciousness, elastic standards of honesty.
[2] Seligman, *Races of Africa*, p. 136.

culturalists and pastoralists. The nomadic pastoralists are those who have best preserved the physical characteristics of the race. The sedentary Fulani are more negroid in appearance than either the nomads or the semi-sedentary farmers, sometimes because they are in fact Fulani-speaking Negroes, or else because they have intermarried with Negroes.

In some parts of West Africa the Fulani have attained a dominant social and political position. During the European Middle Ages they penetrated peacefully into the country that later became Northern Nigeria and here their influence steadily grew until about 1802 when a Fulani sheikh named Othman dan Fodio launched a religious war which won him an empire over a large part of West Africa and the remote hinterland. Although this empire later decayed, the Fulani remain the ruling class in much of Northern Nigeria, and constitute the aristocracy of Guinea.

The Bantu play but a small part on the West African scene. They live in Cameroon, on the north-western frontier of the Bantu world, and generally speaking occupy the forest areas, while their Sudanic-speaking neighbours prefer the mountains and the grasslands. There are also in this racial borderland certain tribes who have mixed characteristics and are called semi-Bantu.

Finally it must be mentioned that there are throughout the region between the forest and the desert large groups of strongly hamiti-cized negroid pastoralists, descendants, it must be supposed, of the people of the ancient sub-Saharan empires. Such, for instance, are the people of the Chad territory.

A number of foreign races have made their home in West Africa. Liberia, as we have seen, was settled by emancipated Negroes from the United States in the first half of the nineteenth century. These people, though of African descent, were entirely alien to African conditions and formed an exclusive society in the coastal towns, while professing to exercise sovereignty over the indigenous tribes of the interior, who resented their presence. During the last twenty years or so there have been genuine efforts on the part of the Afro-American rulers to replace this 'colonial' situation by co-operation with the local tribes, while the financial position has improved under the stimulus of American enterprise, and there has been some expansion of social and economic services. Sierra Leone, like Liberia, was originally settled by immigrant Negroes but the presence of the British Government prevented a reproduction of the Liberian situation here. Nevertheless the 'creoles' in the former Colony claim social superiority over the indigenous peoples in the neighbouring territory though of course unable to exercise political sovereignty over them. The Akus are to the Gambia what the creoles are to Sierra Leone, descendants of liberated slaves.

Another important group of foreigners are the so-called Syrians (they are in fact mostly Lebanese) who play the same part as the Asians in East Africa. But they are far less numerous than the East African Asians, nor are their roots in the country so deep.

Finally the Europeans, mostly officials, technicians, traders, miners, missionaries and teachers, who are in a different category from the others. The great majority are transients, that is to say they do not expect to end their lives here. After working in West Africa, either for themselves, or like the officials and the missionaries, for others, they will in due course retire to their homes in Europe. Unlike Kenya or Algeria, West Africa has no *native* European population.

## Aspects of Culture

The strong, highly organized, settled, predominantly agricultural true Negro societies of West Africa have, as was briefly indicated in Part I,[1] evolved a culture that has several most remarkable characteristics. The most noteworthy of these was the system of secret societies and a strong artistic tradition that finds its chief expression in sculpture. Most secret societies were associations in some ways corresponding to the English conception of a friendly society, a group of people who have come together for mutual benefit, and who derive a certain social distinction from membership. Some of these societies were exceedingly powerful and had important religious, judicial and social functions. Such, for instance, was the Poro Society of Sierra Leone, which had a very wide membership and which may, according to one author, have been at one time an association for protection against slave traders.[2] Another was the Egbo Society among the Ibibio of Nigeria, so influential and widespread as to have assumed the character of a government. How far these societies have retained their power and influence in the face of modern political, social and educational developments is difficult to estimate.

African sculpture is confined to a well defined geographical area which corresponds to the basins of the Niger and the Congo, and

[1] p. 20.
[2] Newland, H. O., *West Africa*, pp. 193-4.

hence to the regions of West Africa and Equatoria in this book. Why this should be so is not easy to explain but it is worth observing that the people of the sculptural zone are mainly sedentary agriculturalists who have been settled in their present homes for a long time, while the people of East and South Africa follow a pastoral or semi-pastoral economy and arrived where they are now comparatively recently. The climates and vegetation of the several regions are also dissimilar, a great part of the area where sculpture is practised corresponding to that of heavy rainfall and thick forest.[1]

At one time sculpture flourished throughout West Africa, but the art has now declined and is only perpetuated in a few places. The change is due to the decay of those institutions with which sculpture was most closely associated, the tribal customs and the tribal religion. Modern changes in the conception of chiefship and in the role of the chief have also deprived artists of the patronage which was formerly in many cases their stimulus and inspiration.

There are two different styles in West African sculpture, that of the western Sudan and that of the Guinea Coast. This classification is a very broad one, and certainly does not imply that the two styles fall rigidly into separate categories. Like the frontiers of race, climate and vegetation, the artistic frontiers are ill-defined and not easily perceptible.

The western Sudan is a predominantly Moslem area, and iconoclasm is an essential tenet of Islam. It is perhaps for this reason that pagan art in this area shows a tendency towards asceticism and restraint and is highly formalized. It consists largely of human and animal figures and of masks carved in wood, many of the forms being of a geometric design characteristic of the Moslem art of decoration.

The Guinea Coast, which in this context runs from Senegal to Cameroon, has a much more varied artistic tradition. It is also an ancient one, as is proved by the discovery over a large area in the neighbourhood of Nok in Nigeria of terra-cotta figures from a culture dating from the latter part of the first millennium B.C. There is also some evidence that the Nok culture survived long enough to influence the art of Ife, which flourished after the first millennium A.D. Since the latter is believed in turn to have affected the development of the art of Benin, there is therefore perhaps a

[1] Exceptionally, there are fine sculptors among the tribes in the north of Portuguese East Africa.

continuous thread in the artistic tradition of this part of Africa that goes back for over two thousand years. It is indeed from Ife and Benin that are derived the best known examples of West African art. Ife produced admirable bronzes of outstanding naturalism and elegance, terra-cottas, elaborate shrine furniture from quartz and granite, and megalithic monuments. The bronzes and ivories of Benin are the product of an art which was essentially associated with the ruler and his court and which seems to have reached its *apogée* in the fifteenth and sixteenth centuries. The earliest examples known to us are thin and naturalistic and in style not far removed from that of Ife. Later, representation became static and stylized and the early simplicity became overlaid by a profusion of decorative detail. By the nineteenth century the art of Benin had fallen into decadence.                    *(Plate* 73)

The art of metal casting was by no means confined to Ife and Benin. Small bronze gold-weights are the most representative examples of Ashanti art, although Ashanti metal work reaches its highest level in the small bronze urns and vessels made for cere- monial use. In Dahomey a restricted family guild worked as re- tainers of royalty and nobility and cast human figures and animals representing the fauna of the country and scenes from daily life.

Throughout the region there is a distinguished tradition of wood carving, a special feature being the carving of masks connected with religion and with the rites of the secret societies, decorative sculpture, clay modelling, and appliqué work on cloth.

Though it is to trespass on the next chapter a word may be said here of the art of Equatoria. This region is peopled with few ex- ceptions by Bantu, but there do not seem to be any fundamental differences in aesthetic between their art and that of the true Negroes of the Guinea Coast. Wood carving predominates and reaches perhaps its peak in the rich and varied production of the Ubangi-Congo river system. In particular the art of the tribes commonly grouped under the name Bushongo,[1] between the Kasai and Sankuru Rivers, is distinguished by boldness of design, descriptiveness, and superb craftsmanship.

## History

The end of the Scramble for Africa saw West Africa practically

[1] J. Vansina prefers to call them Bakuba, as 'Bushongo' is properly applicable only to the Bambala tribe (Ethnographic Survey of Africa, Central Africa, Belgian Congo, Part I, *Les tribus Ba-Kuba et les peuplades apparentées*).

divided between Britain, France and Germany. Portugal retained a small footing in Portuguese Guinea and there was also the Afro-American colony of Liberia, administered by the descendants of former slaves. The largest share fell to France, with Britain well behind in the second place, and Germany third. The Federation of French West Africa, as it ultimately emerged, consisted of seven colonies: Mauritania, Senegal, French Guinea, the Ivory Coast, Dahomey, Upper Volta,[1] French Sudan and the Niger Colony. British West Africa consisted of the Gambia, Sierra Leone, the Gold Coast, and Nigeria.[2] France, with her three colonies of Mauritania, the Sudan and the Niger, occupied the whole of the vast hinterland and reached the sea in four great wedges represented by the coastal zone of Mauritania and the other five colonies. From the Senegal these wedges were separated from each other by the British, German and Portuguese dependencies and Liberia.

Although the maps of the period of the Scramble show vast areas of West Africa coloured in this shade or that, so reflecting the claims of the Powers, the realities of the situation on the spot were very different. European influence was by no means as extensive as the maps suggest. Many of the people of the great hinterland marked out as colonies and protectorates were still quite unaware of their new status and not at all disposed to submit to European government. Yet the Slave Trade could not be stopped, nor peace and good order secured, nor economic development begun, unless effective administration were first established. So the main preoccupation of the colonial Powers in the years following the Scramble was to induce the African people to recognize the new authority. The subjugation of the Gold Coast by the British was completed in 1901 by the annexation of Ashanti as a Crown Colony. In Nigeria the British first revived the idea of the chartered company with powers of government and entrusted the extension of British authority to Sir George Goldie's Royal Niger Company. Goldie brought the slave-trading states of Nupe and Ilorin under control and succeeded in keeping Germans and French out of Northern Nigeria, but in 1900 the government took over the administrative responsibilities of the Company,

---

[1] Upper Volta was suppressed as a separate unit in 1932 but reinstated in 1947.

[2] In 1906 the governments of Lagos and the Protectorate of Southern Nigeria (the former Niger Coast Protectorate) were amalgamated to form the Colony and Protectorate of Southern Nigeria. In 1914 Northern and Southern Nigeria were amalgamated to become the Colony and Protectorate of Nigeria.

which continued, however, to function as a commercial concern. In the same year Sir Frederick Lugard was given the task of forming an administration in Northern Nigeria and was fully occupied till 1906 in consolidating his position in the great Fulani emirates.

The establishment of European government in the French colonies took even longer. There were military operations in Guinea and on the Ivory Coast as late as 1915, while the Niger Colony was not transferred from military to civil administration until 1920. There was a reallocation of territory after the First World War when the German colonies of Togoland and the Cameroons, as they were then called, were divided between Great Britain and France as mandates from the League of Nations. They continued to he held by the same Powers after the Second World War as trusteeships under the United Nations. The British administered their sections of Togoland and the Cameroons as part of the Gold Coast and Nigeria respectively. French Togoland was at one time brought into fairly close association with French West Africa but its autonomy was restored in 1946 and it became an 'associated territory' under the constitution of that year.[1] The French Cameroons was originally attached to French Equatorial Africa for purposes of administration, but was organized as a separate unit when France was entrusted with the mandate. It also became an 'associated territory' under the 1946 constitution.

When France collapsed in 1940 official French West Africa rallied to Vichy. In September 1940 British and Free French forces tried to take Dakar, capital of the Federation, but the attempt failed, and in the event the fear that Dakar might be used by the Germans was never realized. Many Africans did not share the early pro-Vichy leanings of their government and refused to accept the 1940 armistice. Large numbers of men went over to French Equatorial Africa, which had joined the Free French, and thus made no small contribution to the Allied war effort. When the British and Americans landed in North Africa in 1942, Governor-General Boisson threw in his lot with Admiral Darlan and thus brought French West Africa in on the side of the Allies. The British colonies were uniformly loyal and made a notable contribution in materials, money and men.

Both in British and French West Africa the Second World War very much accelerated the movement towards self-government. At a conference held at Brazzaville in Equatorial Africa in 1944 the

[1] See below.

Provisional Government of France gave a new turn to French colonial policy. True to the theory of assimilation the conference repudiated any suggestion of self-government. The aim was to be one of still closer integration, the participation of the dependencies in the reconstruction of the French political system and thereafter in the political life of France. These political advances were to be accompanied by social reforms and economic development. At the same time concessions were made to the local situation in the recognition by the conference of the value of African institutions. The constitution that emerged from these discussions in 1946 was that of a 'union founded on equality of rights and duties', in which the French West African colonies, with others, were described as 'overseas' territories, their people the equal of French nationals, entitled to representation in the institutions of the French Republic and endowed with their own representative assemblies called *Assemblées territoriales.* An 'Investment Fund for Economic and Social Development' was set up in order to promote capital investment. Although this constitution went some way to meet the demands of the élite, it fell far short of establishing the full political equality of Africans and Frenchmen that the theory of assimilation implied. As the years passed, the new African leaders began to demand a much larger measure of self-government and even the substantial changes introduced in 1956 (which virtually substituted a federal relationship for the old idea of assimilation) were soon seen to be insufficient to stem the rising tide of nationalism. The new constitution presented by General de Gaulle after his assumption of power in 1958 radically altered the French system of overseas administration. It enabled overseas territories to become members of a community of autonomous states sharing only foreign policy, defence, currency and some common economic questions. Rejection of the constitution would mean immediate independence and the right of secession was recognized even if the constitution had once been accepted. All the West African territories approved the new constitution by a large majority except French Guinea. The latter was then held to have seceded from France, all French aid was withdrawn and Guinea is now an independent republic. It is described as a 'centralized democracy' which in effect means that the country is governed by Sekou Touré, the president, through a single political party of which he is head. In 1960 the constitution of the Community was amended so as to permit members to become independent republics and at the

same time to retain their membership of the Community. In that year
all members made declarations whereby they became independent.
A number of states soon opted out of the Community but established special relations with it. Those who remained signed 'Community participation agreements'. (Former French Somaliland and
the Comoro Islands are 'French Overseas Territories', and this is
yet another kind of relationship.) The Community has no practical
functions now, but this should not obscure the reality of France's
connections with her former colonies. These are secured by a
number of financial, technical and economic agreements and are
very close indeed.

The political evolution of the British colonies was considerably
simpler, largely because self-determination, including the right to
secession, had long been implicit in British colonial policies. In
Nigeria particularly, Lugard's policy of 'Indirect Rule', that is
administration through the traditional authorities, was an education
in local government designed to enable the people ultimately to
stand on their own feet. At the centre, the first Legislative Council in
British Africa with a majority of unofficial members was set up in the
Gold Coast in 1946. After riots in 1948 a commission of inquiry
recommended radical changes. In the following year an all-African
committee made recommendations which were accepted as a basis
for fuller constitutional development. A new constitution was
published in 1950, elections were held in 1951, and in the following
year a cabinet was appointed with an African prime minister and
African ministers in charge of departments. Further elections and
the victory of the Convention People's Party in 1956 led to the grant
in 1957 of complete independence within the British Commonwealth.
The new nation, which includes the former British trust territory of
Togoland, took the name of Ghana on the strength of a supposed
connection with the medieval empire of that name. Ghana is now a
republic within the Commonwealth.

Ghana was soon followed by other British West African dependencies. Nigeria's three regions became an independent federation
in 1960 and Sierra Leone an independent state in the following year.
The Gambia, a riverine strip surrounded by francophone Africa,
attained full independence in 1965. The way to independence of the
British and French Cameroons was more complicated and will be
described in the next chapter.

Of the former fourteen colonies and protectorates that achieved
independence in the 'fifties and 'sixties, seven have undergone more

or less violent changes of government engineered by the army. The most frequent were in Dahomey, which has suffered five upheavals since 1960. The most tragic is the case of Nigeria, the richest and most highly populated of all West African countries.

In spite of Nigeria's federal structure, regional and tribal interests predominated. Civil government was brought to an end in January 1966 when the prime minister and two regional premiers were assassinated. The army took over under an Ibo officer, General Aguiyi-Ironsi. In July of the same year there was another *coup* and General Ironsi was also assassinated. Lt. Col. (now General) Yakubu Gowon, who comes from northern Nigeria, then assumed control. Nigeria now consists of twelve states, each administered by a governor. Central authority is vested in a supreme military council of which General Gowon is the head.

On 30 May 1967 Lt. Col. Ojukwu, governor of the then Eastern Region, where Ibo form two-thirds of the population, proclaimed the independence of the region and the state of Biafra was born. There followed a war between the federal government and the secessionists which ended early in 1970 with the defeat of Biafra and the flight of Ojukwu. Directly and indirectly the war is said to have cost the lives of two million people.

A smaller, less publicized war has been going on for some time in Chad, where Moslem rebels challenge the Christian Negro government of François Tombalbaye. In Portuguese Guinea there is a liberation movement which the Portuguese at present seem to be able to contain; and towards the end of 1970 there was a mysterious raid on the neighbouring republic of Guinea in which the Portuguese were alleged to have played some part. This the Portuguese strenuously deny. One theory is that the raid was in some way connected with an internal movement against the present government of Guinea.

*Economy*

Although the development of minerals is now tending to modify the picture, the region as a whole still depends primarily on agriculture. The country which lies between the Gulf of Guinea and the semi-arid expanse of the sub-Saharan interior is the richest and most productive of any comparable areas of tropical Africa. Apart from the activities of the Firestone Company, of which more later, and a number of rather specialized plantations elsewhere, all agriculture is in the hands of the natives of the country. In West Africa as

o

elsewhere most Africans are primarily concerned with ensuring their food supply and with certain important exceptions export crops are often just the surplus from their small gardens. Staple food crops include yams, cassava and other roots, pulses, plantains, rice, groundnuts, cereals and large varieties of subsidiary crops such as pumpkins, tomatoes and peppers.

The most spectacular and valuable export crop is cocoa, which originated in South America and was introduced by the Portuguese to the island of São Tomé. After an unsuccessful attempt to grow it on the Gold Coast early in the nineteenth century, a man named Tetteh Kwashi[1] (to whom, if they have not already done so, the people of Ghana should certainly build a memorial) brought six beans from Fernando Po to his native village. From these small beginnings there has grown an industry which accounts for about two-thirds of the value of the exports of Ghana. Cocoa is also an important element in the exports of the Ivory Coast, Togo and Nigeria. Unlike most other edible crops, cocoa is cultivated exclusively for export, and some observers have expressed the fear that the economy may become dangerously weighted in favour of this one crop. These fears are underlined by the prevalence of a deadly virus disease called 'swollen shoot' for which no cure has yet been found and by periodic fluctuations in world prices. Another adverse factor in Ghana is that a high proportion of suitable land is already planted.

Groundnuts are not only a useful African food but an important export crop. Indeed two countries in the region are almost wholly dependent on them. In Senegal and the Gambia groundnuts dominate the economy and provide over 90 per cent of the exports. Nigeria is also a big exporter of groundnuts but having a more varied economy is by no means so dependent on them.

The oil palm likes a fairly high rainfall and though reasonably tolerant of poorish soils prefers rich moist ones. It flourishes in the forest areas near the coast. It was the main source of income in Nigeria before the days of mineral oil. The oil palm is prominent in the economy of the coastal zone. In Dahomey palm products represent three-quarters of the exports.

Coffee is the leading cash crop of the Ivory Coast, where timber is also a steadily rising export. Coffee contributes in varying degrees to the economies of Guinea, Togo, Sierra Leone and Dahomey. Cotton grows in the dry inland territories on irrigated land in the Niger

[1] The name has various spellings.

basin. It is also grown in the extreme south of the Chad Republic, providing a high proportion of the exports of that country, and in the north-central area of Nigeria.

Among other West African products are bananas, shea nuts, kola, piassava, sesame and ginger.

In 1926 the Liberian Government allowed the Firestone Corporation of America to take up a 90-year lease of a large area of land for the establishment of a rubber plantation. The Firestone Plantations cover an area of about 100,000 acres, and produce 83 million pounds (projection 1970) of rubber a year. This and other recently established American enterprises have made an improvement in the economic condition of Liberia.

## Livestock

Large areas of West Africa are infested by the tsetse fly. Varieties of small humpless cattle, believed to be immune to trypanosomiasis, are kept in the forest country towards the coast, but the great cattle zones are in the north, from which there is a considerable trade to the south. The greatest commercial cattle centre in West Africa is Kano in northern Nigeria. Great numbers of cattle are sent from here to Lagos by train and even on the hoof. Sheep and goats are ubiquitous and enormous numbers are kept by the tribes of the western Sudan. There is a thriving export of hides and skins from Nigeria, and in the northern part of that country tanning is an ancient industry. Kano is thought to be the original home of 'morocco' leather.

## Fishing

Sea fishing is practised all along the coast and is a particularly flourishing industry off Senegal and Ghana. Fresh water fishing is an important occupation with several of the inland riverain people, especially among those living on the Senegal River and on the great bend of the Niger.

## Forests

Since the end of the Second World War there has been a great expansion of the timber industry in Nigeria, the Ivory Coast and Ghana. The forests consist largely of hardwood trees yielding beautiful timbers which can be used for the highest quality work. Unhappily there is a conflict between the conservation of forest and the needs of farmers for land, and the tendency is for agriculture to encroach on forest, whatever governments may do to try to conserve the latter.

## Mining

The history of gold mining on the west coast of Africa is an old one and Ghana now ranks about sixth in the world order of gold-producing countries. Ghana gold has been overtaken by other minerals. The most sensational development is oil production in south-eastern Nigeria. Although the flow was interrupted by the Biafra war, it has picked up again and Nigeria will before long be among the world's leading oil producers. South-east Nigeria is also a producer of natural gas. On the Jos plateau Nigeria has an old-established tin mining industry, and at Enugu in eastern Nigeria the only coal mine in West Africa. Nigeria is a major source of columbite, a by-product of tin mining, and to complete the picture there are substantial reserves of iron ore in the northern and eastern areas.

Although Nigerian oil occupies the centre of the stage, other countries in this region have minerals that are actually or potentially important: bauxite and diamonds in Guinea; bauxite, diamonds and rutile in Sierra Leone; phosphates in Senegal; diamonds in Liberia; manganese, bauxite and diamonds in addition to gold in Ghana; manganese on the Ivory Coast and in Upper Volta; phosphates in Togo. The list is not exhaustive. Liberia and Sierra Leone are both important producers of iron ore, and there are substantial deposits of this mineral in other countries of West Africa.

It is to be noted that most of the mineral wealth lies in the countries that face onto the Atlantic Ocean and the Gulf of Guinea. The vast impoverished sub-Saharan territories of the interior are not apparently so fortunate. But the discovery of uranium in Niger should give a new look to the economy of that country. The development of the mines and ancillary services is under way.

## Railways

As in most parts of the continent, the railways of West Africa run inland at right angles to the coast in order to give the most direct access to the interior. Because the British colonies were isolated enclaves in French West Africa, the British West African railways were not interlinked, since none could reach the others without passing through French territory. Each colony had its own railway system, serving none but itself. The French had more room for manœuvre in their vast hinterland and planned their railway system to supplement navigable stretches of the Niger and Senegal Rivers and to link their inland territories to the coastal ports. They succeeded in doing so in Senegal and Guinea, but the two southern railways both stop well short of the Niger. The Ivory Coast railway ends at Wagadugu in Upper Volta and the Dahomey line goes no further than Parakou, 230 miles from the coast.

The Gambia, having its river, needed no railway. In Liberia one line runs from Monrovia to within a short distance of the Sierra Leone border, the other from Buchanan to the north-eastern frontier. Both tap important iron ore deposits.

## Roads

Road making is more difficult and more expensive in West Africa than in East Africa. The cost of unskilled labour is high and the material for road metal rather scarce. Nevertheless both the British and French territories possessed road networks of reasonably good quality by African standards, and the French displayed considerable energy in creating a road system which linked the whole of the interior of French West Africa with the railways.

Intense competition between roads and railways is a feature of the West African transport system, and lorry transport is a most important private enterprise. For short hauls at least it seems likely that this competition will continue, as it is far more likely that roads will be improved than railways extended.

## Waterways

Several rivers of West Africa besides those already mentioned[1] are navigable for part of their length and carry a considerable volume of traffic. Light craft can navigate the lower reaches of the Great and Little Scarcies in Sierra Leone. The Benue can take sizeable vessels according to the time of the year and farther to the east the Cross, Calabar, Imo and Bonny Rivers are used extensively for transport. The Casamance in Senegal south of the Gambia affords access some distance inland. The Bani, affluent of the Niger in its upper reaches, carries traffic for a long distance, and all along the coast of West Africa there are a great number of navigable lagoons and channels.

## The Volta River Dam

At Akosombo in Ghana, on the lower Volta River between the

[1] p. 183.

Akwapim hills and the Togo hills, is the Volta River Dam, which was completed in 1966. The dam has created a navigable waterway northwards of about 200 miles in length. Even more important, it generates hydro-electric power for an aluminium smelting industry, and it will provide electricity for general domestic and industrial use on a very wide scale. The scheme will give a tremendous stimulus to many sectors of the Ghanaian economy.

*Air Transport*

The loss of the Mediterranean–Suez route to the Middle and Far East during the Second World War made West Africa a nodal point on west–east communications. There was a rapid development of airfields in British territory on this new and important supply line, and other airfields were built round Freetown for the defence of the naval base and Atlantic convoys. With the development since the war of international air travel, West Africa is now served by several European airlines, and is within a day's flight of Europe. There is also a good network of internal air services and most big towns are now connected by air.

# CHAPTER EIGHT

# EQUATORIA

THIS is the region of the Congo basin, together with that block of country which lies between the mouth of the Congo River and the Cameroon Mountain and drains directly to the Atlantic Ocean. The Equator runs through the heart of the region but Equatoria does not stretch across the continent, since the highlands of East Africa lie to the east and are of a quite different character. The region therefore comprises the whole of the Congo Democratic Republic and the great land mass of Equatorial Africa. The latter consists of the Congo People's Republic (the Popular Republic of the Congo), Gabon and the Central African Republic. In October 1971 the Congo Democratic Republic, hitherto known as Congo/ Kinshasa after its capital, adopted the ancient name of Zaïre. The Congo People's Republic is commonly called Congo (Brazzaville). The region includes the Cameroon Republic; Equatorial Guinea, once Spanish Guinea, now an independent republic made up of Rio Muni, the island of Fernando Po and one or two other islands; and the Portuguese islands of São Tomé and Princípé.

By far the greater part of the region is francophone Congo/ Zaïre was once the Belgian Congo, and the three countries of Equatorial Africa, with the addition of Chad,[1] formerly made up French Equatorial Africa. The only anglophone area is that section of the Cameroon Republic which was once part of the British Cameroons.

## THE CONGO RIVER AND ITS BASIN

The Congo River, known as Zaïre to the Portuguese who discovered it, forms the largest of African river systems and in this respect is only exceeded in the world by the Amazon. The drainage area is nearly $1\frac{1}{2}$ million square miles and the length of the main stream is estimated at 3,000 miles which places it among the five longest rivers of the world.[2] It rises in Katanga at an altitude of

---

[1] Chad has already been dealt with in the chapter on West Africa.
[2] The other four are the Nile, the Mississipi-Missouri, the Yangtze and the Amazon.

4,659 feet and is called the Lualaba until it reaches Kisangani. It was in the headwaters of the Lualaba that Livingstone thought that he might find the source of the Nile. The Congo River receives innumerable tributaries throughout its length, many of them considerable rivers in their own right and perennial in their flow owing to a well-distributed and fairly high rainfall. Although there are long navigable stretches the flow is broken by many cataracts and falls. (*Plate* 101)

The Congo basin is a vast shallow depression in the African plateau crossed by the Congo River and its tributaries and enclosed by uplands. The lowest part of the depression is in the southwest, where the altitude is about 1,000 feet above sea-level. From here the ground rises more or less gradually towards the north, south and east. The height of the surrounding uplands is by no means uniform. In the north the divide between the Congo and Chad basins is hardly perceptible whereas the eastern side of the rim is marked by the mountainous wall of the Ruwenzori range, with several lofty peaks, the highest reaching almost 16,800 feet. Between these extremes the highlands separating the Congo basin from the Benue, Nile and Zambezi systems and from the Atlantic coastal plain have a range of about 1,500 feet to 6,000 feet. The centre of the depression has a cover of dense rain forest with trees so tall and a canopy of leaves so thick that they exclude the light of day. The floor of the forest is a mat of almost impenetrable undergrowth which gives way to considerable areas of swamp. The higher ground which surrounds the central plain and gradually rises to the mountainous edges is the same more or less wooded savannah that we have observed elsewhere in Africa.

## CONGO (ZAÏRE)

*The Country*

Except for comparatively small areas in the west and north-east the whole of Congo/Zaïre lies within the Congo basin. It is an immense land mass over 900,000 square miles in area, occupying the centre of western Africa between latitudes 5° 20′ N and 13° 40′ S. One peculiarity of the huge territory is that the outlet to the sea is exceedingly small, being only a narrow strip some twenty-five miles across at the Congo River mouth.

About 43 per cent of the country is in the rain forest zone with a rainfall of over 63 inches. This is fairly well distributed throughout the year, with two very short dry seasons and also two periods at the equinoxes when the rainfall is rather heavier than at other times. Constant humidity is accompanied by high temperatures which show little variation throughout the year. In the eastern highlands the climate is cooler owing to the altitude, and the savannah country on either side of the Equator has well-defined wet and dry, hot and cool seasons. North of the Equator the dry cool season corresponds roughly to the European winter. South of the line this season falls in our late summer.

## The People

The people of Congo/Zaïre are largely Bantu and belong to the western branch of that great family. The habitat of this branch coincides fairly accurately with our region of Equatoria, with the addition of Angola, whose African peoples are also Western Bantu.[1] The Congo has seen the rise and fall of several important and extensive kingdoms, of which one was the eponymous Congo, befriended by Portugal in the fifteenth century.[2] Now the Bantu of this area can be regarded as falling into three groups, a western, a southern and a central, each containing a great number of different tribes.[3] They include the Bushongo, in several ways the most developed of the Western Bantu, whose artistic skill has already been mentioned.[4]

In the extreme north-west of the country, occupying most of the Ubangi-Uele basin, is a group of Sudanic-speaking tribes with characteristics which distinguish them both from the Bantu and from the Nilotes of the Sudan. The most important are the Mangbetu and the Azande. The other non-Bantu minority are the Negrillos or pygmies, hunters, trappers and collectors, whose home is the thick tropical forest on either side of the Equator. They are generally on good terms with the neighbouring Bantu tribes, whose languages they speak and with whom they barter game meat for their simple necessities. The population of Congo/Zaïre was 22 million at the end of 1970. (*Plate* 97)

## History

On his second expedition to Africa in 1874-7 H. M. Stanley solved the problem of the Lualaba and other rivers west of Lake

[1] Angola was described in Chapter Two.
[2] pp. 105.
[3] Seligman, *Races of Africa*, p. 186.
[4] p. 192.

Tanganyika and followed the Congo River down to the sea. On his return to Europe he pressed the British Government to take the Congo basin, and when his proposals were rejected, turned to King Leopold II of the Belgians, who readily fell in with Stanley's plans. The King had already shown his interest in Africa when in 1876 he convened a meeting of geographers and others from which emerged the 'International Association for the exploration and civilization of Africa'. When Stanley came home a committee of the Association was set up called the 'Comité d'études du Haut Congo', which later became the 'International Association of the Congo'. The Association was international only in name for it soon passed entirely into the hands of the King of the Belgians. Stanley went back to the Congo as agent of the Association and spent four years building stations and making treaties with the chiefs. All the powers that took part in the Conference of Berlin in 1884–5 gave formal recognition to the Association, and the General Act of the Conference provided, *inter alia*, for freedom of trade in the Congo basin and free navigation of the river. Soon after the conference King Leopold was proclaimed sovereign of the 'Independent State of the Congo' or Congo Free State, which he proceeded to rule as a personal domain and in'no way as a dependency of Belgium.

Serious opposition to the new state came from the Arab slave and ivory traders who had settled in the country west of Lake Tanganyika. This culminated in 1892 in a war which lasted several months and which ended in the total defeat of the Arabs by the State forces.

In order to develop his vast tropical estate King Leopold gave out great concessions based on a monopoly of trade and industry, and it was not long before well-founded charges of gross abuses and oppression began to be levelled against the administration. These had to do with atrocities committed during the collection of wild rubber from the Natives. Following vigorous international agitation the King appointed a commission of inquiry whose recommendations led to some changes in the administration. These were not however of a character to satisfy the critics and in 1908 Leopold finally yielded to the pressure of international opinion and ceded the State to the Belgian Government. At the end of the 1914–18 war the districts of Ruanda and Urundi, formerly part of German East Africa, were entrusted to Belgium to be administered as a mandated territory under the League of Nations. They became a U.N.O. trust territory at the end of the Second World War.[1] During that war and after the fall of Belgium to the Germans, the Congo continued to fight beside the Allies. Congolese troops took part in the Abyssinian campaign and the Congo was also a valuable source of much needed materials.

On assuming responsibility for the administration of the Congo in 1908 the Belgian Government lost no time in correcting the abuses which had brought the Free State Government into disrepute. A sound administration was set up and the resources of the country were vigorously developed. The political aim seems to have lain somewhere between that of the British and the French. There was little tendency towards decentralization, certainly no suggestion of future colonial self-government. Only very limited opportunities were given to Africans to acquire the social or official status of Europeans, and the number of educated Africans is even today very small. Neither Africans nor Europeans had franchise rights. On the other hand the Belgians laid great emphasis on African advance in the field of technology. Every form of skilled employment of a technical nature was open to Africans and the Native became increasingly absorbed into the industrial life of the country with a consequent progressive improvement in his standard of living.

The labour policy of the Belgians was profoundly different from that of the other European powers in Africa. The latter have usually encouraged, or at least tolerated, the migration of labour. Working for wages is regarded as a somewhat abnormal occupation, to pursue which a man travels some distance to a place of employment and stays there for a period of months or years, ultimately, however, returning to his home. Indeed this procedure fits in very well with the African's own attitude towards paid labour. The Belgians on the other hand aimed at the stabilization of labour, that is to say at the creation in due course of a settled population of whole-time industrial workers. This meant the provision of facilities far more attractive and permanent than the compounds and labour lines of other African industrial areas. The Copper Belt in particular has well laid out modern villages, good houses, adequate water supplies and sanitation, hospitals, schools and training centres, everything in fact that from the material standpoint may contribute to a full and comfortable urban life.

The winds of change blew over the Belgian Congo as they did

[1] Chapter Three.

over the rest of Africa. This vast area, where comparatively high industrial achievement stands out in contrast with conditions which are among the most primitive in Africa, which had until recently shown no sign of political consciousness, suddenly developed an overpowering thirst for independence. The Belgian Government quickly acceded to the demands of the leaders, elections were held and independence followed in the middle of 1960. Hardly were the independence festivities over when the country began to fall apart, and it became one of the trouble spots of the world.

To describe adequately the events of the years immediately following independence would require far more space than is available here. To put it shortly, when the Belgians withdrew there was no responsible administration left at all. Law and order broke down, the economy disintegrated and famine set in. The civil population was bullied and plundered by an undisciplined mob that had once been the Congolese army. The country was split into several mutually antagonistic parts under phantasmagoric leaders who in some cases were the tools of foreign Powers. The United Nations, whose intervention had aroused high hopes, were divided in council and ineffective in action. The most important single event in this period was the purported secession of the Katanga province in 1960. Fighting continued until 1963, when Katanga was reabsorbed into the Congo.

After several changes of government, General Joseph Désiré Mobutu seized power as president in 1965 and appointed another army officer as prime minister. In the following year he took over the office of prime minister himself.

Since assuming power General Mobutu has spared no pains to strengthen and confirm his position. He relies heavily for support on the army and the police, though there are no soldiers in his government. He is said to be anti-communist. He does not seem to be a particularly popular personality, but there is no doubt about his genuine concern for his country's advancement; and at least it can be said that since his advent there has been comparative freedom from the confusion and upheavals that marked the early 'sixties.

### Economy—Minerals

Minerals are the most important factor in the economic life of Congo/Zaïre and they account for a high proportion of the country's exports. The focus of the mineral industry is the province of Katanga, an undulating plateau of an average altitude exceeding

3,500 feet, situated in the south-west of the territory. Katanga is especially noted for its copper, mined by Natives long before the appearance of the Europeans, and worked by the Belgians since 1911. The Katanga copper field is one of the richest in the world and makes this province, after the Witwatersrand, the most important commercial and industrial area in Africa. Congo/Zaïre is the world's largest producer of cobalt, and it also produces the greater part of the world's requirements of industrial diamonds. Other important minerals are tin, manganese, zinc, cadmium, uranium, radium and coal. If these were not enough, there have recently been interesting discoveries of mineral oil.

Most mining was formerly in the hands of large companies, almost all Belgian-owned, and the greatest of these was the *Union Minière du Haut-Katanga*. From the mines of the *Union Minière* came 70 per cent of the Congo's revenue. To General Mobutu the *Union Minière* represented the largest obstacle to his aim of economic independence, and at the end of 1966, after considerable argument, the Company's mines were nationalized. This, with the nationalization of other mines and industries, has caused the departure of many Belgian technicians whose expertise was vitally necessary to the economy.

*Agriculture*

Food crops include various cereals, cassava, sweet potatoes, beans and rice. Cash crops are oil palm products, cotton, coffee, rubber, groundnuts and bananas. At one time the collection of wild rubber contributed 80 per cent of the exports of the Congo Free State, and it was indeed with this industry that were associated most of the abuses with which the Free State was charged and which led to the transfer of administration to the Belgian Government. But wild rubber was unable to withstand the competition of the plantation-grown product, which drove it off the market. It was very much the same story with the oil palm. As late as the 1950s half the country's production of palm products came from wild trees. But here as elsewhere it was found that well tended trees are more profitable than wild ones, and Congo/Zaïre now competes with Nigeria as a leading African producer.

To the crops already mentioned should be added sugar-cane, pyrethrum, cocoa, tea, and fibres of various kinds, while the forests covering so much of the country yield valuable timber which constitutes an important export.

*Transport*

The Congo system of river transport is easily the most important and extensive network of inland waterways in tropical Africa. There are 9,000 miles of navigable river and although the main stream and its tributaries are interrupted at critical points by falls and rapids, there are very long stretches of unobstructed waterway, notably between Kinshasa and Kisangani, a distance of nearly 1,100 miles, and from Kinshasa to Port Francqui, about 378 miles up the Kasai River from its junction with the Congo. Navigable portions of the Lualaba are also important links in the chain of communications.

The railways of the Congo were originally designed to supplement the river system, but in recent years the relative importance of these two means of transport changed. With the opening up of new sources of production in areas distant from the rivers, the railways came to be regarded as ends in themselves, indeed as the major arterial lines of communication. Even more recently, with the discovery that within certain limits the cost in the Congo of carriage by road is less than by rail, plans for road construction were given precedence over new railway projects.

The first railway to be constructed was that from Matadi to Kinshasa, 232 miles in length, which provides the interior and its great network of rivers with an outlet to the ocean. A small but important line of 87 miles runs from Boma on the north side of the Congo estuary to Tshela, and serves an area that is comparatively isolated from the rest of the country. In the east there is a combined rail-water system connecting Kisangani with Kalemie on Lake Tanganyika. The Vicicongo railway (*Chemins de Fer Vicinaux au Congo*) taps the Uele River area in the north-east, while the great Katanga mineral field is served by the B.C.K. (*Chemin de Fer du Bas-Congo au Katanga*) which is connected to the Zambia-Rhodesia system and to the Benguela railway running down to Lobito Bay.

## EQUATORIAL AFRICA

*History*

French interest in Equatorial Africa began in the days when France was engaged with Britain in suppressing the Slave Trade. In 1839 a naval officer named Bouët-Guillaumetz obtained the right of residence at two small places on the left bank of the

Gabon estuary and in 1843 similar rights on the other bank. During the next few years arrangements of the same kind were made up and down the coast and in 1849 the French followed the British example in Sierra Leone and deposited a number of ex-slaves[1] at a settlement which they called Libreville. It was not for some years that the French did anything to spread from the coast of Gabon towards the hinterland; not, in fact, until 1875 when the explorer Savorgnan de Brazza travelled up the Ogowe River and crossed over to the Congo basin. In the course of a second expedition in 1880–82 he founded Brazzaville, and using this as a base made treaties with the local peoples which placed large areas north of the Congo River under French protection. Between 1885 and 1891 the French secured most of Gabon and the Middle Congo and then proceeded to expand eastwards towards the Nile and northwards towards the French possessions in North Africa. The spearhead of the eastward advance was Major Marchand's fruitless expedition to Fashoda[2] but the northward movement succeeded, after many years of effort, in securing the whole of the Chad territory and hence through the Niger Colony a continuous empire from Equatorial Africa to the Mediterranean.

After several experiments in government the area was divided into four colonies named respectively Gabon, the Middle Congo, Ubangi-Shari and the Chad territory, joined in a federation with a governor-general whose headquarters were at Brazzaville. In Chad the French met with prolonged resistance from the tribes and the territory was not transferred from military to civil administration until 1920.

When France fell in 1940 the Governor of Chad, a Negro named Eboué born in French Guiana, proclaimed that his colony would join General de Gaulle. The other French Equatorial territories and the French mandated territory of the Cameroons followed this example with the result that Brazzaville became the capital of Free France in Africa and Equatorial Africa became an important base for the Allies. In particular Chad played a most valuable part in the North African campaigns. Eboué himself was appointed to be Governor-General and continued in that office until 1944 when his death robbed France and Africa of a most remarkable man.

The four French colonies availed themselves of their opportunity

---

[1] They had been rescued from a slaving vessel.
[2] p. 53.

under the new constitution of 1958[1] to become autonomous republics within the French community. It was at this stage that the Middle Congo took the name of People's Republic or Congo (Brazzaville) and Ubangi-Shari that of Central African Republic. Gabon, however, retained its former name.[2]

## The Country

The coastline is about 800 miles long and is low and swampy, and fringed with sandspits and lagoons, in this way resembling parts of the coast of West Africa. The southern and longer section is very straight and has few if any good natural harbours. The northern section has several bays and inlets, of which the largest is the Gabon estuary.[3] The ground rises quickly to the plateau, which averages 2,000 to 3,000 feet. Several massifs of greater height tower above the general level. The western slopes are drained by the Ogowe and Kwilu river systems, flowing directly to the Atlantic. The rest of the territory is drained by tributaries of the Congo such as the Mbomu, Ubangi and Sangha. There is dense forest in Gabon and in Congo (Brazzaville). In the north the vegetation is savannah degenerating to thorny bush towards the dividing line between the Chad and Congo basins. The total area is rather less than half a million square miles.

There are two principal climatic belts, the Equatorial and the Sudanic. The former is that of the lower part of the territory and is characterized by temperatures which are fairly constant round 77° and by heavy rainfall, high humidity and a very short dry season. The Sudanic climate is hotter, with a longer dry season, but it has fairly wide daily and seasonal variations. This is the climate of the more northerly part of the region.

## The People

The population is between 3 and 4 million of whom nearly half are in the Central African Republic. Most of the people of the great forest zones of the Ogowe and the Congo, including the Ubangi in its lower course, are Bantu of whom the best known are perhaps the Pangwe (Fang), the most important people of Gabon. Across the upper half of the Central African Republic there are communities of Negroes with a mixture of Hamitic blood, having much in common

---

[1] p. 195.

[2] The reader is reminded that Chad has been included in West Africa.

[3] So called by the Portuguese navigators who discovered it because of a fancied likeness to a gabão or cabin.

with their neighbours in the Sudan and northern Nigeria but distinguished from Negroes with stronger Hamitic strains not only by physical traits but also by the fact that they are primarily agriculturalists and not pastoralists.


*The Economy*

The economic standards of Equatorial Africa were until the last decade rather low. This was due, not to an absence of possibilities, but to a weakness in the foundations on which the countries' economy was based.

In Gabon economic prospects have now undergone a complete change. This has been due to the exploitation of minerals, especially mineral oil, manganese and uranium. Several small oil wells are being worked in the coastal area, where natural gas also occurs. The manganese mine at Moanda is among the largest in the world. Not far from the manganese there are deposits of uranium, and Gabon is also known to possess massive reserves of iron ore. Gold is produced on a small scale.

Congo (Brazzaville) has also benefited from minerals. There is a small oilfield on the coast and it is now in production. There is copper mining near Mindouli on the railway from Brazzaville to Pointe Noire on the coast, and there has for some years been a production of lead, gold, zinc and diamonds. Potentially more important, however, are the very large potash deposits. Mining of these began in 1969. There are also deposits of iron ore and bitumen.

The Central African Republic seems at present to be less well endowed than the other two territories, diamonds being the only mineral to be exploited so far. Other minerals, however, including uranium, are known to be present.

Before the development of minerals in Gabon, timber accounted for 90 per cent of the exports and it is still at the head of the list. Congo (Brazzaville) also relies heavily on timber. In both countries the forests yield oil palm products and rubber, and they both produce cocoa and coffee. Cotton is the dominant crop in the Central African Republic, and it is followed by coffee. Groundnuts are also grown for export and the forestry industry is expanding. Tobacco has proved successful in the Niari valley of Congo (Brazzaville), where there are a number of government-assisted experimental farming projects of various kinds in which both Europeans and Africans participate. There is a plan to dam the Kwilu River at a point about

P

50 miles from the coast. This will provide hydro-electric power for industry, with resultant benefits to the Congolese economy.

Basic foodstuffs are cassava, yams, bananas, maize and other cereals, sweet potatoes and rice. Fishing in the sea and on inland waters provides a useful article of diet. The forest zones are heavily infested with tsetse fly and are therefore unsuitable for cattle. The Central African Republic is less heavily infested, and in the northern part offers better opportunities for cattle breeding.

Until quite recently the only railway was the one that links Brazzaville and Pointe Noire. A new railway has now been built, taking off from the Brazzaville–Pointe Noire line at Mont Belo, and going north to Mbinda. An aerial cableway connects Mbinda with the Moanda mine in Gabon, thus completing the transport chain that gives Gabon manganese an outlet to the sea. Considering the peculiar difficulties presented by the terrain, the road system is remarkably good, and air transport facilities both internal and external are quite well developed.

Inland waterways are about 3,000 miles long but the course is interrupted in places by rapids and by seasonal variations in water levels. The most important is a stretch of 720 miles along the Congo and Ubangi rivers from Brazzaville to Bangui, the capital of the Central African Republic. This is navigable for six months in the year throughout its length, and on the Congo section during the whole year. Gabon has a number of navigable rivers used mainly to float logs from the forest to the Atlantic ports.

CAMEROON

Once 'the Cameroons', this is largely a plateau rising towards the west and falling in the south-east towards the Congo basin. The coastal plain is narrow, with mangrove swamps, sand-bars and lagoons. The Cameroon Mountain rises majestically above it to a height of 13,430 feet. From the central highlands of the territory rivers flow in all directions, some direct to the Atlantic Ocean, some to the Benue, some to the Congo system and some towards Lake Chad. The vegetational pattern is similar to that found in other parts of this region of Africa. There is dense forest in the south, giving way in the north first to wooded savannah and then gradually to dry scrubland where the territory touches Lake Chad. The highlands have a variety of fine mountain scenery. On the coast the rainfall is heavy and well distributed throughout the year.

Duala receives an annual fall of 155 inches. This decreases towards the north and the annual rainfall round Lake Chad is no more than 12–15 inches. (The western side of the Cameroon Mountain receives 400–430 inches a year but the conditions are special.) The temperature is fairly high, being between 72° and 89° in the south and rising considerably higher in the Chad basin.

As we have already seen,[1] this former German territory was divided in two and the parts administered by Britain and France respectively first as mandates from the League of Nations, then as trusteeships under the United Nations. The French trusteeship obtained independence in 1960 but the British Cameroons split into two parts, north and south. The northern part elected to join Nigeria, but the south chose to join the former French-administered territory, by then an independent republic. From this union was formed the Federal Republic of Cameroon.

There had been trouble on the French side while it was still administered by France. A man named Ruben um Nyobe had founded a militant party called the *Union des Populations Camerounaises* (U.P.C.), with a programme of independence and union with the British Cameroons. The U.P.C. was declared illegal in 1955 and Ruben was killed by the French in 1958. Shortly after his death the French announced that the country would be granted full independence in 1960, whereupon one section of the U.P.C. agreed to work in a constitutional manner and was disbanded under an amnesty that was offered at the time. The other section, directed from outside the Cameroons by a Dr. Felix Moumié, a man with strong communist affiliations, continued the campaign even though the country was by then independent and the U.P.C. had been legalized. This section was particularly powerful among the Bamileke tribe on the frontier between the former British and French Cameroons, whose country the mandate arrangements of 1919 arbitrarily divided. The campaign had now lost all association with a political programme and was simply an affair of gang warfare, brigandage and resistance to authority. It is estimated that some fifty thousand people were in revolt against their government and that there was an average of 200 killings a month, often of a most gruesome character. Moumié died under mysterious circumstances in Switzerland in 1960.[2] Since independence the power of the U.P.C.

---

[1] p. 194.
[2] According to press reports, Moumié said before he died that a French organization called the Red Hand had poisoned him.

has declined under heavy government and military pressure, but it remains an irritant and a possible threat to the country's stability.

The Republic has an area of approximately 183,000 square miles and a population of about 6 million. It is divided into two provinces, corresponding to the former British and French territories respectively. The Eastern Province is by far the larger, being ten times the size of the Western. There is a federal government of which the president is head, with a council of ministers and a national assembly. Each province has its own government, with a prime minister and a legislative assembly.

Racially the people are extremely mixed but may be divided into two main groups according to whether they speak Bantu or Sudanic languages. The Bantu live in the southern and central areas and the Sudanic speakers in the north. The northern areas have in the past been frequently invaded by fair-skinned Semites and Hamites, for example the Fulani who founded the empire of Adamawa which straddled the north of the future German Cameroons and the eastern side of northern Nigeria. This empire collapsed with the coming of the Europeans and the partition of the country between the British and the Germans. There are pygmies in the forests of the Sangha River.

The economy of the Cameroon Republic is based on agriculture and the exploitation of forest produce. Apart from food crops, the principal commodities are cocoa, coffee, groundnuts, bananas, rubber, palm products and timber. The most important industrial feature is an aluminium plant completed in 1956. This smelts alumina imported from Guinea, but local deposits of bauxite are being mined on an increasing scale. Hydro-electricity for the plant is provided by means of a dam across the Sanaga River. Cattle and horses are reared in the northern and central parts of the country. The southern part is infested with tsetse fly and pastoral pursuits play little part in the economy.

The transport system is inadequate to the needs of the country. There is one railway from the port of Douala to the federal capital Yaounde; another from Douala to N'Kongsamba. Both these lines serve only the southern part of the country, and produce from the north has to be exported through Nigeria by way of the Benue River. It has now been decided to build a new line northwards from Yaounde which might ultimately be extended to Chad. A first section was nearly completed by the end of 1969. The road system is also being improved. Several rivers in the south are used as waterways and afford access some distance inland.

## EQUATORIAL GUINEA AND THE PORTUGUESE ISLANDS

Equatorial Guinea is the former Spanish Guinea and comprises the mainland territory of Rio Muni, between Gabon and the Cameroon Republic, and a number of islands of which the most important are Fernando Po and Annobon. Spanish Guinea became a fully independent republic in 1968 after a gradual process of emancipation, and is now governed by a president and an assembly. The capital of the country is Santa Isabel on Fernando Po. The total area is a little under 11,000 square miles and the population around 285,000. The most important people on the mainland are the Pangwe (Fang), who are also a dominant tribe in Gabon. The indigenous Africans on Fernando Po are the Bubi, but they are outnumbered by immigrant labourers, mostly Ibo from Nigeria.

Cocoa is the main crop. Indeed it is from Fernando Po that the cocoa bean is said to have been carried to the Gold Coast in 1870. Other exports are coffee, timber, oil palm products and copra.

The Portuguese islands of São Tomé and Principé lie south of Fernando Po and form part of the same volcanic chain. They have an aggregate area of 372 square miles and a population in 1968 of 65,000. At the turn of the century these two islands were the largest producers of cocoa in the world, but they have long since been over-taken and passed by Ghana and Nigeria. However, São Tomé in particular has well developed European-owned plantations of cocoa, coconuts, oil palms and cinchona. Immigrant labourers from the Portuguese colonies in Africa form the majority of the population.

CHAPTER NINE

# SMALL ISLANDS

## ATLANTIC OCEAN

MADEIRA is the largest of a group of islands belonging to Portugal and lying about 400 miles from the coast of Morocco. The islands have an aggregate area of 314 square miles and a population of about 283,000. They are volcanic and rise abruptly from the ocean. Pico Ruivo, the highest point on Madeira, reaches a height of 6,056 feet and some of the other peaks are not much lower. The steep slopes are carefully terraced to prevent soil erosion. Many kinds of fruit grow in abundance, early vegetables are raised for the European market, and the wines, especially the dessert varieties, are famous. Local industries, which include lace making, wickerwork and woodwork, centre largely on providing for tourists whom the agreeable climate attracts to Madeira in large numbers. Funchal on the south of this island is an important port of call for vessels bound for West and South Africa. The population is basically Portuguese but contains Moorish, Italian and Negro elements.

The Canaries are a group of islands belonging to Spain, of which the best known are Tenerife and Grand Canary. They were originally inhabited by a Berber people called Guanche, now extinct, but they fell to Spain in the course of the fifteenth century. The present inhabitants are a little darker than Spaniards but in other respects are indistinguishable from them. The total area of the group is 2,800 square miles and the population about 910,000. Like Madeira, the Canaries are volcanic and rise steeply from the sea. The snow-capped peak of Tenerife reaches a height of 12,000 feet. Lying as they do close to the African coast these islands are more arid than Madeira, especially on the eastern side. However, the soil is fertile, and when irrigated produces an abundance of fruit, vegetables and other crops. Fishing is an important industry and lace making and embroidery are local handicrafts. The islanders lean heavily on the tourist trade. Puerto de la Luiz on Grand Canary and Santa Cruz on Tenerife are considerable ports of call for shipping.

The Cape Verde Islands, 300 miles off Cape Verde on the African mainland, are an old Portuguese colony with a total area of 1,500 square miles and a population of 252,000. There are fourteen islands in all, of which ten are inhabited. They are of volcanic origin, and the highest peak, Fogo, has only recently become extinct. The average annual temperature is high and the rainfall low, but in spite of their aridity the islands produce a large variety of crops, including coffee of high quality, castor seed, tobacco, corn and beans. The majority of the inhabitants are of Negro origin.

## INDIAN OCEAN

Socotra is an island about 150 miles east-north-east of Cape Guardafui, with an area of 1,400 square miles. It was formerly administered from Aden as part of the Eastern Aden Protectorate. When Aden and the surrounding British-protected territories became independent in 1967, Socotra merged in the new-formed republic of Southern Yemen.

The island is mostly mountainous along its axis with granite peaks that rise to a height of nearly 5,000 feet above a limestone plateau of 1,000 to 1,500 feet. The mountains are cool and usually cloud- or mist-covered, but the lowlands are hot and malarious. The island is seamed with gorges which are normally dry but sometimes become raging torrents during the rainy season from November to April. The flora has affinities not only with that of Asia, Africa and the Mascarenes, but also with that of Polynesia and South America.

The population is about 12,000 and consists of two main elements. The coastal people are mostly Arabs and Africans, the latter being largely descendants of slaves from East Africa, though some are the offspring of West African soldiers stationed on Socotra during the last war. The nomadic pastoral inhabitants of the mountainous interior are Socotri proper, some tall and fair-skinned, others shorter and darker. The Socotri speak a language which with Mahri, to which it is related, and the pre-Islamic dialects of Arabia, forms an independent branch of the south Semitic family. Although they were Christians for centuries, the Socotri are now nominally Moslem.

The economy is a poor one. The principal occupations are fishing and raising the small Socotran cattle. The main exports are ghee (clarified butter), said to be the best in the whole of the northern Indian ocean, and mother of pearl. Other exports, of which the volume is small, are the red-coloured resin called dragon's blood, aloes' juice, lichen, ambergris, civet musk, dried shark, pottery, pearls, rugs, skins, and tobacco. Agriculture is precarious, and the islanders are compelled to import foodstuffs such as maize and rice. Dates are an important article of diet.

Socotra was known to the Greeks and Romans and appears in the *Periplus of the Erythraean Sea* as a busy trading station. During the European middle ages it was a notable haunt of Indian pirates. It was seized by the Portuguese in 1507 but abandoned in 1511. With the opening of the Suez Canal Socotra lay right astride the sea route to India and thus became of some importance to Great Britain. From 1876 onwards the Sultan received a subsidy from the government in Aden and in 1886 he formally placed himself under British protection. In effect this meant that the Sultan's government had complete control of all internal matters, British supervision being limited to foreign affairs.

Abd-el-Kuri is a small island lying between Socotra and Cape Guardafui inhabited by pearl divers and fishermen. Other islands in the group are Kal Farun and The Brothers.

# The Nile

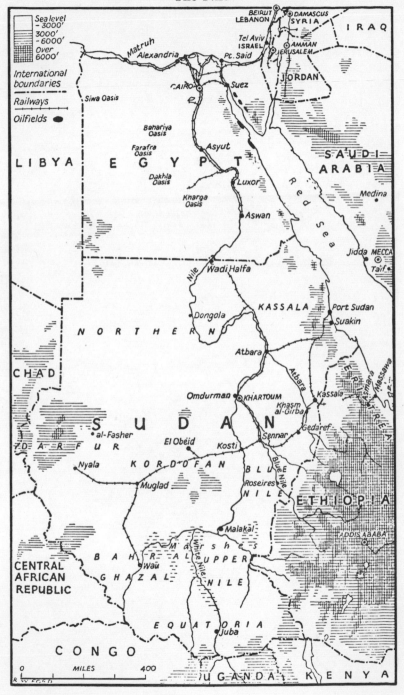

Sea level
- 3000'
3000'
- 6000'
Over
6000'

International
boundaries
Railways
Oilfields

BEIRUT    DAMASCUS
LEBANON    SYRIA
IRAQ
Matruh    Tel Aviv   AMMAN
Alexandria    ISRAEL    JERUSALEM
Pt. Said
CAIRO    Suez    JORDAN

LIBYA    E  G  Y  P  T
Siwa Oasis
Bahariya
Oasis
Farafra    Asyut
Oasis
Dakhla    Luxor    SAUDI
Oasis    ARABIA
Kharga
Oasis    Aswan    Medina

Red Sea

Jidda  MECCA
Taif

Nile    Wadi Halfa

N  O  R  T  H  E  R  N    KASSALA    Port Sudan
Dongola    Suakin
CHAD    Atbara    Atbara
Omdurman    KHARTOUM    Kassala
S  U  D  A  N    Khasm
al-Girba    Gedaref
al-Fasher    ERITREA
D  A  R  F  U  R    El Obeid    Kosti    Sennar    Asmara    Massawa
Nyala    K O R D O F A N    BLUE    Roseires
Muglad    NILE    ETHIOPIA
Malakal    ADDIS ABABA
B  A  H  R    A  L    M a r s h e s
CENTRAL    G  H  A  Z  A  L    U  P  P  E  R
AFRICAN    Wau    NILE
REPUBLIC    White Nile
E  Q  U  A  T  O  R  I  A
Juba

0    MILES    400
R W FOLD
CONGO    U  G  A  N  D  A    K  E  N  Y  A

## Rivers of West Africa (p.183)

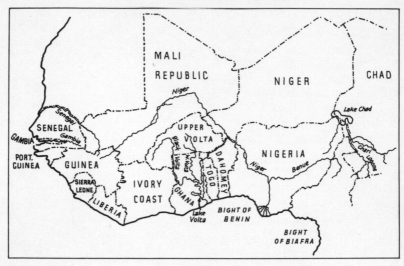

## Congo/Zaïre Rail-River System

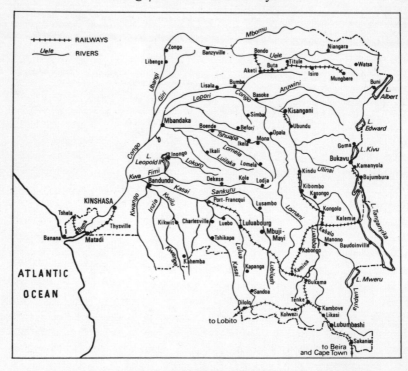

# CONCLUSION

IF there is one thing that we should have learnt by now it is that in discussing Africa we should never underestimate our ignorance. It is true that in the last hundred years much light has been thrown on a continent that until modern times was little known to the outside world. But this light has, as it were, only illuminated the surface. Since the end of the Second World War scholars of every kind have descended upon Africa in great numbers and there has been a welter of publications on almost every aspect of African life. Yet the authors themselves would admit that their researches cover but a narrow field and that the results reach only a small public. We simply do not know what the majority of Africans think and feel, what they are told and what they believe, and our approach to all we read and hear must therefore be exceedingly cautious, in the recognition that the material on which it is based is often flimsy and second-hand. Today a curtain has fallen on large areas of Africa and it is impossible to know what is going on behind it. Parts of the continent are as mysterious and perhaps as dangerous as when the early explorers first tramped through them. A sceptical appraisal of all reports and commentaries is therefore more than ever necessary.

## Retrospect

In 1970 we look back on the first decade of African independence. For some the last ten years represent an exciting, wholly gratifying era of self-fulfilment, of pride in achievement, of international acceptance, of action on the world stage, of expansion of the African personality. To the vast majority of ordinary folk, simple peasants struggling along as best they can in a harsh environment, the decade has probably made little difference. To several millions the 'sixties have brought misery and death.

Perhaps the most remarkable though not the most surprising phenomenon of the post-independence years, at least in the former British dependencies, has been the speed with which western-type democracy has faded out. Enormous trouble was taken to equip the new nations with parliamentary institutions on the Westminster

model. These arrangements, so laboriously contrived and earnestly
debated, have been replaced in most cases by a government based
on a powerful, sometimes an all-powerful, party. Furthermore the
new rulers have deliberately set themselves to sweep away the old
tribal loyalties and with them the powers of the traditional authorities that were so lovingly fostered by the British. In local as in
central government the Party calls the tune. Tribalism, it is said,
is a cause of instability, and is conducive to rivalries and power
struggles between opposing factions.[1]

Whatever the recipe for stability, Africa has not found it yet.
Between 1960 and 1969 there were some thirty successful military
*coups d'état* in the independent states, besides a number of civilian
plots and conspiracies. Since then there have been more. These
upheavals were due to a diversity of causes: maladministration and
extravagance, corruption in high places, acts of oppression, non-
fulfilment of impossible promises made during the independence
campaigns, racial and religious antagonisms, sometimes just plain
personal ambition. One cause that we can reject is that usually cited
by displaced presidents: African 'counter-revolutions' are *not*
brought about by 'imperialist' plots and foreign agents.

The great racial questions that agitate the continent are now
polarized, with South Africa and Rhodesia at one extreme and independent black Africa at the other. The gulf between the opposing
ideologies is unbridgeable, although trade links exist and there is a
hint of more. In East Africa the vague hopes that were expressed of
reasonably homogeneous multi-racial societies have not been
realized.

There have been several wars, two of which might have been
foreseen and perhaps avoided. The United Nations' decision to make
the Moslem Eritrean lowlands part of Ethiopia contained a conflict
ready-made; and the southern Sudanese, haunted by memories of
ancient wrongs, gave ample notice of their fear of government by
Arab Moslems in Khartoum. Other arrangements could have been
made in both cases and much suffering thereby avoided.

The war in Chad is like the Sudan in reverse. Here we have
Moslems in rebellion against a Christian Negro government, the
latter helped, of all things, by the French Foreign Legion.

The Portuguese are fighting a war in each of their African territories against various groups of nationalists. The result may well

[1] There has been a tendency to denounce as tribalism quite legitimate minority
interests.

depend on how far they can count on the loyalty of their own civil populations, and on the continued readiness of neighbouring African governments to support the guerillas.

The Nigerian war deserves more space than can be devoted to it in a short summing-up. Religious differences, inter-racial suspicions, opposition between different types of society, economic rivalry, these all played a part in starting it and foreign support to both sides helped to keep it going. For our purpose, however, the war was a tragic illustration of the tenacity with which independent Africa clings to the old colonial boundaries. These were drawn nearly a hundred years ago by European Powers often with little regard for ethnic, social or even geographical considerations. Tribes were cut in half, separated from their farmlands, their grazing, their shrines, and even from the seat of tribal government. These artificial divisions, one would have thought, could only work as long as there was in existence an overriding colonial Power. Yet the new states, so far from welcoming a chance to rationalize their frontiers, appear to regard the old ones as inviolable and condemn any attempt to derogate from them as secession or worse. When the seceding tribe or province has most of the wealth of the country, as Katanga has the copper and south-eastern Nigeria the oil, the struggle takes on a special significance. It is ironical that, as was mentioned in Chapter IV, the Somali, whose habitat is poor and who possess all the social, cultural, and political homogeneity of nationhood, should be fated to live against their will under four different governments.

Apart from the artificial nature of their boundaries, many African states are the wrong shape and size. Some are too small both in area and in population; some are too large for their population and are badly situated; and some have too large a population within a small area. There are few in which population, area, position and physical conditions are nicely balanced.

## Association and Co-operation

The obvious answer is the development of viable units by fusion and federation. That Africans themselves recognize this is shown by the experiments that have already taken place. The most ambitious is the Organization of African Unity, established at Addis Ababa in Ethiopia in 1963. It was designed to promote unity and solidarity among African states and Madagascar, and to combat colonialism.

Besides this organization of continental scope, African states have also formed regional groupings concerned mainly, but not exclusively,

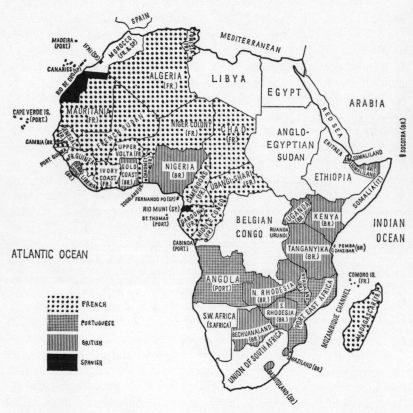

This map represents the position as it was in the early 1950s. The powers administering dependencies are shown by the various hatchings. The distinction between colonies, protectorates and trusteeships is not shown on the map, but may be found in the text.

# Regions and Territories

Madeira.

Canaries.

Cape Verde
IS.

GAMBIA
PORT. GUINEA

SIERRA
LEONE

MOROCCO

MEDITERRANEAN

ALGERIA

LIBYA

EGYPT
(U.A.R.)

NILE VALLEY

SPANISH SAHARA

MAURITANIA

NIGER

WEST

MALI

UPPER
VOLTA

SENEGAL

GUINEA

IVORY
COAST

LIBERIA

TOGO
DAHOMEY

GHANA

NIGERIA

CHAD

SUDAN

ETHIOPIA

ERITREA

FR. TERR. OF THE
AFAR & ISSA

Socotra

HORN OF
AFRICA

CAMEROON

CEN. AFRICAN
REPUBLIC

Fernando Poo

RIO MUNI

São Tomé

GABON

CONGO (B'ville)

EQUATORIA

CONGO
(Kinshasa)

UGANDA

RWANDA

BURUNDI

KENYA

EAST

TANZANIA

Pemba
Zanzibar

SOMALIA

*Atlantic*

*Ocean*

ANGOLA

CENTRAL

ZAMBIA

RHODESIA

MOZAMBIQUE

S. W.
AFRICA

BOTSWANA

SOUTHERN

SWAZILAND

REPUBLIC OF
SOUTH AFRICA

LESOTHO

MADAGASCAR
(Malagasy)

------------- Territorial boundary

——————— Regional boundary

with economic co-operation. Of the nine principal organizations of
this kind,[1] six consist of francophone countries. The most important
is probably the *Organisation Commune Africaine, Malgache et
Mauricienne* (OCAM), founded in 1965 to 'accelerate the political,
economic, social, technical and cultural development of member
states'. OCAM has fifteen members[2] and includes, as the name
indicates, Madagascar and Mauritius.

In addition to these large groupings there are a great number of
offices and agencies for co-ordinating such matters as scientific
research, communications, social services, labour and industry and
so on.[3]

Apart from direct inter-territorial links, there are several organizations which give African statesmen opportunities to meet and to work
together, or at least in which they have a common interest. Thus the
former British dependencies are members of the Commonwealth,
though the connection is becoming tenuous. A network of connections with France does something of the same kind for the former
French colonies. Finally splendid opportunities for consultation and
collaboration are provided by the United Nations, to which the new
nations almost automatically belong.

*The Economy*

When listening to the economists' usual assessment of Africa,
which is invariably pessimistic and based on some such concept as
income *per caput*, it is well to bear in mind that most Africans have
access to benefits that are not easily calculable in terms of cash. These
include the use of land, grazing, fuel and water; milk, meat and other
products of domestic animals; the proceeds of hunting, fishing and
collecting; small luxuries like beer and tobacco; materials and the
help of neighbours in domestic undertakings like house building;
communal support in sickness and old age. These are things that in
advanced industrial societies are bought at considerable expense by
the individual or by the community. The rural African can obtain
them cheaply or provide them for himself by his own labour. Even
so the African standard is not high and is still only comparable, say,
to England in the Middle Ages or to the less prosperous parts of

[1] Counting as one the European Economic Community, with which many
African states have made agreements.
[2] Plus Mauritania, which left the organization but remains a member of its
technical committees.
[3] For regional organizations see *Africa South of the Sahara 1971*, pp. 72 *et seq.*

Europe in the last century. It is however higher than that of a large part of India, if only because Africa is less crowded.

It is admitted that African standards must be raised and there is general agreement that this can be done by improving agriculture and public health, by the spread of education, the exploitation of minerals, the development of industry and communications, the wise use of natural resources such as water, forests, fisheries and wild game, and the conservation of the environment. The question we have to ask is where are the men and the money to come from for such an enormous and complex task? How, for instance, is the infrastructure for a mining industry to be provided? Where are the scientists who will combat this or that pest or disease? Who will supply the men and the materials to build a road here or a harbour there? How are African teachers and technicians to be trained? The answer to these questions lies in foreign aid.

## Aid to Africa

During the colonial era the dependencies looked to the metropolitan Powers to provide such finance as they required. In the case of Great Britain colonial finance was dominated by the Gladstonian budget long after the Grand Old Man had left the scene. But the situation improved in the 1930s and the concept of support to needy colonies received great impetus in the years following the Second World War. Economic assistance was channelled through the Colonial Development and Welfare Fund, which gave money for many far-sighted and useful schemes.

The volume and scope of aid changed dramatically with the coming of independence. There were several reasons for this. To begin with, independence itself was expensive: new buildings, foreign representation, compensation to expatriate officials for whom there was no longer a place, all these and other things cost money. The war, by increasing general awareness, had created a demand for higher standards, and nationalist politicians campaigning for independence had done nothing to diminish expectations. In the United Nations the emergent states found a forum where they could make their needs known to a sympathetic world audience. The following years, therefore, saw a vigorous development of aid through the United Nations' Economic and Social Council, and at the same time a marked extension of bilateral aid, that is aid given directly by one country to another.

There is hardly a field that aid does not cover and the range of

R

objects is almost unlimited: railways in Tunisia, hydro-electricity in
Ghana, agriculture in Ethiopia, forestry in Kenya, oil palm cultivation in Dahomey, mining in Botswana, universities and higher
education in many countries.[1] Aid can take the form of grants, loans,
materials, experts, teachers and technicians. Not only nations figure
as donors. Substantial help is given by great industrial corporations
like Ford, by charitable and religious foundations, and by welfare
organizations such as Oxfam. The American Peace Corps and the
British Voluntary Service Overseas are forms of aid.

Not unexpectedly there has been waste. Some of this was due to
ignorance and lack of discrimination on the part of the donors. The
Tanganyika Groundnut Scheme, a blunder on the part of the British
Government, was a case in point; and it appears that the story of
Russian snow ploughs in Guinea is true.[2] Some schemes were too
hastily undertaken and others were insufficiently supervised, while the
early days of independence saw an absurd extension of the Cold War
to Africa, when the Powers competed with each other in giving aid
in order to gain the friendship of the emerging nations. The new
African governments, for their part, were sometimes careless of their
own resources. Luxury hotels, sports stadia and other expensive
prestige installations were put up with money that was needed for
more basic services. However this was in the early days. Since then
proper organizations have been created, rules and precedents have
been established, a great deal of experience has been gained, all with
the result that aid is now administered in a more reasonable and
fruitful way.

The most dramatic form of aid is that given to Egypt by Russia in
building the Aswan High Dam. This is remarkable not only for the
size and importance of the undertaking but also for the influence and
strategic advantages which it has brought to Russia. Another sensational instance is the Tanzam railway, which Communist China is
building between Tanzania and Zambia.

The supply of arms and the training of African armies is perhaps
the most questionable form of aid. These armies are much more
likely to be used to suppress internal commotion than to fight a
foreign foe, and it would be better for the international conscience
if states that feel that they need big armies should train those armies
and supply the arms themselves.

After some years of aid on the present scale there is disappointment

[1] See *Africa South of the Sahara 1971*, pp. 48 *et seq.*
[2] Little, *Aid to Africa*, p. 21.

among the donors and a loss of impetus. Measured against the size of the problem (we are not now speaking only of Africa) so little seems to have been accomplished after so much effort. At the same time aid-giving countries have problems of their own. America, the richest of all, has the Vietnam war and agonizing social troubles. Britain is in serious economic difficulties and is faced with the complicated uncertainties of the Common Market. Disenchantment and a mood of withdrawal from Third World commitments is reinforced in Britain by the attitude of those African leaders who seem to make a point of taking an anti-British position on every international platform. Would-be investors in African countries are also alienated by the abrupt nationalization of foreign businesses.

As we now recognize, early expectations were too high. The time scale was foreshortened, the human potential overvalued, the magnitude of the task underestimated. Aid is a long-term affair and will spread over many years. When people understand that there can be no quick results they will be more patient. As to snubs and discourtesies, we must remember that abuse of America and Great Britain is the small change of Third World politics. Aid will certainly outlast the present politicians.

## Intellectual Achievements

One of the most remarkable social phenomena in Africa since the Second World War has been the growth of the demand for education. This has been reflected in a considerable expansion of educational facilities in all grades during the 'sixties. Primary education has become almost everywhere an article of national faith and personal ambition, and the increase in enrolment has been astonishing. The advance in secondary education has not been quite so marked, but it is still significant, with emphasis on vocational and technical disciplines and teacher training. At a still higher level there has been a proliferation of universities, and there can be few countries in Africa now that are not endowed with one or more places of higher education of one kind or another. Several African universities enjoy a high reputation and have employed, and produced, distinguished scholars. Higher educational institutions are still compelled to rely heavily on expatriate staff, and it will be some time before the output of nationals is great enough to replace them. There is also a general shortage of good teachers at lower levels.

The last ten years have also witnessed a considerable flowering of African literature. It is a literature that is expressed in the English and the French languages, but the themes are truly indigenous. The most common of these is the impact on the African of contact with white civilization, and the conflict in the individual between acquired European values and inherited traditions and beliefs.

The multiplicity of African languages would seem to militate against the emergence of a true vernacular literature. This obstacle is not present in countries where Arabic is the only, or at least the dominant language, where writers are already heirs to a distinguished literary tradition. But even in black Africa the difficulty is not so great as appears at first sight. Several languages, for example Swahili and Hausa, are coming forward as standard languages among millions of people. They both already possess a respectable classical literature in Arab script that is comparatively little known even inside Africa. They must surely in time become the media of a modern literature that will be African in language as well as in spirit! A few writers have pointed the way: Shaaban Robert in East Africa, Alhaji Abubakar Imam and Hampaté Bâ in West, and others will doubtless follow. Meanwhile African languages have an important part to play in journalism, school books and broadcasting.

## Prospect

While too confident of what aid could do for Africa and how soon, we have been too despondent about African resources. We hear it repeated *ad nauseam* that Africa is poor, and so at present it is. But we do not hear enough about potential riches. There is great mineral wealth in sight and there is no doubt more to be discovered. The rivers represent vast sources of unused power; the land, now so sorely abused, could be made to yield more than it does; industry is in its infancy and there are valuable assets such as forests, fisheries and wild game. Short of some unforeseeable catastrophe, there are good reasons to be cautiously optimistic about the economy.

As to politics the crystal ball is cloudy. Power is a heady wine, but even allowing for that, the exuberant politicians of the last decade have done some startling things. It does however seem that the era of messianic leaders is drawing to an end. Several of these charismatic personalities, who were effective enough while engaged in throwing out a sagging colonial government, have now been toppled from power in their turn, and replaced by less theatrical, more realistic characters. To that extent the outlook is reassuring.

We may look forward confidently to an expanding awareness of African culture and to the increasing influence of Africa on the arts and literatures of the nations. Africa's exciting music and colourful dance styles have been enthusiastically adopted by the young. In literature African novelists, poets and playwrights command a world audience. In academic life the study of Africa is everywhere an established part of the curriculum. Considerable cross-fertilization has taken place by the movement of teachers between Africa and other continents.

We can say with certainty that Africa will continue to change rapidly and that the future still holds many surprises. It would be rash to try to predict what these will be or how they will affect Africa itself and the rest of the world. The author of this book can see no further into these matters than anyone else. We must all be content to await the answers from 'the grand Instructor, Time'.

# READING LIST

Books on Africa are legion and it is impossible to compile a list that will satisfy everybody. Most of the books in the following list are in English and some of them contain bibliographies that will suggest further reading.

## GENERAL

Church, R. J. Harrison, *Africa and the Islands* (London, 1967).

Davidson, B., *Old Africa Re-discovered* (London, 1959).

Europa Publications, *Africa South of the Sahara 1971.*

Fitzgerald, W., *Africa, a social, economic and political geography of its major regions* (London, 1967).

Grove, A. T., *Africa South of the Sahara* (London, 1970).

Hailey, Lord, *An African Survey* (London, 1957).

Hall, R., *Discovery of Africa* (London, 1970).

Hallett, R., *Africa to 1875* (Michigan, 1970).

Hance, W. A., *African Economic Development* (London, 1967).

Legum, C., and Drysdale, J., *Africa Contemporary Review* (Africa Research Ltd). This is an annual publication.

Little, I. M. D., *Aid to Africa* (Oxford, 1964).

Oliver, R., and Fage, J. D., *A Short History of Africa* (Harmondsworth, 1962).

Perham, M. F., *The Colonial Reckoning* (London, 1962).

Perham, M. F., and Simmons, J., *African Discovery, an anthology of exploration* (London, 1949).

Seligman, C. J., *Races of Africa* (London, 1957).

Suggate, L. S., *Africa* (London, 1968).

Werner, A., *The Language Families of Africa* (London, 1925).

Wingert, P. S., *The Sculpture of Negro Africa* (Columbia, 1951).

## REGIONAL

Southern Africa

Ashton, H., *The Basuto* (London, 1952).

Barker, D., *Swaziland* (H.M.S.O., London, 1965).

Brookes, E. H., *Apartheid* (London, 1968).

Coates, A., *Basutoland* (H.M.S.O., London, 1966).

Cole, Monica, *South Africa* (London, 1961).

Cope, J., *South Africa* (London, 1967).

Macmillan, W. M., *Bantu, Boer and Briton* (Oxford, 1964).

Marquard, L., *The Peoples and Policies of South Africa* (London, 1952).

Paton, A., *South Africa and her people* (London, 1970).

Pollock, N. C., and Agnew, S., *An Historical Geography of South Africa* (London, 1963).

Schapera, I., *ed., The Bantu-speaking tribes of South Africa* (London, 1953).

Sillery, A., *The Bechuanaland Protectorate* (Cape Town, 1952)

Stevens, R. P., *Lesotho, Botswana and Swaziland* (London, 1967).

Thomas, E. Marshall, *The Harmless People* (London, 1959). The 'harmless people' are the Bushmen.

Walker, E. A., *A History of Southern Africa* (London, 1957).

Wellington, J. H., *South West Africa and its human issues* (Oxford, 1967).

Young, B. A., *Bechuanaland* (H.M.S.O., London, 1966).

The Year Book (*State of South Africa, economic, financial and statistical year book for the Republic of South Africa*) is full of facts and figures.

The year book and guide published by the Union Castle Company is also useful.


CENTRAL AFRICA

Abshire, D. M., and Samuels, M. A., *Portuguese Africa, a handbook* (London, 1969).

Chilcote, R., *Portuguese Africa* (Englewood Cliffs, 1967).

Debenham, F., *Nyasaland, Land of the Lake* (H.M.S.O., London, 1955).

Hall, R. L., *Zambia* (London, 1965).

Hanna, A. J., *The Story of the Rhodesias and Nyasaland* (London, 1960).

*Handbook to the Federation of Rhodesia and Nyasaland* (London, 1960).

Lockhart, J. G., and Woodhouse, C. M., *Rhodes* (London, 1963).

Mason, P., *The Birth of a Dilemma* (London, 1958).

Mason, P., *Year of Decision* (London, 1960).

Pike, J. G., *Malawi* (London, 1968).

Posselt, F. W. T., *A Survey of the Native Tribes of Southern Rhodesia* (Government of Southern Rhodesia, 1927).

Thompson, V., and Adloff, R., *The Malagasy Republic* (Stanford, 1965).

Wheeler, D. L., and Pélissier, R., *Angola* (London, 1971).

Young, K., *Rhodesia and Independence* (London, 1968).

Some of the best material on Madagascar and the Comoro Islands is in French. *Madagascar* by Hubert Deschamps in the 'Que sais-je?' series (Presses Universitaires de France) is simple and is easy to obtain. A more advanced and specialized work is Massiot, M., *L'Organisation de la Republique Malgache* (Librairie de Madagascar, 1970). One may also read with profit: Decary, R. and others: *La France de l'Océan Indien* (Series 'Les Terres Lointaines' published by the Société d'Editions Géographiques, Maritimes et Coloniales, 1952).

## EAST AFRICA

Coupland, R., *East Africa and its invaders* (Oxford, 1939).

Diamond, S., and Burke, F. E., *The Transformation of East Africa* (New York, 1966).

East Africa Royal Commission 1953–1955 Report (H.M.S.O., Cmd. 9475).

Harlow, V. T., Chilver, E., and Smith, A., *History of East Africa*, vol. II (Oxford, 1965).

Huxley, Elspeth, *White Man's Country* (London, 1953).

Ingham, K., *The making of modern Uganda* (London, 1958).

——, *History of East Africa* (London, 1962).

Ingrams, W. H., *Zanzibar* (London, 1931). Reprinted by Frank Cass, London, 1967.

Lemarchand, R., *Rwanda and Burundi* (London, 1968).

Lofchie, M. J., *Zanzibar : Background to Revolution* (Princeton, 1965).

Mangat, J. S., *A History of the Asians in East Africa* (Oxford, 1969).

Marshall MacPhee, A., *Kenya* (London, 1966).

Mitchell, Sir P. E., *African Afterthoughts* (London, 1954).

Moffet, J. P., ed., *Handbook of Tanganyika* (Tanganyika Government, 1958).

O'Connor, A. M., *An Economic Geography of East Africa* (London, 1966).

Oliver, R., *The Missionary Factor in East Africa* (London, 1952).

Trimingham, J. S., *Islam in East Africa* (Oxford, 1964).


## THE HORN OF AFRICA

Hess, R. L., *Ethiopia* (Cornell, 1970).

Lewis, I. M., *The Modern History of Somaliland* (London, 1965).

Longrigg, S. H., *A short history of Eritrea* (London, 1945).

Trevaskis, Sir G. K. N., *Eritrea* (London, 1960).

Thompson, V., and Adloff, R., *Djibouti and the Horn of Africa* (Stanford, 1968).

Ullendorff, E., *The Ethiopians* (London, 1960).


## THE NILE VALLEY

Duncan, J. S. R., *The Sudan* (Edinburgh, 1952).

Gaitskell, A., *Gezira* (London, 1959).

Holt, P. M., ed., *Political and Social Change in Modern Egypt* (London, 1967).

——, *A Modern History of the Sudan* (London, 1962).

Longrigg, S. H., and Jankowski, J., *The Middle East : a social geography* (London, 1970).

MacMichael, Sir H., *The Anglo-Egyptian Sudan* (London, 1934).

Mansfield, P., *Nasser's Egypt* (Harmondsworth, 1965).
Vatikiotis, P. J., *The Modern History of Egypt* (London, 1969).


MEDITERRANEAN AFRICA AND SAHARA
Barbour, N., *ed.*, *A Survey of North West Africa* (London, 1959).
——, *Morocco* (London, 1965).
Berque, J., *French North Africa* (London, 1968).
Bovill, E. W., *The Golden Trade of the Moors* (London, 1958).
Brace, R. M., *Morocco, Algeria, Tunisia* (Englewood Cliffs, 1964).
Gautier, E. F. (trans. D. F. Mayhew), *Sahara, the Great Desert* (Columbia, 1935).
Gerteiny, A. G., *Mauritania* (London, 1967).
Knapp, W., *Tunisia* (London, 1970).
Samir Amin, *The Maghreb in the Modern World* (Harmondsworth, 1970).
Sylvester, A., *Tunisia* (London, 1969).
Wright, J., *Libya* (London, 1969).
    There is naturally a large literature on North Africa in French. The two following little books are simple to read and easy to find. Both are in the 'Que sais-je?' series (Presses Universitaires de France).
Ageron, Ch.-R., *Histoire de l'Algérie Contemporaine* (1969).
Verlet, B., *Le Sahara* (1958).


WEST AFRICA
Adloff, R., *West Africa: the French-speaking nations* (New York, 1964).
Boateng, E. A., *A Geography of Ghana* (Cambridge, 1966).
Church, R. J. Harrison, *West Africa* (London, 1968).
Fage, J. D., *A History of West Africa: an introductory survey* (Cambridge, 1969).
Flint, J. E., *Nigeria and Ghana* (Englewood Cliffs, 1966).
Fyffe, C., *A History of Sierra Leone* (London, 1962).
Gailey, H. A., *A History of the Gambia* (London, 1968).
Lewis, R., *Sierra Leone* (H.M.S.O., London, 1954).
Lewis, W. Arthur, *Politics in West Africa* (London, 1965).
Liebenow, J. G., *Liberia* (Cornell, 1969).
Lusignan, G. de, *French-speaking Africa since Independence* (London, 1969).
Niven, Sir Rex, *Nigeria* (London, 1967).
Smith, Sir B. Sharwood, *But Always as Friends* (London, 1969).
Thompson, V., and Adloff, R., *French West Africa* (London, 1958).
Ward, W. E. F., *A History of Ghana* (London, 1966).
    S

EQUATORIA

Bouquerel, Jacqueline, *Le Gabon* (Presses Universitaires de France, 1970). The 'Que sais-je?' series.

Carter, Gwendolen, *ed.*, *National Unity and Regionalism in eight African states* (Cornell, 1966). See the article 'Four Equatorial states' by J. A. Ballard.

*Guide du voyageur au Congo Belge et au Ruanda-Urundi* (R. Dupriez, 1949).

Johnson, W. R., *The Cameroon Federation* (Princeton, 1970).

Kalck, P., *The Central African Republic* (Pall Mall Press, 1971)

Slade, Ruth, *The Belgian Congo* (London, 1960).

Schebesta, P., *Among Congo Pygmies* (London, 1933).

Schweitzer, Albert, *On the Edge of the Primeval Forest* (London, 1961).

Thompson, V., and Adloff, R., *The Emerging States of French Equatorial Africa* (Stanford, 1960).

Torday, E., *On the trail of the Bushongo* (London, 1925).

Trezenem, E., and Lembezat, B., *La France Equatoriale* (Société d'Editions Géographiques, Maritimes et Coloniales, 1950). 'Terres Lointaines' series.

Young, C., *Politics in the Congo* (Princeton, 1965).


SOCOTRA

Botting, D., *Island of the Dragon's Blood* (London, 1958).


The following publications not included in the above lists may also be consulted:

*Africa.* Journal of the International African Institute.

*Bantu Studies* (now *African Studies*). A journal published by the University of the Witwatersrand.

*Ethnographic Survey of Africa.* A series published by the International African Institute.

# INDEX

Abd al Wahid, dynasty, 28
Abd el Kader, 48
Abd el Kuri, 220
Abdulla, Khalifa, 50, 157, 158
Abidjan, 183
Abyssinia, see Ethiopia
Adamawa, 216
Addis Ababa, 147, 153
Adwa (Adowa, Aduwa, Adua), 150, 151
Afar, and the Issa, territory of the, see Somaliland
Africa, 3–56; the unknown continent 3–4; physical features, 4–6; climate, 6–7; people, 8–13; population, 8; culture, 13–14; religion and political life, 16–17; justice, 18; subsistence, 18–19; the arts, 19–20; languages, 20–2; history, 22–56; exploration, 42–6; Scramble and partition, 47, 52–3, 99, 104, 106, 126, 192–3; Colonial Powers, 54–6; prospect, 232–3
African Association, 43
African Lakes Company, 98
Africans, see Africa, also under regions and territories, subhead people
Afrikaans, 63
Afrikaners, 62, 63, 71
Afro-Americans, 189–90
Agriculture, see Africa, subsistence, also under regions and territories, subhead economy
Agulhas, Cape, 4
Ahaggar Mountains, 168, 169
Aid to Africa, 229–31
Air Services, see under regions and territories, subhead economy
Akan, 186–7
Aksum, 24, 148, 149
Alaotra, Lake, 113, 116
Al Azhar, 156
Al Ksar al Kebir, 33

Albert, Lake, 5, 6
Alexander the Great, 24, 25–6, 168
Algeria, 166, 171, 172, 174–5, 178–181; see Mediterranean Africa
Algiers, 48, 171, 172
Almohades, 28, 29
Almoravids, 28, 29
Aluminium, 216
Amhara, Amharic, 148, 151–2
Amin, General, 132, 138
Amr ibn al Asi, 24
Andersson, C. J., 44–5
Angola, 91, 92; people, 94; history, 105–7; economy, 110, 111; see Central Africa
Angoni, 96
Angra Peqüena (Lüderitz Bay), 78, 81
Animal husbandry, see Africa, subsistence; Nilo-Hamites, Nilotes; also under regions and territories, subhead economy
Annobon, 217; see Equatorial Guinea
Apartheid, 65, 74–6
Arabi Pasha, 49
Arabic, 21
Arabs, 8, 27–8, 34–5, 42–3, 50–1, 99, 122–3, 145, 157, 169, 206
Art, see Africa: Ethiopian, 152
Arusha Declaration, 134
Asbestos, 69, 89, 108, 111
Ashanti, 41–2, 187, 193
Asians, 12–13, see Indians
Asmara, 153
Assab, 153
Association and co-operation, interstatal, 225–6
Aswan, 155; Aswan High Dam, 162–163
Atbara River, 155
Atlas Lands, 166; mountains, 167
Atrocities, Congo, 206
Augustine, St., 26
Azande, 205

239